Six More Wins:
A Team, A Town, A Rebound, and a Championship!

Jim Maggiore

Foreword by Tim Heiman, Broadcaster for the Binghamton Mets

Copyright © Jim Maggiore

All Rights Reserved: No portion of this publication may be reproduced, stored in any electronic system or transmitted in any form or by any means, electronic, mechanical, photocopy, recording or otherwise, without written permission from the author. Printed in the United States of America. Although every precaution has been taken in the preparation of this book, the publisher and author assume no responsibility for errors or omissions. No liability is assumed for damages resulting from the use of material contained here.

ISBN 978-0-692-39878-4
Cover Design courtesy of Greg Smith (greg@gregksmith.com)

Cover Photos: Clockwise, from top to left: Team championship photo (courtesy of Bruce Adler and the Binghamton Mets); Cody Satterwhite and Xorge Carrillo celebrate the Game 5 Northern Division clincher at Portland; Pedro Lopez gives Kyle Johnson a hug during the on-field celebration after clinching the Eastern League Championship on September 12, 2014.

Back Photo: Steven Matz walking off the field in the eighth inning of Game 3 of the Eastern League Championship Series.

Printed in U.S.A.
Superior Print on Demand
165 Charles Street
Vestal, New York

First Edition: April 2015

Acknowledgements

Thanks goes to the following people for making this book possible.

- B-Mets General Manager Jim Weed and his staff, who provided media credentials to the author and made themselves available for numerous interviews.
- The Board of Directors of the Binghamton Mets Booster Club, who were supportive every step along the way.
- The people who offered comments on the drafts of this work: John Bernhardt, Justin Cohen, Vince Fiacco, Kevin Healy, Mike McCann, Richard Tylicki, and Denis Wickham, and Lynn Worthy.
- Tim Heiman, who provided all of his pre-game 2014 interviews for the author to use as part of his research. Thanks too goes Gabe Altieri, Heiman's intern for 2014.
- Lynn Worthy, the beat reporter for Binghamton Mets, whose stories proved an invaluable source of information.
- An extra note of thanks goes to Bruce Adler, whose championship photo appears on the cover and Eileen Plunkett, who contributed the photo of Hugh Grant and Marc Lawrence.
- One more extra note of thanks to Denis Wickham and John Bernhardt, for going above and beyond with their review comments. Thanks too, to John, for all of his stories!
- Finally, thanks to Alice Maggiore, who donated numerous editing hours for this work!

Note: All photos, unless otherwise indicated, were taken by the author.

Dedication: This book is dedicated to my favorite double-play combination of all time: my daughters, Alice and Emily!

Other Books by Jim Maggiore

Jim Maggiore has been a resident of the Greater Binghamton Area since graduating from Binghamton University in 1978.

His writings and photographs on baseball have previously appeared in the *Binghamton Press & Sun-Bulletin*, and various editions of the *Binghamton Mets Baseball Program*. This is his fourth book. Previous books written by Maggiore include:

1. *Celebrating 100 Years of Baseball in Greater Binghamton: Tales from the Binghamton Baseball Shrine* (coauthored with Michael J. McCann)
2. *Spring Training with the Washington Nationals,* by Fonthill Media.
3. *Golf in Broome County* (coauthored with Michael J. McCann), by Arcadia Publishing.

You can keep up with Jim's work at his author's blog, Jimmaggiore.wordpress.com.

For information on ordering copies of this work, go to bmetsboosters.wordpress.com

Contents

Foreword 7
Prologue: Warming Up in the Pen… 9
Chapter 1. From Binghamton to the Big Leagues 11
   Syndergaard's Sizzling Spring Debut 13
   The Road to Flushing Passes through Binghamton 19
Chapter 2. Six More Wins 25
   Welcome Back 28
Chapter 3. April: Our Team. Our Town. Our Pride. 32
   Francisco Lindor Shines 36
   A Forgotten Snow Globe 41
   Move Over Babe, Here Comes Henry! 43
   That Must Have Been that New Kid, Mays 45
   Binghamton's Crash Davis 49
   Back Home 53
   Binghamton's Voice of the Game 58
   Our Team. Our Town. Our Pride. 62
Chapter 4. Binghamton is Our Hometown 65
   Eddie is Back 67
   From Bat Boy to the "Mad Hatter" 70
   Bosnia to Iraq to Egypt to Kuwait, Then Back Home .. 73
   George Plimpton Redux 77
   Walking Distance 79
   A Baseball and Binghamton Lifer 82
Chapter 5. The Art of Pitching 85
   "Soup" Debuts 94
   Closing as an Art Form 96
   The Education of Matt Bowman 100
Chapter 6. "Big Plaw's Gonna Rip a Double… " 109
   Four Games, 41 Runs 115
   A Visitor from Flushing 119
   Celebrity Watch at the Park 121
   Second Half Changes 124
Photo Gallery 131
Chapter 7. Hunting the Sea Dogs 147
   Playoff Preview 148

Meanwhile, at Citi Field…...153
Striking Distance 155
A Bronx Grinder...157
Lara and Matz and a Split...159
Chapter 8. A Team, a Town, and a Rebound 163
First the Team…...164
Now the Town…...167
And Now a Rebound… 169
Chapter 9. A View from the Press Box................................187
RubberDucks and Spiedie Races..192
Just Get Started..195
From the Kiss Cam to a Spot Start for deGrom 197
Chapter 10. "Etch-A-Sketching" to the Playoffs.................200
Lopez Passes Tamargo while Tovar and Centeno Shine 204
The Kid with the Red Shoes...206
Portland Goes on a Winning Streak 209
Get Out the Etch-A-Sketch®..214
Chapter 11. A September to Remember 222
Portland Silences the Sign Man..226
A Few Feet Short..228
Grinding it Out 231
The Winner Goes to Richmond….......................................234
If it's Monday, We Must be in Richmond?.........................239
The Biggest Double Play of the Year.................................241
Peavey and Carrillo Step Up 242
Matz Breaks the Rules, then the Bats of the Squirrels 244
Epilogue..255
Appendix A. Player Profiles 261
Appendix B. Game-by-Game Log..272
Appendix C. Twitter Handles and Walk-Up Music............278
Notes 281

Foreword

It is not often that a city is treated to a storybook season from its hometown team. The Binghamton Mets did that in 2014.

It is even more extraordinary that that team caps that storybook season with a storybook ending. Jayce Boyd did that with his pinch-hit, walk-off double to clinch the Eastern League Championship Series.

And it is unquestionably rare that someone, for the love of baseball, infatuation with his team and pride in his city, labors for more than a year to turn that storybook season into an actual book. Jim Maggiore has done that with *Six More Wins*.

Jim has loyally served the B-Mets Booster Club in support of the team and has gone above and beyond the call of duty by penning this tale of the unforgettable 2014 Binghamton Mets. From the frigid days of April when five inches of snow blanketed the field just hours before Opening Day to that memorable September night when Steven Matz pitched the game of his life and 6,000 fans celebrated the B-Mets first title in two decades.

Using a collection of interviews with players, coaches, members of the front office and fellow fans, Jim has given readers the opportunity to see the championship season from multiple perspectives. He takes you inside the minds of those who saw the game from the field, the dugout, the seats and the radio booth, painting a picture of a team's journey from the disappointment of 2013 to the euphoria of 2014.

Enduring wet May nights and humid August evenings, Jim has done a masterful job of chronicling the season, with all its peaks and valleys. As a long-time resident of the Southern Tier, Jim has poetically woven the story of the B-Mets' success on the field with the resurgence of the city of Binghamton and its many proud residents.

Among the many storylines coinciding with the championship season, the city of Binghamton celebrated 100 seasons of professional baseball in 2014. Jim does a wonderful job of putting the B-Mets' title in perspective for a city rich in baseball tradition.

In addition to detailing the action on the field, Jim takes a step away from the diamond and chronicles the lives and stories of those strongly attached to the team, from the members of the B-Mets' tight-knit front office to the long-time fans who have been with the team from the very beginning.

Prior to the season, manager Pedro Lopez requested "six more wins." His team delivered.

However, the full story of the 2014 Binghamton Mets and their Eastern League championship is more than those half-dozen victories. It is the tale of a proud and resilient community on the rebound. It is the account of a rekindling love affair between a town and its team. It is a narrative of a team and a city that after getting knocked down, get back up again, dust themselves off and persevere in the face of adversity.

Overall, it is a reminder that baseball is more than just a game.

I know that you will enjoy the adventure.

Tim Heiman, Director of Media Relations and Broadcaster for the Binghamton Mets

Prologue: Warming Up in the Pen...

The story of the 2014 Binghamton Mets is one that will be discussed in this town for years to come. It is a story of resiliency—the 2013 team was swept from the first round of the playoffs by Trenton and before the 2014 season even started manager Pedro Lopez was calling for "Six More Wins."

This phrase became the mantra of the season, with fans nodding at each other in anticipation as the team stepped up its winning ways in early June, culminating in a five-game winning streak in the playoffs to bring home the first Eastern League Championship for Binghamton since 1994.

The *Six More Wins* moniker brought with it many subplots, including numerous players "stepping up" to fill the inevitable holes that popped up during the summer of 2014. The team lost its three best hitters within the same week in June, but amazingly, that is when the team started to play its best baseball. And when Dilson Herrera, the team's sparkplug, got the call to Flushing right before the playoffs began, the team went on to win six of its next eight games to win the championship!

Throughout the early months of the season the team struggled to leave .500 in its rearview mirror, with more than a few players struggling to hit their weight. Patience and perseverance were preached to the players by Lopez and his coaches, as they told the players to "trust the process" and the hits and wins would follow—and they did!

It's not a stretch to say the team's success in 2014 is a metaphor for the city of Binghamton and its surrounding areas. The Greater Binghamton Area has had more than its share of recent disappointment and heartbreak. Yet, Binghamton, like its championship team, is on the rebound. This book captures how a baseball team symbolizes the rebirth of a community and how the symbiotic nature of a minor league team and its town helps both to survive.

Baseball has always connected generations, as stories of the game's history have filtered from generation to generation.

The sport provides the perfect backdrop for reflection, providing an ebb and flow of action that allows time for serious discussion.

I was only about nine years old when I remember having one of my first serious discussions with my dad. We were at Shea Stadium, in 1965, watching the Mets play the Milwaukee Braves. It was my first baseball game and I was in awe of my surroundings. I remember telling my dad how great it would be to have season tickets. He looked at my gleeful face and offered, "Well if you work hard, you can go to college and get a good job and then you will be able to afford season tickets."

From that point on graduating from college became a goal. The conversation took no more than the time it took to have the teams change sides between innings, but it was a conversation whose theme carried me through my Long Island youth, as well as my graduation from Binghamton University. And yes, I even got those season tickets—to the Binghamton Mets!

As with the people discussed in "Binghamton is Our Hometown" chapter, I am happy to call Binghamton my home and am excited about the increasing number of Binghamton University students who are discovering downtown Binghamton. "Back in the day" when I went to Binghamton, the university was a cocoon, separated from the surrounding area. Now, with its educational facilities expanding into the city and its neighboring areas, and with its hosting of community events like the recent premiere of Hugh Grant's new movie, *The Rewrite*, the university has become a symbolic beacon for the area.

As you read these pages and get to know the players who brought home Binghamton's 2014 championship, you'll also learn about the heritage and happenings of the Greater Binghamton Area, and a few of its denizens.

I know I speak for all my neighbors when I say the Binghamton Mets are our team, Binghamton is our town, and we cannot be more proud! Enjoy the read.

Jim Maggiore, February 2015

Chapter 1. From Binghamton to the Big Leagues

Geographically, Binghamton is fewer than 200 miles from Flushing and a fearless driver can make it from NYSEG Stadium to Citi Field in three hours, but the professional development trip from Binghamton to Flushing is far longer, as the road from AA to the majors is littered with obstacles.

2014 marked the 23rd season of the Binghamton Mets, as well as the 100th year of minor league baseball in the Greater Binghamton Area. During its 100 years of supporting baseball, the Binghamton area has sent 748 players to the big leagues, including approximately 250 just since baseball returned to Binghamton in 1992.

Binghamton's distinction of being an affiliate of the Mets and/or Yankees for fifty-seven years sets it apart from other minor league cities. From 1932 to 1968, Binghamton was a farm club of the Yankees, breaking with this tradition only for the 1962-1964 seasons, when the area was affiliated with the Kansas City Athletics and Milwaukee Braves, respectively. During those "Yankee" years, the Greater Binghamton Area often hosted an exhibition game between the Yankees and the hometown Triplets. Such greats as Babe Ruth, Lou Gehrig, Joe DiMaggio, Bill Dickey, and Mickey Mantle played at Johnson Field, which hosted baseball from 1913 to 1968.

After the 1968 season, Johnson Field was demolished to make room for State Highway 17 and, without a stadium, the Binghamton area went without minor league baseball from 1969 to 1991. Baseball returned for the 1992 season, when the New York Mets purchased a Double-A franchise and moved it to Binghamton. The Mets were delighted to have its AA franchise in Binghamton, only 188 miles from Shea Stadium. The close geographical distance was not only convenient in transporting minor leaguers to the big club, but also made it easier for front office personnel to monitor the progress of its prospects, as well as scout the talent of opposing teams in the Eastern League. Finally, it also extended the reach of the New York Mets; the more upstate fans identified with the prospects at Binghamton, the more fans who might be enticed to make the trek to Flushing.

That 1992 team won the Eastern League Championship, defeating the Canton-Akron Indians, three games to two. Right hander Bobby Jones pitched a complete game in the final game of the championship series, winning 5-2, striking out nine and not walking a batter while retiring the final 16 hitters in a row. Tom Wegmann, a teammate of Jones on that '92 team recently recalled that "You just knew that when Jones got the ball that year you were going to win. He was lights out and you could tell he was going to become a major league pitcher." Jones won 12 games for the 92 B-Mets, and posted an astonishing 1.88 E.R.A. for the 158 innings he pitched. He went on to win 74 games for the New York Mets from 1993 – 2000, including a one-hit shutout of the Giants in Game 4 of the National League Division Championship in 2000.

The New York Mets owned the franchise for two years before selling it to a quintet of local owners early in 1994. Today, with its farm clubs spread across the country, from Las Vegas, where the AAA team plays, to St Lucie, Florida, where the high Class A team resides, and with various farm clubs in between, the Mets continue to relish having a team in central New York State. Since the autumn of 2010, when Sandy Alderson and his assistants, John Ricciardi and Paul DePodtesta, began running the front office of the New York Mets, Alderson or members of his immediate cabinet have been annual visitors to Binghamton.

When Alderson visits Binghamton, he prefers to sit in the stands and mingle with the fans, turning down his standing invitation to enjoy the game from the owner's skybox. Alderson enjoys visiting with the front office staff and owners, but when it comes to watching the game, he prefers the open air of the stadium. Jeff Wilpon, one of the owners of the New York Mets, has also made fairly regular trips to Binghamton and through the years has been known to gush to friends and acquaintances over the talent he has seen. During one of his visits in 2014, Wilpon met with catcher Kevin Plawecki, showing him how highly the organization regarded his talent.

The athletes who played in the Big Apple and also played between the white lines of the diamond in Binghamton comprise a who's who in New York City baseball, including such names as Whitey Ford, Thurman Munson, Joe Pepitone, Bobby Richardson, Edgardo Alfonzo, David Wright, Johnny Blanchard, Preston Wilson, and Tom Tresh, just to name a starting nine! You can name a pretty good pitching staff behind Ford too, including the likes of Vic Rashi, Matt Harvey, Ralph Terry, and Jon Niese! And for a bullpen you can start with Jim Coates, Jason Isringhausen, Heath Bell, Jeurys Familia and Jenrry Mejia. This list does not include the numerous athletes who have joined the Binghamton nine for a rehabilitation assignment from injury, including Billy Wagner, Steve Trachsel, and Moises Alou.

Since 1992 it sometimes appears as if the N.Y. Mets organization has been compelled to prove that the gap in play between AA and the majors can be as small as that of the one the fearless driver experiences. For every year the AA Binghamton Mets have been in existence, the team has sent an average of 11 players to Flushing. The reasons for this unusually high number are varied, not the least of which is that Binghamton has been fortunate to host talented youngsters. Another significant factor is that the N.Y. Mets, with the exception of the Omar Minaya era, have largely eschewed free agency for the last quarter of a century, relying on its farm system to be a feeder to the big leagues. The Alderson regime has been especially interested in increasing the overall level of play in the minor leagues, foregoing free agency to use the annual baseball draft to rebuild the farm system. A constant refrain of the Alderson era has been "Be Patient. Remain loyal. We are not that far away."

Syndergaard's Sizzling Spring Debut

Alderson's reliance on rebuilding through the farm system shows itself not only in the increased number of prospects in the pipeline, but in the "buzz" generated by scouts and the improving won-lost records of the teams in the minor league system. The story lines of recent spring training camps have focused on the upcoming talent instead of the returning veterans. An example of this was in full display on March 3, 2014, when the N.Y. Mets opposed the Atlanta Braves in Walt Disney World, the spring training home of the Braves. The media buzz was not about David Wright, New York's star third baseman, or about the Mets' chances of having a winning record. Instead, the pre-game stories were filled with stories of a prospect nicknamed "Thor."

At approximately 12:35 PM, when Noah Syndergaard popped out of the visitor's dugout at Disney's Champion© Stadium and started his stroll toward the left field bullpen, all eyes were on him. The unsophisticated fans called out for Noah's autograph, "Noah, can you sign a few?", "Noah, got a minute?"

The diehards, however, knew calling out for an autograph on the day a pitcher starts is futile. An unwritten rule of baseball is that on the day a pitcher starts, he remains focused on his assignment and does not stray by signing autographs. Ron Darling, in his book *Complete Game*, describes his demeanor on the days he pitched:

"Leave me alone. That's the message I put out to the world on days I was due to pitch. Even to my wife and kids, the message was much the same: leave me alone so I can do my thing and prepare for battle."

As Syndergaard headed toward the bullpen area, scores of Mets fans shouted out words of encouragement, "Go get 'em Noah!", "Good luck, Noah!"

Ten minutes later, after he had stretched, Syndergaard began warming up. He had attracted a large crowd, as fans adorned in blue and orange lined the bullpen railing.

Noah Syndergaard warming up in the bullpen for his debut in a major league uniform at Lake Buena Vista on 3/3/2014.

      This is Syndergaard's first appearance in a major league game. He is the Mets' top prospect, coming to the Mets with Travis d'Arnaud as part of the for R.A. (Robert Allan) Dickey trade in February 2013. The 2014 edition of the *Baseball Prospect Handbook*, published by Baseball America, says Syndergaard has a ceiling of being a # 2 starter for a championship team.

      In 2013, the then 20-year-old Syndergaard was brilliant in his debut season in the Mets' organization, going 9-4, striking out 133 batters over 118 innings as he split his time between high Class A (St. Lucie) and AA (Binghamton). At Binghamton he was simply brilliant, going 6-1 with a 3.00 E.R.A, with one bad start inflating his E.R.A, as he was dominating in 10 of his 11 starts.

      His signature pitch is a fastball that sits at 94-95 and touches 98 mph, and he commands both sides of the plate and both planes (high and low) of the strike zone with it. He also has a big breaking curveball, which Terry Collins called the "hook from hell" the first time he saw Syndergaard throw. It seemed as if the only time Eastern League batters could touch Syndergaard was when he left his changeup up in the zone. Scouts got wide-eyed looking at him on the mound, realizing that if the only negative thing you can say about a twenty-year-old who throws heat is that he has an inconsistent changeup, you are watching a potential franchise star.

Syndergaard was named the best pitching prospect in both the Florida State and Eastern League in 2013 and prognosticators and pundits are targeting the development of his changeup as the key in having Syndergaard improve his success rate against left hitters, as lefties hit .296 against him in 2013, while right-handed batters hit a feeble .196.

Syndergaard does not disappoint Collins, the fans, or the scouts on this day. The only things hanging are the heads of the Braves as they return to the dugout. His first pitch is 98 mph and Jason Heywood, the Braves leadoff hitter, just waves at it for strike one. Syndergaard goes on to strike him out and allows only one base runner in two innings of work.

At the end of the game, the Braves are effusive with their praise. Evan Gattis, the Braves' catcher remarks on Syndergaard's stuff: "He's real. He should turn out to be pretty good."

Justin Upton chimes in, "Harvey's Harvey, but him (Syndergaard) and Wheeler are definitely a close second."

Syndergaard expressed relief after his debut, feeling a bit of the pressure of carrying great expectations on his shoulders, as he tells Adam Rubin of ESPN: "That's a lot of weight coming off my shoulders right there."

Indeed, if the Mets' travails were a film noir, Syndergaard's talent would be the stuff "dreams are made of," the famous line issued by Humphrey Bogart to close the fabled film, *The Maltese Falcon*.

Syndergaard is just one of the ex-Binghamton players that Sandy Alderson hopes will be the foundation for good fortune for his organization. Righty pitcher Rafael Montero spent half the year in Binghamton in 2013 before being promoted to Las Vegas and opened almost as many eyes as Syndergaard, going 7-3, with a 2.43 E.R.A. In 67 innings he struck out 72 batters and only walked 10.

Syndergaard and Montero are targeted for the Las Vegas rotation at the start of 2014 and in spring training, beat reporters and media personnel are estimating that both could be in Citi Field before mid-season. Though they are two of the biggest recent prospects emanating from Binghamton, they are far from alone. Of the 64 players invited to spring training in 2014, no fewer than 40 of them played in Binghamton. The N.Y. Mets' 40-man roster alone contains 27 players who came up through Binghamton and the 25-man roster includes 16 ex-Binghamton Mets!

Players in the lower minors look forward to spending time in Binghamton; they know playing well there has become a calling card to Citi Field.

There is optimism among Mets fans for the years 2014 and beyond, due to the large number of pitching prospects that have arrived (e.g., Matt Harvey, Jon Niese, Zack Wheeler) and the ones that are about to make an impact (Jake deGrom, Noah Syndergaard, Jeurys Familia, Rafael Montero, and Jenrry Mejia).

2014 has brought back the memories of 1994, when the regime of Steve Phillips touted the players from Binghamton's 1994 championship team as leading the way to respectability, including: Bill Pulsipher, Jason Isringhausen, Edgardo Alfonzo, and Rey Ordonez. Alfonzo, now a spring training and minor league instructor for the New York Mets, recalled that team fondly when, on the back fields of St. Lucie in spring training, he was approached by some fans from Binghamton.

"Hi Edgardo, I came down all the way from Binghamton and remember you and that great team in 1994!"

"Ah, Binghamton, what a great team," Alfonzo said with a smile as he paused to sign autographs. He rattled off names as if twenty years were twenty minutes.

"We had a guy named Pulsipher and he was not too bad was he? What a game he pitched in the playoffs!"

"Yeah, he just threw a no hitter in the playoffs," recalled the Binghamtonians, proudly remembering that Pulsipher no hit the Harrisburg Senators in the first round of the playoffs.

#	Name	#	Name	#	Name	#	Name
0	Omar Quintanilla*	27	*Jeurys Famila*	49	*Jon Niese*	72	Kevin Plawecki*
1	Chris Young	28	*Daniel Murphy*	50	*Rafael Montero**	73	*Adam Kolarek**
2	Anthony Seratelli*	29	*Ike Davis*	52	Carlos Torres	74	*Cory Vaughn**
3	Curtis Granderson	30	Andrew Brown	53	Jeremy Hefner*	75	*Cory Mazzoni**
4	Wilmer Flores	32	John Lannan*	55	*Noah Syndergaard**	76	*Chasen Braford**
5	David Wright	33	*Matt Harvey*	56	Scott Rice	77	Brandon Nimmo*
6	Matt den Dekker	34	Joel Carreno*	58	*Jenrry Mejia*	79	*John Church**
9	Kirk Nieuwenhuis	35	Dillon Gee	60	Brandon Allen*	80	*Logan Verrett**
11	Ruben Tejeda	36	Juan Centeno	61	Miguel Socolovich	81	*Jack Leathersich*
12	Juan Lagares	38	Vic Black	62	*Erik Goeddel*	82	Matt Clark
13	Josh Satin	39	*Bobby Parnell*	63	Steven Matz		**Field Staff**
15	Travis d'Arnaud	40	Bartolo Colon	64	*Danny Muno**	10	Terry Collins
16	Daisuke Matsuzaka*	43	Ryan Reid	65	Cesar Puello*	7	Bob Geren
19	Zach Lutz	44	Kyle Farnsworth*	66	Josh Edgin	18	*Tim Teufel*
20	Anthony Recker	45	*Zack Wheeler*	67	Dustin Lawley*	26	Tom Goodwin
21	Lucas Duda	46	*Jeff Walters*	68	Erik Campbell*	51	Dave Hudgens
22	Eric Young	47	Jose Valverde*	70	*Wilfredo Tovar*	59	Dan Warthen
23	Taylor Teagarden*	48	*Jacob deGrom*	71	*Gonzales Germen*		

The 2014 Spring Training Roster. *Italics* indicate a former Binghamton Met. An asterisk indicates the player was not on the 40-man roster for 2014 spring training.

Alfonzo was smiling now, making eye contact with the fans. "That was a great year, a great team." Alfonzo stated he probably would be visiting Binghamton a few times during the season as part of his duties as a roving minor league instructor and he was looking forward to his return. When Alfonzo was elected to the Binghamton Baseball Shrine in 2004, he was unable to attend, so his next visit to Binghamton would be his first since that championship season of 1994.

Binghamton Mets' hitting coach Luis Natera recognized the fans from Binghamton and joked with them "I'll be going back to Binghamton, I need to buy a house there," he said with a big smile, as he anticipated his return to Binghamton for his seventh consecutive season.

Author's Note: In June 2014, Natera was promoted to assistant hitting coach of the New York Mets, breaking his run in Binghamton. Ironically, in 2015, however, he returns to Binghamton as its hitting coach once again.

The Road to Flushing Passes through Binghamton

The jump from A to AA is considered by many to be the biggest jump in talent in professional baseball, even bigger than the jump from AAA to the big leagues. When a player performs well at AA, he is pegged as having "major league talent." The key then becomes harnessing that talent and refining the mental part of the game to bring out the talent on a daily basis. Baseball is a grind; nothing emphasizes that point more than the minors.

In Class A, the pitchers rely on their fastball, and focus on commanding it. They are taught that good control goes far beyond having a good innings pitched-to-walk ratio. They are told to locate the fastball on both sides of the plate, and taught when to throw a four-seamer up in the zone or a two-seamer low in the zone. The primary goal of a pitcher toiling in Class A is to show the organization that he has COMMAND of the fastball. Once he masters that, he can move up the ladder and generally, in AA, is where he will be asked to start to show command of his secondary pitches.

Whereas a pitcher can be successful in Class A with one "plus" offering, in AA to achieve success, the pitcher needs to show two or three pitches, so that hitters cannot just "sit" on the fastball. The focus is on his being able to command these secondary pitches within the strike zone.

When the call to AAA comes, consistency and command are the tickets in demand. And with the pressure to get immediate returns on players before they can turn to arbitration or free agency to increase their salary, often an organization prefers a prospect's stay in AAA be short.

On the hitting side of the ledger, the progression follows a similar path. In Class A the batter shows he has the ability to hit a fastball and ideally, shows a command of the strike zone from a batter's point of view. Having a good knowledge of the strike zone means far more than not chasing pitches. The more a batter can zero in on the type of pitch he can handle, the more chances for success he has. In AA, the hitting task becomes more difficult, as the pitchers mix in more curveballs, changeups, and off-speed deliveries to keep the hitters off balance. The hitters can no longer just afford to "sit" on a fastball. They have to show the ability to "grind out" an at bat, take a pitcher's pitch in the zone for a strike, or if they have two strikes, show the ability to foul off a pitch to keep alive.

For the New York Mets, Binghamton's AA team has been an instrumental stop on the road to Flushing. Many of the current Mets proved themselves as they toiled at Binghamton. For David Wright, who played in Binghamton for the first two months of the 2004 season, it was where he first started to believe he could make the big leagues, as he hit ten homers, knocked in forty runs and hit a whopping .363!

For Daniel Murphy, it was teaming with Nick Evans and Mike Carp to form a formidable 3-4-5 in the lineup and, just as important as his 13 homers, 67 RBIs and .308 batting average were that year, was his two-week stint at second base. Murphy, then a third baseman and knowing that David Wright was firmly entrenched there, was happy to show the Mets his versatility in manning second. His play at second in 2008 under manager Maki Oliveras gave him the confidence to make the transition to second after earlier attempts to convert him to a left fielder failed in the big leagues.

2012 was the second year in Binghamton for Juan Lagares, but it was his first year in the organization as a full-time center fielder. His sterling defensive play for manager Pedro Lopez enabled Mets' brass to realize his future was as a center fielder. Up until that 2012 season, Matt den Dekker was considered the premier defensive outfielder in the system. Though den Dekker is no slouch in the outfield, Lagares has proven his defensive prowess, as he won a Rawlings Gold Glove award in 2014.

Lucas Duda was drafted in the seventh round of the 2007 baseball draft and in 2009 he found himself playing left field and first base for Binghamton, where he showed both power and patience at the plate and hit at a .281 clip. Double A was a test for Duda, as he needed to increase his power and show he could hit southpaws as well as hit breaking pitches. Duda showed mixed success in that '09 season, hitting homers at a disappointing rate of one for every 43 at bats, but seeing his strikeout ratio decrease from once every 3.7 at bats to one for every 4.3 at bats. His on base percentage rose, from .358 to .380. Though not showing enough power to warrant a promotion to AAA, Duda's return to AA in 2010 was a short one, as that year he showed drastic improvement. In only 161 at bats he hit six homers and his on base percentage was an off-the-charts .411 clip. He continued his torrid pace at Buffalo, then the AAA affiliate of the NY Mets, and was in the big leagues by the end of 2010.

Matt Harvey's stay in AA was the least successful of his stops in professional baseball. Highly touted after pitching for the University of North Carolina for three years, Harvey was the seventh pick of the 2010 amateur baseball draft. After pitching dominantly in the Florida State League in 2011, going 8-2 in 14 starts and striking out 92 hitters in 79 innings, Harvey found the transition to AA baseball a challenging one. In 12 starts he went 5-3 with a 4.53 E.R.A, with his strikeouts-to-innings pitched ratio decreasing and his walks-to-innings pitched increasing from his work in the Florida State League. For Harvey, his stay in

Binghamton in 2011 was all about developing his secondary pitches. Though the Mets wanted to see results, they were more interested in seeing Harvey develop as a pitcher, learning to trust his secondary stuff. The organization knew the fastball was there, they wanted to see more of the curve, slider and the changeup. Harvey showed enough that the Mets promoted him twice in 2012, first to Buffalo and then to the big leagues, where he seemed to find another level.

Once he got to the big leagues, it all changed for Harvey. "I no longer had to focus on developing pitches," he explained. "I could now just focus on getting the hitters out." Once in the big leagues, Harvey relished the notion of challenging hitters with high fastballs. By moving his fastball both up and down in the zone, Harvey kept the hitters off balance. Also, the years in the minors spent developing his secondary pitches now gave him the luxury of being able to throw his sliders and changeups when major league hitters were looking for fastballs. And finally, Harvey's mental approach to the game became keener. This was the big leagues, and now "The results really mattered," he explained. The spotlight was on him and his personality filled the circle.

Ironically, the best pitcher on that Binghamton team of 2011 was none other than Collin McHugh, a soft-tossing right hander who threw about six to eight miles slower than Harvey. In August of 2011, Sandy Alderson visited NYSEG Stadium and more than one fan remarked to him that "That McHugh, he has been the best pitcher on this team!" McHugh was dominant, going 8-2 with a 2.89 E.R.A, while striking out 100 batters in 93 innings, and walking 32. McHugh, only an 18th-round pick in the 2008 amateur draft, apparently did not "wow" the organization enough, however, as he was traded for Eric Young, Jr. in 2013.

All McHugh did in 2014 was have a year every bit as good as the National League Rookie-of-the-Year, Jacob deGrom, going 11-9, with a 2.73 ERA in 154.2 innings pitched, with 157 strikeouts for Houston. If the Astros had remained in the National League, McHugh might very well have beaten out deGrom for rookie of the year honors.

While at Binghamton, McHugh honed in on those things on the mound that he could control and forgot about things that he couldn't. In his blog, *Another Day Older, Another Day Wiser*, Collin related a lesson that Phil Regan, the pitching coach at St. Lucie had taught him earlier that year, before his promotion to AA. McHugh explained, "Our pitching coach challenged us to make a list of five goals for the year. He stressed the importance of having tangible milestones to continually look towards during a long, grinding season." So Colin dutifully came up with his list: 1) Win 10 games; 2) Throw 150 innings; 3) Walk fewer than 38 guys (his prior year's total); 4) Strike out nine hitters per nine innings; 5) Not miss a start due to injury.

"Taking out a red pen, reminding me of my English 101 critiques, Regan crossed out # 1, 2, and 5. He then said something so profound. 'Control what you can control. Don't try to control things over which you have no control.' " McHugh has taken that advice to heart, focusing on the execution of his pitches, the *process of pitching*, and not worrying about what happens after that.

McHugh is still remembered fondly by the staff and fans. "He's just one of the all-time good guys," remarks group sales director Eddie Saunders. "He was appreciative of all those little things we did that made his job easier and was always eager to stop and chat. Just a regular, unassuming guy, who remained an everyday guy even though he realized that when he put on a uniform, he became 'superman' to a lot of the fans."

No doubt there is a book in McHugh's future. His blog offerings are informative, insightful and provocative. During his stay in Binghamton, I spoke to him a few times about the work of Dirk Hayhurst, the then minor league pitcher who had written the best-selling book, *The Bullpen Gospels*. Though he hadn't read the book yet, he was aware of Hayhurst's success and he admitted he thought about writing a book someday. When we discussed some of his blog entries, he was always appreciative that someone had taken the time to read his work and was interested in discussing it.

There are many rungs on the minor league ladder for the Mets—from the rookie leagues of Kingsport and the Gulf Coast

League to short season Brooklyn to low-A Savannah, to high-A ball in St. Lucie, to AA in Binghamton and AAA in Las Vegas. Binghamton sits not only at the crossroads of Interstates 81 and 86 in New York State, but also at the crossroads of the prospect ladder for the Met organization. Frank Sinatra added to the luster of New York City with his famous description of the city as "If you can make it here, you can make it anywhere…New York, New York…"

Binghamton's version of the song, etched in the minds of all those who inhabit the clubhouse is "Binghamton…if I do well here, I can make it in New York!"

Chapter 2. Six More Wins

On Monday, January 13th, 2014, the New York Mets unknowingly gave Binghamton baseball fans their year-long theme for 2014. With the announcement that the coaching staff from the 2012 and 2013 teams would return for its third season at NYSEG Stadium, the year's focus became clear—Six More Wins.

The press release for the Binghamton Mets nailed it in its first sentence. "Fresh off one of the best seasons in Binghamton Mets history, the New York Mets announced Monday that manager Pedro Lopez, hitting coach Luis Natera and pitching coach Glenn Abbott will return to guide the Double-A club in 2014."

In the world of AA baseball, where teams dramatically change from year to year, and often from the first half of the season to the second half, Lopez, Abbot, and Natera provided a bedrock for success and a yearning for the team to not only be repeat winners of the Eastern League's Eastern Division, but to be victors in the playoffs as well. In 2013 the Binghamton Mets needed six wins in the playoffs to become Eastern League Champions, but they failed to get even one.

The coaching trio remembered how they exited the playoffs, losing three straight to the Trenton Thunder, the affiliate of the N.Y. Yankees, in the first round, where the turning point came in the very first game. The B-Mets took a 5-3 lead into the bottom of the ninth with closer Jeff Walters on the mound. Walters quickly got Mason Williams looking at a third strike and Ramon Flores on a groundout to first—two outs no one on, a two-run lead and the best closer in the league on the mound.

Lopez, Abbot, and Natera were smiling inside with anticipation.

But the baseball gods had other ideas and Trenton started to live up to its moniker as a rain of base hits fell at *Arm and Hammer Stadium* in New Jersey. Jose Pirela doubled; Gary

Sanchez singled, knocking in Pirela. "No problem," thought Walters, still only one out to go. Then the season turned on a bleeder as Tyler Austin hit a seeing-eye single on a grounder up the middle. "Still need only one more out," thought Lopez in the dugout, never considering a pitching change. When Casey Stevensen followed with a double to left to tie the game, the fans in Trenton turned the stadium into a full-fledged storm.

"OK, we get the next guy" and then win it in extra innings," thought Abbot.

But outfielder Ben Gamel singles and the Thunder win.

Two outs, nobody on, but five straight hits doom the Mets. Trenton leads the series, 1-0.

The Mets and Darin Gorski are hard-luck losers the next night in Trenton, as Mikey O'Brien pitches the game of his life and beats the Mets, 2-1.

The next night, the series comes to *New York State Electric and Gas* (NYSEG) Stadium, and the concrete yard at the corner of Henry and Fayette Streets is packed. Binghamton's denizens are determined not to see the season die this night. Lopez is so sure the Mets will win that he does not even think about packing for the off season. He and his team still had six more wins to get!

NYSEG Stadium was electric that night, with the Binghamton faithful feeling just like Lopez. A fan behind the home dugout held a huge cutout of the face of Allan Dykstra, the team's cleanup hitter and MVP. Somehow, though, the B-Mets do not score a run, despite getting 11 hits and six walks. The team loses 3-0. Some Binghamton fans are still smarting over the umpire's calls that went against the Mets that night, especially the runner's interference call against second baseman Danny Muno in the bottom of the seventh. A benches-clearing fracas ensued, ending with the ouster of Lopez, Muno, and shortstop Wilfredo Tovar.

Two innings later the whole team is sent packing.

The 2013 season is about to die for the B-Mets, as the 7th-inning melee draws to an end.

Lopez spent a lot of time in the home clubhouse that night, replaying the game in his mind and trying to shake the sadness from within. In talking with beat reporter Lynn Worthy he offered that he would gladly trade the individual honors he received this year in exchange for a championship ring.

Lopez's trophy case was impressive as he was named "Eastern League Manager of the Year," as well as having *Baseball America* recognize him as the "Best Managing Prospect" in the Eastern League. Though the organization rewarded him by having him spend the final month of the season with the N.Y. Mets in Citi Field, Lopez could not shake the memory of being swept by Trenton. He had fallen six wins short of his goal for the team, to win both rounds of the playoffs for the Eastern League Championship.

Now, in January of 2014 it looks as if Lopez and his coaches will have a roster populated with many who swallowed that bitter playoff loss. An abundance of pitching prospects in the upper tiers of the New York Mets' system and a logjam of outfielders in AAA guarantee the return of a veteran team to Binghamton.

With the additions of Curtis Granderson and Chris Young to the big league team, few outfield spots are open in Vegas, where Matt den Dekker, Kurt Nieuwenhuis, and Cesar Puello are the leading candidates to man the outfield on an everyday basis, which means many of the outfielders from the 2013 team will find themselves back in Binghamton in 2014. At this point the N.Y. Mets appear to have few openings in their projected 12-man pitching staff either, leaving pitchers such as Rafael Montero, Noah Syndergaard, Jacob deGrom, Cory Mazzoni, Jeff Walters, and Logan Verrett to toil for Vegas. That logjam dictates the Binghamton pitching staff will be filled with many AA veterans as well.

The returning veterans to Binghamton will be supplemented with a number of rookies who had promising seasons last year in St. Lucie, many of them manning the infield.

Though snow covers the frozen ground of Binghamton and sub-zero days fill the January and February calendar, the hearts of baseball fans in the Southern Tier are warm with thoughts of six more wins for the coming season.

Welcome Back

On Wednesday, April 2nd, 450 people pack into the ballroom at the Doubletree Hilton Hotel in downtown Binghamton, just a few blocks from NYSEG Stadium, where the B-Mets open the season the next day against the Akron RubberDucks. Binghamton Mets President Michel Urda addresses Binghamton's faithful fans from a dais at the front of the room.

Attendees have chosen this welcome home dinner over the dedication ceremony of a local high school baseball stadium whose invited guests included Hall of Famers Johnny Bench, Joe Morgan, and Goose Gossage. Tom Tull, chairman and chief executive officer of *Legendary Entertainment*, a Hollywood-area film production company that has produced such films as

Batman, and *42*, funded the $2.2 million project for a state-of-the-art baseball facility that included a synthetic-turf surface, dugouts, press box, and bleachers.

Tull was a member of the Maine-Endwell 1988 graduating class and he is honored to be giving something back to his hometown. He tells the *Binghamton Press & Sun Bulletin*:

"I'm very proud to have come from this area. There's a work ethic here, people are nice here, genuinely nice human brings. I'm very proud of the fact that I grew up here and this is an incredible day for me to stand here and look at the field."

Tull played football and baseball during high school and the school's current baseball coach, Gary Crooks, is the same coach for whom Tull played two varsity baseball seasons. Tull takes an extra added measure of pleasure in dedicating the field as *Gary Crooks Field.*

Back at the welcome home dinner, shortly after Tull delivers his remarks 10 miles to the west, Urda elaborates how baseball can be a place to heal. Only two days earlier, Johnson City police officer Dave Smith, an 18-year veteran of the force, had just started his tour of duty when he was called to check on a disturbance at the nearby Southern Tier Imaging building. He arrives on the scene at approximately 7:05 A.M.

Within minutes, he is dead.

A deranged man approached his car as soon as Smith pulled into the parking lot and, as Smith tried to calm the man from the seat of his police car, the man wrestles Smith's gun away and shoots and kills him. In a hail of gunfire, the killer is in turn killed by Smith's backup. Two men are dead and there is no hint of an answer to the question of "Why?"

Police Chief Joseph Zikuski conducted his emotion-filled press conference on Monday with a voice that cracked and eyes that swelled with sadness. Commenting on Smith, Zikuski said, "He was a good officer, he's going to be greatly missed."

Neighbors of the shooter cannot believe what they are told.

"He was a really wonderful neighbor," neighbor Holly VanderBunt, told *Press and Sun Bulletin* reporter Jon Harris. "We're just in total shock."

Tomorrow hundreds of people from the community will attend Smith's funeral; he is the first Johnson City police officer to lose his life in the line of duty since 1925. Urda recognizes the pain of the community. "We have been through a lot the past few days. Tomorrow I hope baseball can start the healing process," he states. "The ballpark can be our oasis of peace."

This is not the first time that baseball has served to heal the community. In recent years, all too often baseball has had to provide an escape for tragedy. Almost five years to the day, on April 3rd, in 2009, another deranged man killed 13 people in Binghamton's Civic Association Center before killing himself. This mass murder and suicide saw national media descend upon Binghamton as the nation tried to understand the shooting.

And in June of 2006 and September of 2011, the area became the victim of devastating flooding from the Susquehanna River.

At NYSEG Stadium, moments of silence were held, donation stations were set up, and the community reflected and took solace in the playing of a game as part of its recovery from these national stories of frustration and despair.

Urda ends his speech on an optimistic note, looking at manager Pedro Lopez and saying "Six more wins!" For as good as 2013 was, Urda hopes for a championship team in 2014.

When Lopez takes the podium, he does not shy away from the challenge. He has already filled in Urda of his goal for winning six more games, and Urda has gladly taken up the rallying cry.

"When we were looking over the roster last night, Abby and Louie and I looked at one another and we realized, this is a better team on paper than the one we had last year." Lopez is looking into the audience now, pausing for effect. He is genuinely excited about the makeup of this team, with 16 players returning from last year.

Lopez repeats his feelings to the audience, "On paper, this team is better than last year's." Seven of the fourteen position players are returning: catchers Xorge Carrillo and Blake Forsythe; infielders Matt Reynolds (one game in 2013) and

Wilfredo Tovar; and outfielders Darrell Ceciliani, Travis Taijeron, and Cory Vaughn.

The members of the pitching staff carry the theme of a veteran-laden roster even further. The fifteen pitchers slated to start the season at Binghamton include: Hamilton Bennett, Matt Bowman, Chasen Bradford, TJ Chism, John Church, Angel Cuan, Darin Gorski, Adam Kolarek, Rainy Lara, Jack Leathersich, Greg Peavey, Tyler Pill, Hansel Robles, Cody Satterwhite, and Jon Velasquez. No fewer than nine of these pitchers spent time with Binghamton in 2013: Bennett, Bradford, Church, Cuan, Gorski, Kolarek, Leathersich, Peavey and Pill.

The returning veterans will be supplemented with a number of rookies who had promising seasons last year in St. Lucie, including shortstop/second baseman Matt Reynolds; first baseman/DH Jayce Boyd; and third baseman/left fielder Dustin Lawley. The roster is rounded out with perhaps its two most important additions, two veteran minor league hitters who are hoping to use AA to get a shot at the big leagues: infielder/outfielder Brian Burgamy and first baseman/outfielder Matt Clark. Though neither played in the minors last year, both had excellent years in professional ball: Clark had a great year in Japan and Burgamy hand an excellent season playing in independent ball.

Chapter 3. April: Our Team. Our Town. Our Pride.

Opening Night on Thursday, April 3rd, started with a special treat for the fans—the temperature for the 6:35 first pitch did not reach 60 degrees, which meant the attendees could turn their ticket stubs in for a free pass to a game the following Monday or Tuesday, fulfilling an offer made by Urda during his speech at the welcome home dinner the night before.

Lefty Darin Gorski, returning for his third year in Binghamton, took the mound against Akron's Cody Anderson, the fifth-rated prospect for the Cleveland Indians. Gorski is the prototypical "crafty lefty," throwing his pitchers in the range of 75 mph to 87, topping out at 89, relying on command and control to be effective. Gorski is a minor league version of Tommy Glavine, relying on location instead of velocity for getting his outs. Selected by the New York Mets in the seventh round of the 2009 amateur draft out of Pennsylvania's Kutztown University, 2014 marks Gorski's sixth year in the Mets' organization. He began 2013 in the starting rotation of AAA Las Vegas, but hurt his shoulder after starting only three games and has been trying to get back to AAA ever since. He has lost a few miles off of his fastball, topping out at 89 mph now instead of 91.

Though he was selected as the Mets' organizational pitcher of the year as recently as 2011, when he won 11 games for St. Lucie, time is not on Darin's side. He'll turn 27 after the season and this year is critical for him. A logjam of prospects at Las Vegas has sent Gorski back to Binghamton and he takes a rear seat to the likes of Montero, Syndergaard, deGrom, Mazzoni, and Verret. Any thought of turning Gorski into a reliever this year was quickly forgotten due to the number of lefty relievers who have had success in the minors, including Jack Leathersich, Adam Kolarek, and TJ Chism, all of whom find themselves in Binghamton to start the season.

Gorski is a popular player who carries a perpetual smile, with a wide-eyed demeanor that shows he just loves to play the game. He is a fan favorite, always having time not only to sign autographs, but to engage in friendly banter as well.

Gorski is the only lefty in the rotation that starts the season, as behind him are righties Rainy Lara, Tyler Pill, Hansel Robles, Greg Peavey and Matt Bowman. The organization watches the number of innings pitched each season by its young pitchers, holding them to a 30-35% increase in the number of innings pitched on a year-to-year basis. Consequently, the six-man starting staff for the Binghamton Mets is ideal.

It turned out that the free ducats for the low temperature were the only thing Mets fans would celebrate on this Opening Night, however, as the Akron RubberDucks beat them, 7-1. The game was a lackluster effort by the Mets, as they mustered only four hits while their pitchers walked 11 and hit a batter.

The game took an abrupt turn for the worse when the bullpen took over, as the game was close for six innings, with the RubberDucks holding a scant 2-1 lead. But in the final three innings the Binghamton bullpen did a quick imitation of the early-season New York Mets bullpen, displaying a lack of control and effectiveness. Lefty TJ Chism and righty John Church combined to turn a close game into a rout, giving up five runs on five hits, with three walks in the final third of the game.

The B-Mets tonight make 18 outs on the ground and strike out five times, never getting a runner past first after they scored their run in the first. Simply stated, it is one of those losses that you want to flush from your memory immediately after the game is over. Or, as veteran infielder Brian Burgamy would say, "Get out the Etch-a-Sketch®, turn it upside down and shake it out!"

There were only two bright spots the entire night—Darrell Ceciliani's first inning triple and Jack Leathersich's striking out the side in the eighth inning.

Earlier in the day the New York Mets lost their third straight to the Washington Nationals, 8-2, and New York Mets' manager Terry Collins did not mince words as he exhorted on the need to get better performance from his bullpen in his post-game press conference.

"It was tough….We've got to come out of that bullpen and we've got to start throwing some strikes. When we're successful, it's because you make the other team swing the bat. Not that they can't get a hit, but when you're behind in the count, you're going to get in trouble in this league."

Zack Wheeler held the Nationals to three runs in six innings, but his bullpen gave up five runs in the final three innings, walking three and pitching behind in most counts, letting the Nationals turn the game into a laugher. Though the bullpen meditations were from Collins, they might just have well have come from B-Mets' manager Pedro Lopez.

When pitchers work from behind, it's usually just a matter of time before the hitters make them pay. If the batter is sitting with a 2-0 or 3-1 count, he not only can look for a fastball, but he can look for a fastball in a location that he likes, and if the pitch isn't where he wants it, he can let it go by, or as they say in the broadcast booth, he can "spit on it."

In amateur ball and lower levels of the minor leagues, *being selective at the plate* translates to making sure you are not swinging at pitches out of the strike zone. But as you move up the minor league ladder, being selective means looking for pitches that you know you can handle and letting the others go by, even if they are a called first or second strike.

Hall of Fame pitcher Don Sutton, during a recent interview during a Hall of Fame induction weekend summed up the importance of pitching ahead in the count and having command: "I was told at a young age there were two secrets to pitching: the first was to be able to throw your fastball to get ahead in the count, 0-2, and the second was that you also had to be able to throw something other than a fastball for a strike when you were behind, 2-0."

The following afternoon the B-Mets start arriving at the park at around 1 p.m. Though the game starts at 7, the unofficial time for players to report is between 1 and 1:30 p.m., as every player has pre-game work to do. The pitchers stretch and run, and throw bullpens on scheduled days and then shag flies in the outfield. The position players usually stretch and review scouting reports, then take batting and infield practice. As the players saunter in from the parking lot, the warmth and sunshine of Florida are distant memories. The day is packaged in gray, from the low slate sky to the asphalt roads that absorb a seemingly nonexistent sky. There is no snow, but there is rain and it is cold, the wind is strong and it is a day that shuns baseball.

Mercifully, the game is called shortly after the gates open.

No doubt today is the type of day the minor leaguers dread; it is a night that holds only the promise of television in their overcrowded apartments. There will be no going out to eat at a nice restaurant, not unless their parents came into town for opening weekend, for minor league salaries are "minor" in every way. A rainout might be welcomed in the dog days of the season, giving the players' bodies a chance to rejuvenate, but so early in the season, the players need repetition to establish a rhythm in their new surroundings. The rainout tonight just means they've got to be at the park by 9 a.m. tomorrow for a 1 p.m. doubleheader.

As I leave the park along with the handful of fans that challenged the weather, I recall when rainouts used to bring a smile to my face, as in the 1960's when the Mets' television announcers, Lindsey Nelson, Bob Murphy, and Ralph Kiner filled the airwaves with stories of baseball seasons past. Kiner seemed to have a story for every day he walked the earth, and there were plenty of those. He was 92 years old when he passed away in January of 2014.

Growing up a Mets fan on Long Island meant listening to stories of how Ralph dated Hollywood legends Elizabeth Taylor and Janet Leigh and how Bing Crosby, then owner of the Pirates, would arrange for dates for Ralph. It also meant learning how the area behind the left field fence at old Forbes Field evolved from "Greenberg Gardens" to "Kiner's Korner." And, if the rain delay became an extremely long one, then WOR TV would cut away to an old baseball movie like "Fear Strikes Out," with Anthony Perkins portraying Jimmy Piersall and Karl Malden his stern father; or the original "The Kid from Left Field," starring Dan

Daily. Diehard baseball fan that I was in my youth, I actually enjoyed rainouts, as it gave me a window to vintage baseball movies and old-time chatter that otherwise I would have missed. Today, if a rainout happens, the TV station returns you to normal programming, depriving today's youth of a history lesson.

The passing of time is not always progress.

Francisco Lindor Shines

On Saturday the sun did not make an appearance, but neither did rain or snow, so the weather was good enough for the Mets and RubberDucks to get in two games. The B-Mets beat the Akron RubberDucks, 6-3, in the first game, but lose the second, 3-0, giving them a 1-2 record at the season's start. But the scores of the game are insignificant; this day turns out to be the Francisco Lindor show as the 20-year-old shortstop shows why he is the top-rated prospect for the Indians and ranked the #13 overall prospect in baseball by Major League Baseball. On a day that saw the temperature sitting at 39 degrees in the second inning of the first game, Lindor had the congregation shouting his name in appreciation mid-way through the second game.

In the first game, Lindor hit a two-run homer and in the nightcap he went 2-4, giving him a three-for-eight day with two RBIs, a homer and a run scored, not to mention a .385 batting average to start the season. Lindor's hitting, however, was not what was most memorable about his day. It was his defensive wizardry in the second game that put an exclamation point on his prospect status. In the bottom of the second, with one out and outfielder Travis Taijeron on first, second baseman Matt Reynolds hit a ground ball up the middle that had Binghamton fans thinking runners on first and third, but Lindor had other ideas. He ranged far to his left, dove behind second, snared the ball and then, with Taijeron bearing down on Akron second baseman Joe Wendle, Lindor somehow managed to flip the ball to Wendle from his glove to get a force out.

Respectful applause concluded this play on an April day that imitated a Saturday afternoon closer to February 5th than

April 5th. In the bottom of the sixth, Lindor gave an encore performance, surpassing his earlier fielding gem. Brian Burgamy, the Mets' first baseman, led off the inning with a hard ground ball up the middle and once again, Lindor was off and running. When he was behind second, Lindor stretched to his limit, gloved the ball, and, as his momentum carried him to right field, he turned and threw to first, nailing Burgamy. As the applause rippled through the stadium, Lindor trotted back to short, letting a small smile ruin his stoic face. His play led to a 1-2-3 inning for the RubberDucks and the Mets could not be blamed for thinking it's hard to come back when anything hit up the middle turns into a 6-3 putout!

Dave Wilson, the play-by-play announcer for the RubberDucks, became an immediate believer in Lindor's ability almost as soon as he saw him play.

"Every day you see him play, he brings to the table that he may show you something you have never seen before," gushed Wilson in an interview with B-Mets announcer Tim Heiman. "He has the mindset that there is no ball he cannot get to; it's unfair to compare him to the all-time greats, but you see him up the middle and you think of Ozzie Smith or Dave Concepcion."

When Lindor came up to hit in the seventh, shouts of "Way to go Francisco" were heard from about a dozen fans sitting behind home. If one didn't know better, one would have thought the Francisco Lindor fan club was visiting NYSEG Stadium.

Lindor's bat has no magic in it now, however, as he flies to center. Within minutes of Lindor's out, Enosil Tejeda retires the Mets in order in the bottom of the seventh to close out the win for the RubberDucks.

Lindor's sense of humor and accommodating nature were evident after the game as his post-game actions might have even outshone his accomplishments on the diamond. For starters, when he entered the dugout after the win, he remained in the corner of the dugout and signed autographs for the twenty or so fans gathered at the corner. One seventy-five year-old fan even climbed over three rows of seats and scrambled onto the dugout roof so he could hand a card to Lindor to sign!

Sure enough, about 45 minutes later, when Lindor popped out of the visitor's clubhouse, he had an encore performance. As a dozen or so fans approached him, he turned from the clubhouse door, broke into a semi-sprint, ducking behind three or four of his teammates. He looked like a running back looking for a hole in the line of scrimmage.

The autograph hounds stopped in their tracks, thinking Lindor had had enough of them for one day. Almost as soon as he started to run, however, Lindor stopped and walked back to his fans with a big smile on his face. One by one, the fans formed a line for Lindor's autograph. Francisco smiled and signed one copy of everything put in front of him. When someone asked him what he thought of his fans yelling out his name in encouragement, he said "I loved it!" Encouraged by his acknowledgement, the fans continued to engage in small conversation.

"Nice game today, Francisco!"

"What did you enjoy more, hitting a homer or making those fielding gems?"

Lindor's lips formed a resplendent smile as he succinctly responded, "home run." He walked with a bounce back to the bus, knowing he had put in an almost perfect day, both inside and outside the diamond's white lines.

The next day, Sunday, the fans in Flushing were buzzing from Ike Davis' grand slam that brought home a victory for the New York Mets. Those Binghamton residents who brought copies of the *New York Daily News* this morning no doubt needed to take a double take at the back page to remind themselves that they were reading the *Daily News* and not *Binghamton's Press & Sun-Bulletin*. Filling the entire back page was a picture of a grinning Ike Davis, flanked on his left by Juan Lagares and on his right by Ruben Tejeda, all former B-Mets!

In inimitable tabloid style, the headline blared "SLAMMY DAVIS," evoking memories of Sammy Davis, Frank Sinatra, and Dean Martin and the Hollywood "Rat Pack" days of the '60's. The three teammates formed a rat pack of their own as they celebrated Davis' pinch-hit heroics against J.J. Hoover to give the Mets a 6-3 victory over the Cincinnati Reds.

The front office staff of the Binghamton Mets even got into the act by posting the following question in the concourse area behind home plate before the game: *Did You Know that with his walk-off grand slam yesterday, former B-Met Ike Davis became the first Met to do so since former B-Met manager Tim Teufel in 1986?*

Only a few hours after Binghamtonians had digested the grand news from the big city over their morning cups of coffee, the Binghamton gates opened at 11:30 A.M., a half-hour earlier than usual for an Easter egg hunt for the young fans. The Mets would be on the road Easter Weekend, so the Easter Bunny was on hand today to get pictures taken with the toddlers and youngsters that were scrambling around the premises, looking for the pastel-colored plastic eggs placed in bushes and shrubbery down the left-field line.

The eggs from the Easter Bunny foreshadowed the goose eggs that Hansel Robles, the Mets' 24-year-old right hander, threw at the RubberDucks this afternoon. Robles was dominant, throwing five innings, giving up only two hits and striking out eight while walking one. Though Jack Leathersich and Chase Bradford each gave up two runs later in the game, the Mets held on for a 5-4 win. Robles' deliveries ranged from 80 to 96 mph, with most of his deliveries settling in the 89-91 range.

Throughout the day Robles commanded both sides of the plate. He showed consistent late break on his fastball when he kept it low in the zone, as the Akron hitters were reaching and lunging for his outside pitches. Robles worked quickly and sprinkled in a few sliders and changeups while holding yesterday's hero, Francisco Lindor, in check as Francisco struck out in the first and popped out to the catcher in the third.

Francisco Lindor proves he is only human as he pops one up and Kevin Plawecki gets ready to haul it in.

Robles was a model of efficiency, working quickly, with no wasted time between pitches. After receiving the sign from Plawecki, Hansel simply rocked back, turned his right foot toward third and lifted his glove and hand to his chest before releasing the ball with a release point at about 10 o'clock.

In watching Robles dominate Akron this afternoon, fans wondered how Robles dropped from being *Baseball America's* #12 prospect in the Mets' organization entering 2013 without even making an appearance in the top 30 in the 2014 prospect rankings. Robles posted solid numbers last year in the minors, going 5-5 with a 3.78 E.R.A. and striking out 71 batters in 95 innings. Solid as these numbers were, however, they were a drop off from Hansel's previous year. In 2012, Robles dominated the NY-PENN League, as he led the league in E.R.A. and was fifth in strikeouts.

2014 is critical for Robles, as he needs to reestablish his prospect status. Working against him is that youth is no longer on his side, as he'll turn 25 in August. Also, he does not feature that one dominant pitch—his biggest strength is his command of the fastball, but skeptics are eager to point out that he will need more than fastball command to climb the baseball ladder. With a still-developing slider and a seldom-used changeup, scouts wonder what final form his secondary pitches will take. The relatively low release point he has effectively eliminates Robles from developing an above-average curveball, as a key for success with the curveball is a straight, over-the-top delivery. Finally, Robles' short stature works against him—scouts like to see size in their pitchers, allowing them to throw on more of a downhill plane.

Those who saw Robles pitch on Sunday, however, came away impressed with his poise, fastball command, and most of all, his results. Robles's season at Binghamton in 2014 will be an intriguing one; while Syndergaard and Montero are the current cornerstones of the New York Mets' pitching prospects, and Steven Matz, at St. Lucie, is turning heads as well, Robles has a chance to be the Mets' sleeper prospect of the year.

A Forgotten Snow Globe

The first Monday of the season brings another rainout for the Mets, bringing their season to a symmetrical status: two wins, two losses, and two rainouts.

When the first pitch of the fifth game of the season is thrown on Tuesday night, April 8th, the temperature is 45 degrees, but a strong wind makes it seem at least ten degrees colder. I count 133 diehard fans in attendance, though the attendance will be announced as 1051, as the daily attendance figures include "all tickets sold," including season ticket holders, not just those in attendance.

On this night I find myself thinking of a painful joke Mike Urda told at a Welcome Home dinner a few years back.

Urda began his statement in a matter of fact style. "Being an owner of a minor league team has so many rewards, you get to meet great people, get to know the players up close and get to see great baseball!" Then he raised his voice a little. "And from a money standpoint, it is true that you can accumulate a small fortune."

Urda paused, looked at the ballroom and then said, "But of course, what they don't tell you is that you have to start with a large fortune!" The crowd gave him applause and some knowing glances. During April and May in any minor league town in the Northeast, the weather becomes an obstacle to keeping the books in the black.

NYSEG Stadium is enveloped with a low ceiling of charcoal grey clouds as the leadoff hitter for the Erie SeaWolves, Jamie Johnson, steps into the batter's box. Looking onto the field from a box seat behind the plate, I feel as if I am ensconced in a forgotten snow globe that has had its dome painted a dull and dreary gray. Though no snow falls, tonight's sky is left over from winter and only the calendar proves it's April. Greg Peavey is on the mound for the B-Mets, making his first start of the year. This is his third tour of duty with Binghamton and after pitching in 39 games for AAA Las Vegas last year, he can be forgiven if he thought he'd never see NYSEG Stadium again. No longer considered a prospect, he is now seen as the prototypical "organizational player," someone who gives the touted prospects a measuring stick against which to perform.

Shaggy haired and slender, with a boyish face and perpetual smile, Peavey is a picture of a latter-day Huckleberry Finn. He has a fastball that is purely major league average, sitting in the 90-91 mph range.

He and his wife had their first child, Graydon, earlier this spring. Besides balancing his pitches, Peavey now has to balance fatherhood and baseball. He can hit 93 when he reaches for something extra and he throws his curveball at 78 mph, giving him an outstanding range of 15 mph between his slowest and fastest pitch. He pitches to contact, as he does not have a dominating "out" pitch. He mixes in his curve and slider in with a fastball, which he throws about 75% of the time.

Peavey is another one of those youngsters you find yourself rooting for very hard. He is down-to-earth and knows the odds are not in his favor, but he has tasted what it feels like to be the proverbial "phone call away" in AAA. He has just enough raw talent that he just might make it to the majors someday, pitching "beneath the radar" of the top prospects to get there.

In the bottom of the third, the crowd gets livelier, making noise now as the two-for-one beers start to have an effect. Frigid air and all, fans like their beer. You can hear the buzz of the sixty or so conversations, but cannot make out the words, as it seems as if everyone in the stands is talking, as if moving lips can heat the extremities. The bases are loaded now and Wilfredo Tovar steps into the batter's box, with the crowd shouting out snippets of encouragement.

"You can do it number 2!"

"C'mon, Wilfredo!"

The video screen now does its part, putting up a "clap your hands" image, urging the fans to make noise. Tovar watches two balls go by and the situation becomes promising. On the next pitch, however, Tovar finds himself swinging at a low breaking ball and sends a weak pop up to first. Tovar follows the ball into the opponents' glove, then throws his bat against the ground. Going into the fourth inning, the score is tied at two.

In the bottom of the fourth, veteran minor leaguer Matt Clark deposits a low fastball over the right-centerfield fence, giving the Mets a 4-2 lead. It is one the Mets would not relinquish, as they win on this night, 7-2. Peavey takes 4 innings to get in his 75 pitches, and he leaves with a 4-2 lead.

Move Over Babe, Here Comes Henry!

With the game well in hand I put my score sheet away and plop myself next to Kevin Healy and his wife, Cyndy, who are two of Binghamton's finest fans. The scoreboard tells us a lie, saying it is 45 degrees in the 8th inning. Kevin, Cyndy and I engage in small talk, though our discussion is larger than the crowd. Then, between innings I ask Kevin if he knows what today is. He looks at me with a grin from ear to ear, "Of course I do!"

He looks at me with disappointment. "Did you really think I wouldn't know?" Cyndy now leans over and with a smile that matches Kevin's, states, "We were there, in Atlanta!"

I look at them in with a tilted head and furrowed brow, feigning disbelief, knowing that they are not playing with me, that they were sitting in Atlanta's *Fulton County Stadium* when Aaron hit the home run that caused broadcaster Milo Hamilton to shout, "Move Over, Babe, Here Comes Henry!" I ask them both to tell me how in the world they wound up being eye witnesses to one of baseball's best moments.

Cyndy picks up the story.

"We were dating way back then and we were visiting my relatives in Atlanta and of course, with the Braves being home and the chance to see history, we had to go to the game." She looks at Kevin and smiles now. "And he got mad at the person behind us because he was playing his transistor radio too loud."

Like runners in a relay, Kevin now picks up the story.

"There we are watching the game, and you know, I want to soak in the ambience of the stadium and what not," starts Kevin. In his next sentence, he emphasizes the n*o*. "I don't need *no* transistor radio telling me what Aaron is gunning for. Well, after Aaron's first at bat, I turn around to complain and…"

Cyndy can't let him finish the story. "And then he realizes they guy with the radio was blind!"

Kevin nods his head in agreement, "Yep, he couldn't see anything, but he wanted to soak up everything about the game. He wanted to be there to witness history, just like we did," explained Healy. "Obviously I never asked him to lower the radio," concluded Healy.

I look at them both and ask what it was like when Aaron lifted the ball into the Braves bullpen.

"We knew it was gone the minute he hit it," Healy excitedly explained, reliving the moment as if it were yesterday. "We stood and cheered for as long as possible. It was great, one of the best moments I ever had at a baseball game!"

I now look at Cindy and Kevin with a hangdog face, imagining what it must be like to witness such a great milestone. Healy is reading my mind.

"But you know, after the homer, it was all downhill. After the tribute at home plate, the stadium cleared out. They all wanted to see him get the record, but once he did it, everyone went home. I think when the final pitch was thrown, there were only about 10,000 fans in the park."

"Yeah, you know, everyone remembers that homer, but no baseball fan can tell you what the final score was or who won the game," I countered to Kevin.

We are not the only ones to recount this event. Tim Heiman, up in the broadcast booth, uses his "Where Are They Now" segment to talk about Al Downing, who pitched for the Binghamton Triplets in 1962 and 1968 and who threw the pitch that "Hammerin' Hank" deposited over the left field fence.

"Today we remember Al Downing, who had a great year for Binghamton in 1961, going 9-1 before being called up the big leagues to help the Yankees win a World Championship. Though he was a four-time all-star and won 20 games in the big leagues, he is best remembered for throwing the pitch in 1974 that gave Aaron his 715th home run and allowed him to pass Babe Ruth for the all-time home run record."

Downing, ever the gentleman, has a great line for when he is asked about that night now. "I never say 7:15 anymore. When someone asks me the time. I say it's a quarter after seven."

For the record, the Braves won, 7-4 that night, and the announced attendance was 53,775.

That Must Have Been that New Kid, Mays

The next night, at 5:45 p.m., 50 minutes before the first pitch, I find myself sitting next to Harold "Tuffy" Schalk. The temperature is 47 degrees and though a wind is blowing, it is a forgiving one tonight, as its intensity pales to that of the night before.

Tuffy is a true diehard, in his 76th year and still collecting autographs. He is often at the stadium before the visitors' bus arrives, so he can get the autographs of all the rising stars. He had the autograph bug at an early age, waiting outside Ebbets Field for player autographs as a youth. Schalk is like all autograph hounds and fishermen—no matter how many autographs he gets, he only thinks of the one that got away.

And in 1951, when he was 13, he let a big one get away. He remembers the day as if it were yesterday.

He was waiting outside the visitors' clubhouse on Flatbush Avenue as the New York Giants were arriving at the park. He had been waiting a few hours and had gotten a good haul of autographs when he decided it was time to grab a bite to eat. As he walked away from the clubhouse door, he saw a young man quickly get out of a cab and hurriedly cross the sidewalk in front of him. Tuffy did not recognize him but he had the earmarks of being a ballplayer. He was a kid, no more than 19 or 20, in great shape, and had an athletic gait as he headed toward the clubhouse.

It wasn't until after the clubhouse doors closed that it dawned on Schalk, "That must have been the new kid... Mays."

Though Schalk saw the game that day and saw Mays play many more times before Schalk settled in upstate New York, Schalk never did get Willie's autograph.

An outing with his granddaughter over a decade ago rekindled Schalk's quest for player autographs. He was sitting in the stands at Oneonta, watching the Class-A Oneonta Tigers warm up. His granddaughter, then 10-years-old, was having an easy time getting autographs. "When I realized how agreeable the players were and how easy it was to talk with the players, the interest in collecting autographs returned big time," explained Schalk.

In a nondescript game on this Wednesday night, the Mets defeat the SeaWolves, 7-2, behind another impressive debut by a "non-prospect" starter, Matt Bowman. On the depth chart for right handed pitchers in the Mets' organization, *Baseball America* ranks Bowman number 18, and he doesn't even come close to making the overall top 30 list. But Bowman is an ace tonight, giving up only one run on three hits while striking out four, and making Princeton proud.

In 2012 Bowman was signed off the campus of Princeton University after being drafted in the 13th round. With his closely-cropped hair and clean-shaven face, Bowman would look at ease back in Princeton with books under his arm. He travels to and from the stadium with a backpack, reinforcing his collegiate image. His windup is often compared to Tim Lincecum, as he twists his body in the middle of his delivery to get maximum drive from his right leg. He did not pattern his delivery after Lincecum, though. "Perhaps the reason why I wound up with a delivery like his is because we're both kind of short and both right handed, so we're just trying to get all we can out of our delivery," Bowman explains when asked about his pitching symmetry with Lincecum.

Matt Bowman and Darrell Ceciliani in a relaxed moment on the chow line during a post-game picnic.

    With more starts like the one he had tonight, Bowman may make the scouts notice and join Will Venable, Chris Young, David Hale, and Ross Ohlendorf as recent big leaguers who have hailed from Princeton.
    After the game I go to the bar and restaurant across the street, *Amici's*, which can be seen as a microcosm of how to rejuvenate a city. The small restaurant, which has seating for approximately 80 people, is in its third year of business, located approximately 100 feet behind home plate at NYSEG Stadium. It

replaced a dingy bar called Ron's in 2011 and the corner of Henry and Lewis Street looks a lot brighter these days. Three color TVs can be seen through the tinted windows and serve as a beacon to the baseball fans leaving the stadium. On this night, however, there were only 29 fans in the stands at the conclusion of the game at 9:26 p.m. By 9:30 I am the only one sitting at the bar.

The bartender, Shane, is eager to talk about any topic at all, as tonight is a lonely night for bartending. "When the weather heats up, this place will be hopping," he states. "We definitely see increased business both before and after the games during the summer, but right now this homestand was a slow one, it was just too damn cold."

Get Shane talking about rejuvenating the city and he gets animated. "That's what building this place was all about. An eyesore was torn down and we put a nice pizza bar in its place."

On the window sill sits a small card that highlights the goals of a local company hoping to turn the *Traditions Hotel and Spa*, located about six miles west of the stadium, into a gaming casino and resort destination.

Traditions is on the property that used to be known as the IBM Homestead, where IBM held its meetings for its "100 percent days" and the building was also used as a guest hotel for dignitaries like Franklin Roosevelt, before he was president. Noted celebrities like Bing Crosby golfed there as well

Turning *Traditions* into a gaming casino is one of the many ideas being discussed by business people and community leaders about revitalizing the Greater Binghamton Area. The decision about which proposals will be accepted by the state commission is targeted for late October, right around the time the new World Series Champion is crowned.

I finish my Guinness, leave a tip on the bar, and say goodnight. It is 10 p.m. and with temperature in the mid 30's, there aren't going to be any more visitors tonight. As I leave *Amici's*, I note the B-Mets' team bus is parked outside the clubhouse and the clubhouse attendants are loading it up with the players' equipment. The Mets have finished their first home stand with a 4-2 record and two rainouts. The first road trip of the season will take them to New Hampshire and Portland, just in case the team hasn't adjusted to playing in temperatures below forty degrees.

Binghamton's Crash Davis

In the early hours of the morning, the bus should be able to make it to the team hotel near Northeast Delta Stadium in Manchester, Vermont, in a little over 5 hours, meaning the players will get to rest their heads in a bed at approximately 5 A.M. The route takes them from Albany, N.Y, to the Massachusetts towns of Chicopee and Worcester and Lowell, then it crosses the New Hampshire border and goes through Nashua before landing in Manchester. After about eight hours of sleep, the players will rise, get a bite to eat, and hop on the team bus to the park.

The B-Mets spoil opening night for the Fisher Cats, cruising to a 9-1 win, with Gorski holding the Fisher Cats to one run in six innings while striking out ten. Dustin Lawley and Brian Burgamy hit their first homers of the season and Matt Reynolds goes 3 for 4 at the plate, hitting from the ninth spot in the order. The New Hampshire fans came out in full force, with 5, 946 fans showing up to enjoy the game and the unexpected warm weather of 62 degrees.

The Mets' stay in New Hampshire turns out to be a pleasant one, as they win three out of four games. The first three games of the series had unseasonably mild temperatures, with the lowest temperature being the 62 degrees on opening night. The hitting attack is led by Burgamy, a switch hitter, who gets his first three homers in the first three games of the series and goes 5 for 11, raising his average to .276. "I'm in a good place. I started slowly, but digging my way out of it now," he tells Tim Heiman before the third game of the series. "I'm feeling pretty good now."

Burgamy was the quintessential nomad in 2013, playing for four different teams. "Last year was fun, I hit all year, so that made it fun," he states. Burgamy started with the York

Revolution in the Atlantic League and when he hit well there, the Mexican League came calling. "From a financial point of view, playing in Mexico was an obvious choice," explains Burgamy about his decision to play outside the U.S. Then after the Mexican season was over he was recruited to play for the independent St. Paul Saints, where he hit eight home runs in 24 games. Finally, he finished the year back in the Atlantic League, with the Sugar Land Skeeters, once that team made the playoffs. All told Burgamy hit 32 homers and knocked in 101 runs.

"I'm just thankful to get a second chance in organized ball," summed up Burgamy regarding his choice to sign with the Mets. He admits it has taken a while to mature as a hitter.

"When I first started in organized ball, I knew it all, I was on top of the world," he explained. "And then, when I did get suggestions, I took all the tips word for word, trying to do all of the suggestions, instead of selecting the suggestions that would work for me, given the type of hitter I was. I never really learned what my strengths were until I stated playing in independent ball, in the Atlantic League in 2009."

Burgamy is the "Crash Davis" of this team, as his 80 home runs in Independent League play recall the Kevin Costner character of *Bull Durham*, who was a prolific minor league home run hitter.

"Love of the game is what keeps me playing, long after many of my peers have had to give up the dream," explains the 5'10" utility infielder.

The ability to play 1B, 2B, and 3B contributed to his being signed by the Mets, as his versatility and power brought two needed ingredients to the organization. Burgamy's career also shows the importance of confidence, because in addition to learning patience and selectivity, his confidence fueled his production.

For the final game of the series, on Sunday morning, April 13th, despite the game-time temperature reaching only 44 degrees, Burgamy was looking forward to facing the Fisher Cats' hard throwing right hander Aaron Sanchez, no matter the high probability of some broken bats and stinging hands. Sanchez was Toronto's # 1 rated prospect and the 23rd-rated prospect in all of baseball entering the 2014 season. The scouts love the 6' 4" body of the 21-year-old Sanchez, not to mention his 98-mph fastball, the sink on his two-seam fastball, and the movement on his curveball and changeup. He was selected by the Blue Jays as the 34th overall pick in the 2010 draft, four picks ahead of Syndergaard and ahead of such already established major leaguers as Brandon Workman and Andrelton Simmons.

Though he has only pitched to a 15-16 record in the minors, Sanchez has shown his promise by striking out 265 batters and holding hitters to a .219 average. If he has an Achilles' heel, it is control. Entering the season Sanchez has walked 134 hitters in 256 innings, averaging close to five walks per nine innings. But scouts are quick to point out that is what minor league innings are for, to refine control and improve command. Sanchez is one of the elite prospects in baseball and is expected to dominate AA and finish the year in AAA, if not the majors.

Today, in his home debut, Sanchez's promise and his "heel" are evident, as he gives up four hits, walks four, hits three batters and gives up three runs in 3.2 innings. Burgamy got one of those hits in his first at bat against him, then struck out swinging in the third. As unsettling as Sanchez's command was, the Mets did not break through until the 3rd inning and when they did so, they did it without a hit.

After Sanchez walked Matt Clark to lead off the inning, he then hit Dustin Lawley and Cory Vaughn. As if to put an exclamation point on his development needs, Sanchez walked right fielder Travis Taijeron to force in the game's first run. Backup catcher Xorge Carrillo then hit a sacrifice fly to center and second baseman Wilfredo Tovar followed with a soft single to right to give the Mets a 3-0 lead. Entering the bottom of the third, though no ball had been hit hard against him, due to his lack of command, Sanchez was down by three runs.

Hansel Robles was the antithesis of Sanchez on this day, hurling five shutout innings and displaying excellent control while allowing only four hits and striking out six in his five innings to lead the Mets to a 6-0 win. On paper, Robles had no right outpitching Sanchez, and the Mets had no right winning this game, but they won handily, with Robles turning in his second consecutive outstanding start of the season.

This is the kind of game that builds confidence. Baseball is often a game of momentum and with this win over a stellar pitching prospect, B-Mets hitters emanate a quiet confidence. The Met hitters displayed their patience throughout the game, drawing ten walks, with veteran minor leaguer and DH Matt Clark receiving five free passes on this day!

As the Mets pack up their belongings and board the bus for the trip to Portland, four regulars, Darrell Ceciliani (.367), Matt Clark (.345), Travis Taijeron (.316), and Wilfredo Tovar (.370) are hitting over .300. Matt Reynolds is not far behind at .290. Overall offensive confidence is also buoyed knowing that stalwarts such as Dustin Lawley (.182) and Cory Vaughn (.107) will start to heat up soon. Throw in the fact that the team E.R.A. is 3.07 and the Met staff is second in the league in strikeouts and you sense the players' growing confidence.

The bus ride to Portland is one of the shortest the B-Mets will have during the year, as it's under two hours, traveling across New Hampshire on Highway 101 for about thirty miles before turning north on Interstate 95 for the final hour. Portland's Hadlock Field is one of the most pleasant of AA stadiums, with its left field wall being a replica of Fenway's green monster and its crosswalk in front of the stadium showing white bats within a white rectangle.

Awaiting the Mets in Portland is southpaw Henry Owens, the second-rated prospect in the Red Sox' organization, with only shortstop Xander Bogaertes ahead of him. Owens is a scout's dream: 6-feet-7 inches tall, a fastball over 90 miles per hour and a changeup so good his fastball is his second best pitch. He doesn't turn 22 until July 21.

Having dispatched of Sanchez only the day before, the bats of the B-Mets are undaunted in facing Owens. In the third inning Burgamy and Clark each hit a two-run homer off Owens to give the Mets a 4-2 lead. For both, it is their 4th homer of the season, as they share the team lead. Greg Peavey nurses the lead for five innings, allowing only one hit and two runs on a Sean

Coyle home run in the second inning, which followed a walk to Stefan Welch.

In the bottom of the sixth, though, Peavey tires a bit, allowing a leadoff single to Mookie Betts. Peavey then walks his fourth and fifth batters of the game, shortstop Deven Marrero and first baseman Travis Shaw. Pitching coach Glenn Abbot comes out to the mound to check on Peavey, giving lefty reliever Adam Kolarek more time to warm up. But when Peavey gives up a long sacrifice fly, Lopez brings in Kolarek to pitch to lefty-hitting first baseman Stefan Welch.

Kolarek, after getting ahead with a first-pitch strike, leaves one up in the zone and Welch hits a long double to center that gives the Sea Dogs a 5-4 lead. From there the Sea Dogs turn it into overdrive. Blake Swihart, the promising catcher and fifth-ranked prospect in the organization, singles hard to left on a 1-0 pitch, knocking in Welch. Then Swihart, the 2011 first-round draftee, steals second. On a 3-1 count third baseman Sean Coyle singles to center, bringing home Swihart. Then Coyle steals second. Then he steals third and eventually comes around to score on a single by lefty Peter Hissey.

It is an embarrassing inning for the Mets as Lopez's strategy of bringing in the Kolarek to face the Sea Dogs' bottom half of the lineup fails miserably and the Sea Dogs score six runs and go on to beat the Mets, 9-4.

The next two nights are brutally cold in Portland, with snow flurries filling the air. Both games are postponed, giving the Mets as many rainouts as they have losses in the young days of the season. The Mets board the bus back to Binghamton with a 3-2 record on the road trip. With an overall record of 7-4, they are tied for first with Portland in the division. The six hour bus trip takes them south down I-95 and west along I-90 and New York's I-88.

Back Home

The next night, Thursday, April 17th, New Hampshire visits NYSEG Stadium, as Matt Bowman takes the mound under cloudy skies with a temperature of 55 degrees. Bowman, who won't turn 23 until May 31st, is superb on this night, as the B-Mets defeat New Hampshire, 4-1. Needing only 80 pitches to throw seven shutout innings, Bowman strikes out 11 while giving up only 4 hits and walking one.

The hitting stars of the game include Darrell Ceciliani, who goes 3-for-5 with a double and two runs scored; Matt Clark, with two RBIs; and Matt Reynolds, who goes 3-for-4 with a run scored. John Church throws a scoreless 8th inning and Chase Bradford finishes it up by giving up one run in the top of the ninth.

After the game Bowman downplayed his dominance while playing up his humility as he told Ashley Marshall of MILB, "I thought I had a good mix of everything. I established my fastball, my slider and changeup were good and I managed to throw my curveball. Nothing was working particularly well, but Kevin Plawecki called a great game and we were able to mix it up enough to keep them off balance."

Nothing was working particularly well? Don't let the Fisher Cats hear that. Throwing an assortment of pitches that ranged from 78 mph to 93, Bowman was in and around the strike zone all night and the Fisher Cats had numerous swings and misses. Bowman was throwing too many strikes for New Hampshire to take a passive approach so they went down swinging 10 times. He pitched off a fastball that he located on both sides of the plate and kept down in the zone, while also showing a big-breaking slow curve, a sharp slider, and a changeup with late break. He was a strikeout and groundout machine, as he complemented his 11 K's with eight groundball outs.

Interestingly, Bowman was the 410th pick in the 2012 draft and, at first glance, he probably should not even have been drafted that high! At Princeton, he posted a 4-2 record with a 4.66 E.R.A. in his final year.

Since when does a 4.66 E.R.A. in the Ivy League get you drafted?

Ironically, Bowman has dramatically decreased his E.R.A as a pro, as he posted a 2.45 mark at Brooklyn in 2012 and had an E.R.A. of 3.05 in 2013, splitting his time between Savannah and St. Lucie. If his first few starts are an indication of what will happen in 2014, Bowman will be climbing up the prospect list of the Mets. In his first two AA starts he has thrown 12 innings, allowed 7 hits and struck out more than a batter an inning.

On the hitting side, Matt Reynolds continued his hot hitting, as he goes three for four, to bring his average to .333. In looking at the first few games of the season, Lopez tells broadcaster Tim Heiman that Matt Reynolds has been the biggest surprise of the season and he contemplates moving him up in the order. Besides the play of Reynolds, perhaps the biggest surprise is that Bowman and two of his pitching colleagues, Hansel Robles and Rainy Lara, do not show up on any top 30 prospect lists of the New York Mets' organization. Through the first two weeks of the season these pitchers have dominated the opposition, showing excellent command of the strike zone as well as a wide assortment of pitches.

By now Lopez realizes one of the biggest challenges he has is finding enough playing time for everyone. He has a roster full of players used to playing every day, but so far he has had to be a master juggler, allocating playing time to everyone.

He has Jayce Boyd and Matt Clark sharing the DH/1B duties and has given time to Burgamy at both 2B and 3B, while splitting Lawley's time between 3B and LF. Center field has been shared between Darrell Ceciliani and Kyle Johnson, leaving the right field slot to be split between Travis Taijeron and Cory Vaughn. Reynolds and Tovar have been rocks of reliance at shortstop and second base, respectively, with Lopez rewarding Reynolds' success at the plate by moving him into the second slot of the batting order. Not only has Reynolds been hitting well, but he has a short swing and goes to right field well, which is ideal for a # 2 hitter in the lineup.

Though a baseball season is a marathon and it has only just begun, the performances of Bowman, Lara, and Robles generate a buzz around Binghamton. Their work, coupled with the early season success of AA veteran Darin Gorski and the superb hitting of newcomers Clark, Burgamy, and Reynolds, has Binghamtonians bantering about 2014 bringing a "September to

Remember" for the Southern Tier of New York. Lopez's mantra of six more wins, besides being a bold mantra, might just be an accurate one, muses more than one follower of the team at this early juncture.

On Friday night, April 19th, a determined Sanchez shows the Binghamton Mets why he is the #1 rated prospect for the Blue Jays as he throws six dominant innings, striking out six and walking only two, leading New Hampshire to a 6-3 win. The Sanchez the B-Mets saw tonight was the antithesis of the one they saw last Sunday when Sanchez walked four and hit three. Tonight he had excellent command, staying low in the strike zone and displaying a lot of movement as he sat at 93-94 mph most of the night and touched 97. He needed only an occasional breaking ball to shut down the Met lineup and retired 14 batters in a row between the first and sixth innings.

The Binghamton Mets, behind excellent pitching from Rainy Lara, took the finale of the three-game series with the Fisher Cats, giving them a 9-5 record. Matt Reynolds cemented the number 2 position in the batting order by going 4-4. Since his move up to the number 2 slot, Reynolds has gone 5-8, raising his average to .383. In his previous two years, Reynolds hit .259 and .226 respectively, so his torrid start has not only caught Lopez by surprise, but the B-Mets fans as well.

"I'm just trying to stay consistent, stay up the middle," explained Reynolds, elaborating on his early-season success. "Last year I think I just put too much pressure on myself and when the results weren't what I wanted, I got down on myself. So I really don't set personal goals, I just try to stay positive throughout the season. I just came into the year with the mindset to get at it each day."

On Monday, April 21st, the B-Mets fans attending the game against the Portland Sea Dogs were in for a real shocker. It is 74 degrees and the sky is a beautiful cerulean blue when the first pitch is thrown! Lefty Henry Owens was given his second start against the Mets in the young season and he was up to the task, stifling the hometown team, holding it to only two hits over five innings. Owens had a shutout and a 5-0 lead entering the bottom of the sixth when the Mets used only two hits to score three runs. Left fielder Kyle Johnson led off the inning by reaching on an error by first baseman Travis Shaw. With Matt Reynolds displaying a patient approach at the plate, Johnson stole second and Reynolds continued his patience by drawing a walk. Burgamy then came up with the hardest hit ball of the night, ripping a double off the left-field wall, scoring Johnson and putting runners on second and third with no outs.

Owens, using his changeup effectively, got Kevin Plawecki to ground out third to first, with the runners holding. Jayce Boyd made it a 5-3 game with a two-run double to the right-centerfield gap. Owens then regrouped, getting Darrell Ceciliani to ground out to short and then inducing Dustin Lawley to swing and miss at a third strike.

After the game Owens said his changeup was his most effective pitch, as he used it to keep Mets hitters off balance, allowing only four hits. Owens had trouble with this command, walking four batters and only striking out three. Though he ran his record to 3-0, his E.R.A. actually rose on this night, to 2.28.

Mike Antellus, the Sea Dog announcer enjoys watching Owens pitch. Before the game, he was a guest of Tim Heiman's on the pre-game show and explained, "Owens needs better command of the curveball, he reminds me of Clay Buchholz in that regard when Buchholz was down here in AA. He just needs to command that curveball more, fine tune that fastball to make all his secondary pitches better. He already has that good changeup."

As impressive as Owen's pitching performance was between the lines, his performance after the game was to be admired more. With approximately two dozen fans waiting outside the visitor's clubhouse, Owens spent about ten minutes signing every item fans put in front of him, all the while engaging in pleasant conversation with the fans and referring to many of the adults in the crowd as "Sir." The phrase most often out of his mouth was "Thank You," in response to the fans congratulating him on a well-pitched game.

Binghamton's Voice of the Game

The next night it was a pleasant 56 degrees at the time of the game's first pitch with clouds hiding the sun. Predictions for thunderstorms and strong winds were prevalent. By the fifth inning the weather had indeed turned, as a strong wind blew in and the rain started to fall. In the middle of the sixth, the wind and rain got stronger. As I sat and watched the game, I pondered leaving in the top of the seventh, but like leaving church, there are some events that I just cannot bring myself to leave early. I was saved from my dilemma by Mike Urda, who came into my row and invited a handful of season ticket holders to enjoy the rest of the game in the warmth of an unused skybox. We did not need to be asked twice!

As the game unfolded and both teams put up zeroes on the scoreboard, those of us in the skybox were treated to the voice of Tim Heiman, the Mets' play-by-play announcer. Listening to Heiman, you realize he comes from the school of Vin Scully, who has been doing the play-by-play of the Dodgers for over half a century and was recognized as the greatest broadcaster in baseball history by Curt Smith, in his book *Voices of the Game* in 2008. Like Scully, Heiman makes you feel as if he were talking only to you. There is no such thing as dead time when Heiman works; he has a stat and a story for every player appearing in the game. Among the nuggets Heiman will share this night:

"The B-Mets are looking to avoid losing back-to-back games for the first time this year."

"The B-Mets bullpen has been magical tonight, throwing 5.1 scoreless innings."

Heiman majored in mechanical engineering at Rensselaer Polytechnic Institute (RPI) in Troy, N.Y., and he got his start in sports broadcasting when he showed up at the college radio station. He went to the meeting thinking he might get a music assignment, perhaps as a DJ or something similar. At the meeting, the leader asked "Is anyone interested in sports?" Once Tim raised his hand, the rest, as they say, is history.

At RPI he broadcasted Division 1 hockey and loved it. Before long he was telling his parents he was thinking of pursuing broadcasting as a career and "junking" his mechanical engineering studies. His parents gave him a choice—he could pursue his broadcasting interest on a full-time basis, as well as be on his own concerning finances, or he could continue to work toward his mechanical engineering degree, pursue his broadcasting interests on the side, and continue to have all expenses paid by his parents.

Tim, an astute youth, chose to have his expenses continue to be paid.

Interestingly, his parents may not have been as surprised by Tim's request as he thought. After he embarked on his professional broadcasting career, his mother showed him his fifth grade essay on what he wanted to be when he grew up. And yes, there it was in black and white—he had written he wanted to be a sports broadcaster!

Upon graduation, Tim continued to show his street smarts by turning down a 60K engineering job to become a broadcaster for the NY-PENN Auburn Doubledays for no salary. He did, however, get free housing—he was the fifth guy in a four bedroom house!

Following his Auburn experience, Tim interned with the Binghamton Mets under Matt McCabe and when McCabe decided to go to law school, general manager Jim Weed offered Tim the full time job of broadcasting B-Mets games.

Tim has never looked back.

Tim's favorite road cities in the Eastern League are Portland and Manchester (New Hampshire). He pointed out that in April and early May, Portland can be cold and dreary, but it comes alive in the summer as a thriving summer vacation destination.

Tim grew up in Smithtown, Long Island, and has fond memories of listening to Bob Murphy broadcasting Mets games on the radio. Tim lists the current Mets' radio broadcaster Howie Rose as his favorite announcer today.

"Being in the right place at the right time has greatly helped me in my career," Tim stated. "Being McCabe's intern proved to be a blessing, as when he left to go to law school, the full-time spot opened for me."

What Tim does not mention is his work ethic and mellifluous voice, two characteristics that will serve him well as he climbs the broadcasting ladder. Tim's attention to detail can be seen in the work he does to ensure he has no dead time on the air; he spends 20 minutes to a half hour preparing an information card on each opposing player for every team. So that's a card for over 20 opposing players, plus at least two coaches and a manager – approximately 13 hours of prep time just to have anecdotes to share on the visiting team for each series. In addition to his information cards, Tim is constantly reading Eastern League and Major league recaps so he can stay abreast of current happenings.

As Dustin Lawley leads off the bottom of the ninth in the 3-3 game, Heiman informs and narrates, "To the tune of 'Sweet Home Alabama,' the Alabama native, Dustin Lawley comes to the plate." No matter that Lawley swings and misses at a low pitch outside the strike zone for the team's 10th strikeout of the game, Heiman is unfazed, showing no hint of fandom on this night. As left fielder Kyle Johnson steps to the plate, Heiman knows the wishes of his listeners, but he dispels the chances of a walk-off homer as he paints the scene.

"On a night like this, the ball is not going to carry, not with the cold and the damp air. It's best to just start a rally and start with getting on base."

As the count reaches 1-1 to Johnson, Heiman tells us of Johnson's hometown while also reminding us of the chill in the air. "It's 1-1 to Idaho native Kyle Johnson, who I had a chance to speak with earlier today concerning playing in the Northeast. Johnson told me this was his kind of weather and the brisk air makes him feel right at home."

Heiman has watched enough games to have a sense of what is to come. A few seconds after he refers to the need to start a rally by doing something small, Johnson gets on base with a hit.

"Darrell Ceciliani now stepping to the plate with Matt Reynolds, the Mets' hottest batter on deck," states Heiman.

While Johnson leads off first, Ceciliani hits a grounder to the right of the first base bag and now it is a foot race to the bag, Heiman conveys the bang-bang nature of the play, Ceciliani out by a hair at first!"

Heiman is at his best, however, in the top of the eleventh inning. As Jon Velasquez enters the game, he reminds us that in his last outing two days ago, Velasquez got touched up, giving up 3 runs in one inning. When Henry Ramos starts the inning with a line-drive single, Heiman sets the stage. Up to the plate steps designated hitter Matt Spring, who has struck out four straight times.

"Up now is Matt Spring, who has a golden sombrero for his night's work, but he can relieve that with one swing of the bat."

As if on cue, reliever Jon Velasquez delivers a flat fastball on a 1-0 pitch and Spring hits a monstrous home run over the left field fence. Heiman expands on the moment: "That ball is outta here. Power when you need it and Spring delivers!"

The Mets go quietly in the bottom of the eleventh and as I walk out of the stadium I realize Spring and Heiman have both delivered on this night. The Mets lose 5-3, and drop three games behind the Sea Dogs, as the Portland nine moves their winning streak to six.

Ask Heiman if he minded the extra inning game and he smiles and explains, "I love what I do. How many people can say they come to a ballpark to work each day?"

The next night the Mets get their fifth postponement of the season, so their record reads nine wins, seven losses, and five postponements.

The night of Thursday, April 24th, brings dry skies and temperatures of 53 degrees to NYSEG Stadium, so it feels like a heat wave as the B-Mets play Portland for the fourth time in the season, still looking for their first win.

Peavey takes the ball for the Mets, opposed by right hander Keith Couch. Peavey pitches well, going seven innings while allowing four runs on seven hits and striking out five without walking a batter. Couch is better, however, allowing only two runs in six innings. But the Mets score single runs in the seventh and eighth innings against reliever Nate Reed and send the game into extra innings. They win it in the bottom of the tenth, when Kyle Johnson, pinch hitting for Taijeron, hits a sacrifice fly to score Cory Vaughn, who had led off the inning with a double and advanced to third on a wild pitch. Closer Chase Bradford gets his first win in relief, throwing scoreless innings in the ninth and tenth, bringing the B-Mets record to 10-7, good for second place in the Eastern League, two games behind Portland.

Portland is a formidable foe in the Eastern League, as six of the top 30 prospects in the Red Sox' organization are with the team, led by their outstanding battery of Henry Owens and Blake Swihart, the number two and number five prospects in the organization, respectively. The sparkplug of the team so far, though, has been second baseman Mookie Betts, who came into tonight's game hitting .452! Betts will not be 22 until October 7th and has shown he can hit for power and steal bases as well, as he had 15 home runs with 38 steals in 2013 in Class A ball.

Infielders Devin Marrero (shortstop, # 15), Travis Shaw (1b, # 26), and Sean Coyle (# 30, 3B) round out the list of prospects. Add in minor league veterans such as Carlos Rivero, Shannon Wilkerson, and Peter Hissey and the Sea Dogs have an excellent balance of youth and experience.

Our Team. Our Town. Our Pride.

The Mets closed out the month with a road trip to Erie and Akron, where they go 2-3 with another two rainouts and finish the month with a 12-10 record, three games behind first place Portland.

While the B-Mets board their team bus for the return trip to Binghamton from their "Baseball in Education" day rainout in Akron on April 30th, general manager Jim Weed sits in the middle of the conference room in NYSEG Stadium, surrounded by three members of the Binghamton Mets Booster Club and his sales ticket manager, Joe Pascarella. The topic for discussion during this working lunch of pizza and soda is how the booster club can help further community support of baseball in the area.

Jim is dressed in tan khakis, with a blue button shirt, participating as an active listener and facilitator. The conference room is painted in a light blue, evoking memories of the Mets' royal blue. Pictures honoring the history of professional area baseball line the walls, including three pictures of the Binghamton Bingos, which was a moniker of the Binghamton franchise at the beginning of the 20th century. There is also an aerial shot of Johnson Field, which served as the home of baseball in the area from 1913 to 1968. Many old timers in the area still consider the Johnson Field years the glory years of area baseball, when the Binghamton Triplets annually fed prospects to the dominant Yankee teams of the 1950's.

On the west wall of the room are three shelves of the more memorable mementoes that have been "giveaways" at the stadium through the years, including a David Wright bobblehead, a B-Mets luncheon tote bag, various B-Mets baseball caps, and a collection of water bottles. On the south wall is a picture of the façade of the stadium, with its gray stone blending in with the sky to make the cement façade almost indistinguishable from the sky. Binghamton is known for being one of the cloudiest and rainiest cities in the nation, and the stadium picture does not dispute this. The conference room is the centerpiece of the B-Mets offices. Here is where all the meetings are held and the players sometimes even come here to escape from the confines of the clubhouse and watch television.

Jeff Smith, community volunteer and retired executive from the local utility company, has come up with a three-page document centered on the question of "What can the booster club do to help increase community support?" As president of the B-Mets Booster Club, I also get to attend the session.

Various ideas are kicked around, from the boosters making sure outlying geographical areas are well stocked with pocket schedules to the booster club sponsoring community nights at the stadium. Weed shows his pleasure with dealing with such a committed group through his active listening and pensive comments.

"We get a few, but not a lot," Weed answers in response to Jeff's question about the number of groups that use the stadium to hold social events. "We've tried to make it as easy as possible for some groups to come out by just telling them to use a promo code when they order tickets for the group discount," expands Joe. "For so many clubs, organizing a night at the park seems like a daunting task, so we've tried to remove all the complexity from it. We do what we can, but in general, we do not get as many groups as we'd like."

One of the action items resulting from the meeting will be the formation of a list of groups that the booster club will approach about having a social night at the stadium. Another action item is for the booster club to sponsor at least two themed nights at the stadium, to help celebrate the 100th year of professional baseball in the Greater Binghamton Area.

"You know, the players come and go, for the most part every year. But the thing that is constant is that this is our town and the more we remind people that this team is really its team, *our team*, the more we can get folks to embrace the team," muses Denis Wickham, one of the original founders of the booster club in 2012.

"That's right," pipes in Jeff. "This is our team, our town, and we need to remind people to take pride in one of the community's assets."

Smith's face lights up. He is constantly looking for ways to spur economic redevelopment. "The first step to economic redevelopment is to hold on to the assets a community has; this team is a jewel for our area that we need to make sure we continue to polish!"

I have been relatively quiet for most of the meeting, a distinct anomaly for me. But now, as I speak, a smile creases my face. "You know, I think we have a slogan for one of our theme nights—'Our Team. Our Town. Our Pride!'"

Everyone nods in agreement as the last of the pizza is eaten. 100 years of baseball in the community. A goal of six more wins. Our Team…Our Town…Our Pride….We walk out of the meeting knowing there is a lot going on in this baseball season besides the play between the white lines.

Chapter 4. Binghamton is Our Hometown

Author's Note: Now we take a respite from action on the diamond to see how the optimism for revitalization comprises the everyday lives and thoughts of a few of Greater Binghamton's inhabitants; their thoughts echo the optimism building among New York Mets fans. The people discussed here range in age from 21 to over 90, with the common denominator being they call Binghamton their hometown.

Two of the most complimentary words used today to describe fans of the N.Y. Mets are "loyal" and "patient." The last eight years have been difficult, ever since Carlos Beltran got caught looking at a 3-2 breaking pitch from Adam Wainwright with the bases loaded and two out in the bottom of the ninth in Game 7 of the 2006 National League Championship Series. That sharp curve from Wainwright foreshadowed the fall of the Mets. Though the New Yorkers had winning seasons in '07 and '08, two late summer fades blocked the team from post-season play. Now the team is tied with the Houston Astros for the major-league lead for most consecutive years of futility, finishing under .500 for six straight years. The Mets record during this span has been dismal, as shown in the following table.

Year	W-L Record	Percentage	Attendance	Manager/General Manager
2009	70-92	.432	3,135,904	Jerry Manuel/Omar Minaya
2010	79-83	.488	2,559,738	Jerry Manuel/Omar Minaya
2011	77-85	.475	2,352,596	Terry Collins/Sandy Alderson
2012	74-88	.457	2,242,803	Terry Collins/Sandy Alderson
2013	74-88	.457	2,136,355	Terry Collins/Sandy Alderson
2014	79-83	.488	2,148,808	Terry Collins/Sandy Alderson
6-Year Totals	452-519	.465	**Average:** 2,429,637	

The loyal and patient fan base, though down from the record attendance of 4,021,534 in 2008 is still well over two million strong. For the first time in six years, Citi Field attendance actually increased in 2014 and the team only finished four games under .500. There is room for optimism in the hearts and minds of the Flushing faithful. In 2015, Matt Harvey and Bobby Parnell are returning from injury and Michael Cuddyear is an additional bat in the lineup.

To put this into further perspective, the N.Y. Mets are where the Binghamton franchise was in 2012, and just as the Binghamton franchise has turned it around, there is hope that many of those players from the 2012 Binghamton team, including Josh Edgin, Wilmer Flores, Juan Lagares, and Zack Wheeler can turn it around in Flushing. The AA Mets clearly turned the corner during the past two years, with a first-place finish in the Eastern Division in 2013 and an Eastern League Championship in 2014.

B-Mets W/L Record	Winning Percentage	Manager
2009: 54-86	.386	Mako Oliveras
2010: 66-76	.465	Tim Teufel
2011: 65-76	.460	Wally Backman
2012: 68-74	.479	Pedro Lopez
2013: 86-55	.610	Pedro Lopez
2014: 83-59	.585	Pedro Lopez
6-Year Totals: 422-426	.498	

Loyalty and Patience. Those are exactly the traits that have driven the approximately 47,000 Binghamton residents and the almost 250,000 Broome County residents to remain as citizens of the Greater Binghamton Area through the past three decades of job loss, unemployment growth, and dramatically increasing property taxes. In looking at the story of many residents of the Southern Tier, a recurring theme prevails. "We'll work through the difficulties and remain in the area."

These people already know what Hugh Grant's character in the recently released film, *The Rewrite*, took the length of the movie to find out. Five minutes into the film, which is set in Binghamton, Grant's character, Keith Michaels, muses, "It's impossible to know what anyone could have to teach here, except to get out."

By the end of the movie, though, Michaels is begging to stay in the town, as he is proud to teach at BU and call this town his home.

The journey of Michaels reminds us of the pride in which Rod Serling proclaimed Binghamton as his hometown in his introduction to the Twilight Zone's *Walking Distance* episode on October 30, 1959:

"Everybody has to have a hometown, Binghamton's mine. In the strangely brittle, terribly sensitive make-up of a human being, there is a need for a place to hang a hat or a kind of geographical womb to crawl back into, or maybe just a place that's familiar because that's where you grew up.

"When I dig back through memory cells, I get one particularly distinctive feeling—and that's one of warmth, comfort and well-being. For whatever else I may have had, or lost, or will find—I've still got a hometown. This, nobody's gonna take away from me."

Eddie is Back

Eddie Saunders, group sales director for the Binghamton Mets, is too young to list Elton John as a favorite musician, but his choice to stay in the Grater Binghamton Area reminds one of John's hit song from 1974—"The Bitch is Back." Saunders had a chance to leave Binghamton in January 2014 and go to work for the Daytona Cubs in the Florida State League as a Director of Ticket Operations. Instead, he chose to stay in Greater Binghamton and work for the B-Mets as a post-graduate intern in 2014. It marked his sixth straight year of employment for the franchise. He started working in the ticket booth as a high school student in 2009 and worked all four years that he attended SUNY

(State University of New York) Cortland to get his Bachelor of Science in sports management.

Why would a 21-year-old with a newly-minted college degree turn down the sunny skies of Florida for Binghamton's slate skies?

"I've lived here my whole life and the B-Mets have always been good to me," explained Eddie. "I was thinking that after I worked another year as an intern, a full-time position might become available. This area is home to me and I love working with the players and staff."

That's Eddie in the middle of this staff photo of the front office for the Binghamton Mets. Back row, left to right: Bob Urda, Richard Tylicki, EJ Foley, Jesse Scaglion, Joe Pascarella, Heath Tracy-Bronson, Lisa Shattuck. Front row, left to right: Erica Foley, Joe Campione, Eddie, Jim Weed, and Connor Gates.

And the players love working with Eddie. In 2013 and 2014 Eddie handled a variety of tasks, including driving players to and from the airport and providing transportation around town. Eddie has his share of funny stories to tell.

"In 2013, they asked me to pick up Chase Bradford from the Binghamton airport. When I got there, they told me the plane was cancelled. So I call my contact in Binghamton and tell them Bradford's not coming. But the clubhouse attendant tells me 'No, they have the wrong information, we know he's coming in tonight!' Well, to make a long story short, turns out Bradford's plane to Binghamton was cancelled, instead he was flying into Syracuse and getting in around midnight. So what was supposed to be a 20-minute excursion turned into a whole night and early-morning affair!"

To top it off, Eddie even had to return to the Syracuse airport the next morning to retrieve Bradford's luggage, which did not make the flight!

Eddie's popularity with the players is symbolized with the term of endearment that outfielder Darrell Ceciliani bestowed on him in 2014. As Eddie did tasks in the clubhouse, Ceciliani started to greet him with "What's up, bitch?" whenever he saw him.

Eddie smirks when he explains that the term is a compliment.

"Yeah, Darrell's a great guy and he appreciated me doing things like picking up his girlfriend from the airport or doing a food run for him. It was his way of recognizing that I kind of went beyond the job description for him."

"Beyond the job description" also characterizes Eddie's affection for his hometown baseball team. As a high school student he had a season ticket and he developed a strong friendship with Mako Oliveras, the B-Mets' manager from 2007 to 2009.

"Mako was a wonderful guy, he went out of his way to greet me and even introduced me to his extended family and friends when they would come to visit," explained Eddie. And last September, Eddie went above and beyond the call of duty to see his B-Mets clinch the division championship in Portland.

"I'd been planning to drive Saturday morning to catch Game 4, but then they announced they were moving that game up to noon. So that messed up my plans, but I listened to the game on radio that Saturday afternoon and when they won, I just had to go to the deciding game!"

So go Eddie did, leaving his house at around 6 P.M. for the drive to Portland, stopping for only a bathroom break and checking into his motel a little after midnight. The next morning, he managed to get up by 9 and was driving around downtown Portland in his KIA Soul and sure enough, he gets a text from Jason Griffin, the B-Mets strength and conditioning coach. Griffin had just dropped off his car at a rental agency and saw Eddie driving around town, and he needed a ride to Hadlock Field. So even on his day off, Eddie was attending to the needs of his players and coaches!

"Watching that final game was great," Eddie remembers. "After the game, Pedro made a special point out of coming of the clubhouse and thanking the contingent of fans from Binghamton who made the trip. That's one of the nice things about working in minor league baseball. The players appreciate what we do and the added recent treat has been the pleasure we have been getting from their play on the field!"

For the 2015 season, Eddie and his colleagues on the B-Mets staff look forward to bringing the excitement from last year's pennant chase to the stadium the whole year.

Eddie remembers the championship night of September 12th as if it were yesterday: "That night they won it, the stadium was packed and electric. It was nice to see the community brought together by one single item—rooting for a championship!"

From Bat Boy to the "Mad Hatter"

Though officially his title is Director of Community Relations for the Binghamton Mets, Connor Gates wears so many hats that he could be also be called the "Mad Hatter" of Binghamton. In addition to his community relations role, where his primary duties include lining up player appearances and being a community advocate, Gates also is a regular National Anthem singer, the coordinator of all on-field promotions, game-day statistician, overseer of the bat boys, and the jockey for "Hickory the Hot Dog Horse," which calls for him to throw hot dogs into the stands each game while walking in a horse costume from the waist down, allowing him to appear as if he were riding a horse.

Gates has been working for the Binghamton Mets since he was a 16-year-old bat boy, a job that he waited six years to attain. He wrote a letter to the B-Mets when he was ten, asking to become the team's bat boy. He had to wait six years, as he was not aware of the child labor laws that would not allow a ten-year-old to begin earning a paycheck. "Four of the greatest years of my life," recalls Gates about his time as a bat boy.

17 years later he still loves what he does. "I'm not crazy about the hours, but every day I come to the park to work I can't believe it—it's as if I'm ten years old all over again," gushes Gates when describing his job. On most game days, Gates is at the park six to seven hours before the first pitch and doesn't leave until a half hour or so after the end of the game. The statistics board in the concourse behind home plate with the corresponding "Did you know that…" fact is his responsibility. For day games, this means being at the park at approximately 6:30 a.m. to scan the internet to get the stats of baseball's leaders to update his board.

In getting people to come to the park, Gates realizes that putting on a good show for the fans is just as important as the show that the team puts on in the field. "Sometimes it's easy to overlook all the planning that goes into all the events we do between innings," expounds Gates.

As Gates puts it, "connections with the players is one of the benefits of this job that is almost as great as any paycheck," and he has plenty of stories to relate about his encounters with players through the years. One of his favorite players is Jose Reyes. Gates just loved watching Reyes race around the bases during the summer of 2002. "I got to drive Jose to the Binghamton airport when he played in the All-Star Futures game in '02 and that turned out to be a memorable moment. At the time Jose did not speak any English and I did not speak any Spanish, so we drove to the airport in complete silence," narrates Gates.

"When Jose was getting his boarding pass, the ticket agent was asking if he had any bags to check. Reye looked at me quizzically, wondering what the agent was requesting. I didn't know how to translate, so I just started raising my voice and wound up basically yelling at Jose, 'DO YOU WANT TO CHECK YOUR BAGS?' After many strange glances from the folks in the airport, I finally came up with a creative way to motion with my hands to find out if Jose had any bags to check."

To this day, whenever Jose sees Gates, whether it is at a major league ball park or spring training, Reyes takes time to greet Gates with a warm hug.

Ex-New York and Binghamton Met Jason Phillips is one of the closest friends Gates has gained from his baseball vocation. With a huge smile creasing his face, Gates goes on to recount one of his favorite stories.

"When Phillips was with the Blue Jays, he had to go to Yankee Stadium for early batting practice and asked me if I wanted to go. Did I want to go? What a ridiculous question. Of course I would go!" Gates' voice rises and his face is animated as he continues his story and the details flow as if the event occurred only yesterday.

"Greg Zaun, Matt Stairs, and Jason were taking batting practice. Mickey Brantley, who had been the Mets' roving instructor a few years earlier, was the hitting coach for the Jays then. He saw me in the dugout and called me out to the field. There I was, seeing BP up close and Matt Stairs came up to me and introduced himself. Then, shortly after Stairs stepped into the cage, a pitch from Brantley came close to his head. Stairs looked out at Brantley, then back to me and back to Brantley again and he yelled, 'You keep that up and Connor's gonna be pitching BP!'"

A typical workday during a home stand for Connor often lasts up to 14 hours and 60- to 70-hour work weeks are standard fare during all home stands. Despite the long days and the fact that he went off to college to study theater, Connor clearly prefers the diamond to the stage. Besides, as the jockey for "Hickory the Horse," he has become a welcome sight for the fans who come out every year.

Broadway may have its long running shows, but NYSEG Stadium has Gates and his horse as the longest running hit on Henry Street.

"It's all in the wrapper this year," Gates explained when he was asked about the secret behind throwing a good hot dog into the stands.

Bosnia to Iraq to Egypt to Kuwait, Then Back Home

Richard Tylicki has to be the only Lieutenant Colonel in the U.S. Army National Guard who doubles as a minor league Director of Stadium Operations. A background like his you will never see again in any Baseball Almanac. He has served as the Director of Stadium Operations for the Binghamton Mets since 1996 and since that time he has also served four overseas tours with his guard unit, totaling close to four full years of overseas duty. Throughout his employment with the B-Mets he has juggled his baseball duties with his reserve requirements of serving one weekend every month and two weeks every year, not including various other meetings.

His first overseas stint was as part of a peace-keeping mission in Bosnia from July, 2002 to March, 2003. He served as a liaison officer between the American troops and the British and Dutch troops. America was at war in Afghanistan at the time and Rich was happy to be serving on a peace-keeping mission. The assignment was not danger-free, however, as Bosnia still had numerous landmines buried in its soil from its civil war of the 1990's.

"Whenever you traveled there, you had to be certain not to ever leave the highway, for fear of coming across a live mine," recounted Tylicki during a recent luncheon at a local sports restaurant.

After his Bosnia tour, Tylicki returned to the Mets for the 2003 season, but shortly after was ordered to report to Iraq for a fifteen-month assignment over 2004-2005. As fate would have it, Tylicki had to turn down a general manager's job for a minor league team in Georgia due to his military commitment in Iraq, which lasted until February 2005. By this time he had a unit of 180 men reporting to him and his unit was paired with the Iraq Survey Group, which was the group that searched for weapons of mass destruction. His unit's duties included providing bodyguards for specific individuals, supplying convoy security support, and providing perimeter security as well, often involving multiple rings of security. In some cases Rich and his men were running inspections not under American control, so at times they had to rely heavily on local police forces.

As captain of the unit, he saw many get injured and often he and his reserves were under enemy fire. One of the toughest things he has ever had to do was make the follow-up call to the wife of the one man from his unit who lost his life. While supplying security around the perimeter of a chemical weapons factory, an explosion occurred, killing that man and injuring five others.

"Of course, having served so many tours overseas, you know death is always a possibility, but you hope and think that you can always escape it," noted Richard.

Looking back, Richard marvels at some of the things his unit was asked to do. At one point some of his men had to climb a smokestack that was 70 to 80-foot high to remove a radioactive source. "Thank goodness that was very friendly territory," explained Richard. "Climbing a smokestack would have made an inviting target."

By March of 2005 he was back at his job in Binghamton. Though the team had two losing seasons in 2005 and 2006, he was happy to be back home, as his stay in Iraq was a long way from the friendly fireworks nights of NYSEG Stadium.

Iraq was followed up with a 12-month stay in Egypt that started in the fall of 2007 and included all of the 2008 season. After Egypt, a two-year full-time assignment followed from November 2011 to November 2013. The first year had Rich based in Pennsylvania, but the second year had him in Kuwait, where he worked on a security and life-support mission. His team's life-support tasks included such mundane but necessary tasks as getting rid of waste on the base, etc. Halfway through his tour in Egypt, Rich received a promotion to major.

Through all the tours of duty Rich has always come back to Binghamton. "It's the area that keeps me coming back," explains Richard. "It is just about the right size, not too small and not too big either!" he states with a smile. "When I lived in Glasgow, Kentucky, it was too rural and in a big city like New York, for instance, you're just a number. Here, I enjoy being recognized in the offseason at other sporting events and having a chance to really make things happen."

Rich is quick to point out that the area is a "sort of a sports mecca" without the big city annoyances. As someone who has spent most of his working life in the sports world, he loves to spend his leisure time watching sports as well and Binghamton is an ideal locale for him to work, as well as to watch.

"There's world class golf here every year, with the *Dick's Sports Goods Open*, and every summer there's world class tennis with the *Levine, Gouldin, & Thompson Challenger Event* at Recreation Park, and of course, there's hockey where the players are only one step away from the NHL," he acknowledges. It doesn't matter that Rich does not name all the sporting events held in the Greater Binghamton Area every year—there are simply too many. So while he makes no mention of the *Chris Thater Bicycle Races*, where top cyclists compete for prize money every year, or the summer training camp of the New York Jets that is held thirty miles away in Cortland, New York, or the Division I sports that Binghamton University hosts, his point has been made.

Rich graduated from Kentucky State University and then received his Masters in Sports Administration at Western Illinois. He always wanted to be employed in the sports arena, as after playing various levels of football, baseball, and basketball in high school, sports was in his bloodlines. Though football is truly his favorite sport, he has been delighted to have made a living within the baseball world.

As the Director of Stadium Operations, he is responsible for all aspects of stadium upkeep and, as with every administrator in minor league baseball, is constantly searching for ways to maximize improvements while minimizing cost. For example, during the two-day Eastern League All-Star break that occurs every season, Rich can be seen power-washing the stadium. "No matter the assignment here, we all try to make the ballpark experience as enjoyable as possible and as bright and refreshing as possible," notes Richard.

Richard Tylicki, in orange B-Mets shirt, conversing with fans during a game in 2014.

Tylicki found his way to Binghamton after the 1994 winter meetings in Dallas, Texas. He had half a dozen job offers, and he came to Binghamton simply because it was the best job offer he had. "Binghamton offered me a place to live that I shared with two other interns, as well as a salary of $500.00 a month, so I was sold on coming here!"

One year has now turned into more than 20.

Seeing the B-Mets win the Eastern League championship this past season was not the only rewarding thing that occurred in the 2014 season for Tylicki. In July, while the B-Mets were on the road and Rich was serving weekend duty at Fort Indiantown Gap in Pennsylvania, Rich was promoted from Major to Lieutenant Colonel. There is no resting on laurels for Rich, however. The offseason priorities for Rich included painting the steel beams in the rafters of the concourse, as well as replacing the ceiling tiles in the ticket office and press box. "The offseason is always full of making improvements that you just can't get done during the season," he explains.

Rich enjoys rekindling friendships during the season, as he can often be seen walking around the stadium and making himself at home, sitting next to area fans and listening to them for any ideas they may have. He is grateful for the bucolic feel of a baseball game on a summer evening. Serving his country or his fellow residents of Broome County, Tylicki seeks to make a difference and draws satisfaction from his work.

Though Rich has had some other offers through the years in sports management, he has always chosen to return to Binghamton. "It's my home now and I'm proud to be able to say that," Rich explains with a smile.

George Plimpton Redux

Michael J. McCann is a full-time Johnson City firefighter, a local baseball historian, lifelong resident of the area, and the coauthor of the book sponsored by the booster club, *Celebrating 100 Years of Baseball in the Binghamton Area: Tales from the Binghamton Shrine*. McCann is often the annual host of the players that return to Binghamton to be inducted into its baseball shrine and Mike has put many of his memories of hosting the players in the book.

"The area is rich in baseball history, not only with players who have made their mark on the diamond, but with those who made their mark off the field as well," notes McCann as he points out the shrine houses broadcasters such as Ron Luciano and Pete Van Wieren in addition to stalwarts of the championship teams of the Yankees in the 1950's and 60's.

Mike is also a sort of "George Plimpton of sports writing" in Binghamton. Plimpton, if you remember, was a nationally known author and journalist who often participated in sporting events and then wrote about his experiences. Two of the many books he authored were *Paper Lion*, which dealt with his experiences as a training camp quarterback for the Detroit Lions in 1963, and *Open Net*, which documented his stint as a goalie for the Boston Bruins in a preseason game.

Well, besides the Shrine book mentioned above, McCann is also the coauthor of *Hockey in Broome County*, *Baseball in Broome County*, and *Golf in Broome County*, all published by Arcadia. Though not actually competing within the fields of play, Mike has been active for all sports along the sidelines as he writes about them. Besides his involvement in the Binghamton Baseball Shrine, he has been a caddy for golfers coming to Endicott to play in the B.C. Open and has also been active in supporting Binghamton hockey through his role in the *Broome Sports Foundation*.

McCann has many stories to tell about the rich history of sports in the Southern Tier; one of his favorites involves golf. "Bob Hope played in the 1973 *B.C. Open*, during the Pro-Am event, which was the inaugural year for the tournament as a PGA-hosted event," explains McCann as he sets up his story.

"Well during the whole time Hope was on the course, it was as if he were performing, his jokes were plentiful. At one point, when he was hitting out of the rough, he remarked 'Hitting here is like hitting off Bing Crosby's toupee!'"

McCann's face lights up as he recounts Hope's visit and the 44 years of professional golf in the area.

"People just don't realize the number of great golfers who have played here through the years—Hale Irwin, Sandy Lyle, Gary Player, Tom Watson, Tiger Woods, they all played here at one time or another," gushes McCann. "And what a boost to the community the golf tournaments have been," adds McCann. "Since the first tournament was held in 1971, it has raised over $14 million dollars that have been distributed to various charities in the area!"

Binghamton is a city on a comeback trail and its sports legacy, which McCann has documented between fighting fires, is part of the bedrock that beckons young and old to become part of the fabric of its comeback story.

Mike McCann poses with his four books about sports in the Greater Binghamton Area.

Walking Distance

Aside from a short sojourn to New Jersey in the late 1960's, Vince Fiacco has lived all of his 69 years in Broome County, growing up in the First Ward of Binghamton, getting married, settling in neighboring Endicott, and raising two children. Now he is happily retired in the home where he and his wife, Vicki raised their children. Retired, but not through working, as he donates his time for various charitable groups in the area.

As with most of his generation, he has worked for multiple companies, due to his areas of expertise being collateral damage when downsizing occurred. He started his corporate career after serving Uncle Sam from 1965 to 1967 by working for AT&T in New Jersey. He remained at AT&T for five years until he decided a return to his hometown was in order and it was time to get his undergraduate degree by using the G.I. Bill.

He graduated from Binghamton University in 1978 and went to work for IBM shortly thereafter, serving as an engineer in the component manufacturing arena. "Back then, if you worked for IBM, you were thought to have it made," mused

Vince. "Whenever we had a significant product announcement, the company cafeteria would serve 'surf and turf' for all the employees; the lines would go on forever. And of course there were the Family Days at the country club every other year. Those were really great!"

Everyone in the area looked with amazement at the IBM Family Days, where arcade rides, food, and top class entertainment were provided free of charge to IBM employees and their families. "Working for IBM was special back in the day, you took a great deal of pride in working for the company," recalled Fiacco.

Pride is a word that comes up often during our conversation. Vince elaborates, "I think this area has seen its worst days pass, but at the same time, it will never get back to the days that Endicott Johnson and IBM reigned supreme. In the end, however, the degree of success we have as a community in bouncing back may come down to the pride and ownership we show in this area in our everyday life."

After 16 years of employment, Fiacco became one of the statistics of IBM's downsizing in 1994; from IBM he found himself working for the aerospace branch of the BF Goodrich Corporation in Norwich from 1995 to 2000. From there he wound up at B.A.E, where he worked until his retirement from the corporate world in 2008.

From IBM to B.F. Goodrich to B.A.E. (British Aerospace and Marconi Electronic Systems), Vince never considered leaving the area. "It was a great place to raise our family, with it being centrally located in New York and also being so close to other big cities like New York and Philadelphia," explains Fiacco. "Besides, while I was a victim of downsizing, there was enough industry in the area where I could stay in my field and earn a living."

Leaving the area was never really an option for Vince, as he married a hometown girl who had steady employment as a nurse at Wilson Hospital and who was committed to the area. Vince never really had a desire to leave his hometown either.

"When IBM let me go, we were a little nervous, but confident that I could find something in the area," explained

Vince. "There was still some manufacturing here, and though things were starting to decline in the 90's, there was still a lot of area industry, including B.A.E, Raymond Corporation, and the like."

Over the years, with IBM pulling back, many smaller businesses that relied on contracts from IBM were forced to leave or close. Replacing the manufacturing jobs have been an influx of retail businesses, culminating in an increase of service jobs. The transition to a service economy, has brought lower paying jobs with it, and a need for employees to be at the respective "brick and mortar" stores for more hours, often resulting in fewer hours to give back to the community.

Vince is a strong believer that the strength of any community lies within its people. "It's a little disappointing right now because a number of organizations that depend on volunteers are struggling. The fire department where I volunteer, West Corners in Endicott, is at about half of past manpower levels," states Fiacco. "Those people who moved out over the years are not coming back. For example, I believe IBM used to employ close to 14,000 people in the area and now it is down to a few hundred."

All things considered, though, Vince believes in the Greater Binghamton Area. "It's been wonderful living in this area my whole life. It truly feels like home and I do think the area has started to rebound. It's nice to see the revitalization start to occur. Binghamton University has had a lot to do with our rebirth."

Vince remembers when Binghamton University started out in Endicott as Harpur College. It is now a thriving university, with 16,000 students and plans to grow to 20,000. Its growth has provided the area not only with well-paying professional jobs, but it has also helped economic growth in downtown Binghamton by opening a satellite center. With the influx of students attending downtown classes, an increase in housing and small business development have increased as well. "Walking in downtown Binghamton is now a real treat in some areas," explains Vince.

The days of Vince's youth were reflective of far simpler times. "I grew up in the First Ward of Binghamton and everything was within walking distance of our house on Dickinson Street," explains Fiacco. "There were movie theaters, swimming pools, playgrounds, mom and pop stores, etc. My parents never owned a car so I remember walking or biking anywhere I wanted to go."

Interestingly, Fiacco's boyhood memories, though a generation later, echo those of Martin Sloan, the protagonist in Rod Serling's *Walking Distance* episode, which is based on Serling's youth in Binghamton. "Whether I was walking with my dad to Johnson Field, or to the neighborhood grocery, everything that I needed or wanted was right here," Fiacco reminisces.

A Baseball and Binghamton Lifer

Baseball fans come in all shapes and sizes and the fan base for Binghamton baseball has included many colorful characters through the years. Perhaps there is no more unique fan populating the stands of NYSEG Stadium today than "Duke" Davis, who has been coming to Binghamton Mets games since the team's inception in 1992. Duke has been a resident of the area since 1934, when his mom and dad moved the family to the area from Ithaca.

Davis, unlike the majority of us who follow our local teams, can truly empathize with today's minor league player, as Davis was a minor league catcher in the Brooklyn Dodgers organization in 1944 and 1945. He was signed by longtime Binghamton resident, Dodger coach and scout, Jake Pitler, in the spring of 1944. Davis reported to the Olean farm team, which was then in the PONY League (now the New York-Pennsylvania League). Davis later also played for Burlington, North Carolina, in the Carolina League. His salary for Olean was $90.00 a month; in 1945 he negotiated his own contract and was quite pleased with himself as he almost doubled his salary, receiving $162.50 from the Dodgers organization.

Duke proudly recalls the day he was offered a contract from the Dodgers as if it were yesterday. "I was sitting at my desk in the office when my manager called and said I had a call from the Dodgers," explained Davis. "When I got to the phone everyone in the office looked up and was listening and everyone heard the Dodgers ask if I could report immediately. I looked at my manager and he looked at me and said 'Davis, get outta here!' Well, the whole office stood and cheered. I was a professional ball player."

"I got a concussion in 1944 playing ball and the big club sent me a get well package that included Pete Reiser's Brooklyn Dodgers cap. I still have that cap today!" Davis says with a smile.

Duke Davis watches batting practice from his usual perch. He's wearing Pete Reiser's cap from 1944!

Talking with Davis is like walking through Binghamton's baseball history. He was working at Ozalid when he got the call from the Dodgers and a supervisor for Ozalid at the time was Binghamton native "Wild Bill" Hallahan, who was a star pitcher for the St. Louis Cardinals in the 1920's and 1930's and started for the National League in the game's first All-Star game in 1933.

"Bill and I used to talk baseball all the time and we had a lot to talk about, you know, pitcher-catcher stuff," Davis beams. After his playing days ended, Davis often caught bullpen sessions for the Triplets. He remembers warming up Whitey Ford in 1949 and being impressed with the big break on Ford's curve.

When Mako Oliveras was the manager of the B-Mets, he had Davis take a turn in the batting cage before a game. At the young age of 85, Davis had the B-Mets' players marveling at his ability to make contact. "I told them it all comes down to hand-eye coordination, no matter the age," exhorted Davis.

Today Davis is a proud member of the *Association of Professional Ball Players of America*, which was formed in 1924 for ex-professional players, with no distinction between the majors or the minors. His card serves as his ticket to all Binghamton Mets games. Recent lifetime members of this organization include ex-NY Mets Carlos Delgado, Shawn Green, and ex-Binghamton and NY Met Jason Isringhausen.

You can usually see Davis at all B-Mets home games, sitting off to the left of home, right behind the aisle. He enjoys his vantage point from this angle. Davis is also a member of the New York State Section 4 Hall of Fame and was honored by the Brooklyn Cyclones in 2006.

Duke celebrated his 92nd birthday on October 11th, and an early present for him was the championship that the B-Mets supplied on September 12th. Duke made it to all three playoff games at NYSEG Stadium. "It was great," said Davis of watching the playoff run in September.

Author's Note: As we close this chapter, we see these people all have the same thing in common. They have proudly chosen the Greater Binghamton Area to be their home and are optimistic about the area's future. Though only six in number, they and their families are representative of the resiliency and commitment of the inhabitants of the Greater Binghamton Area. As Pedro would put it, they currently are "trusting the process" of revitalization, awaiting the results they are confident will come.

Chapter 5. The Art of Pitching

As May begins, the Mets find themselves two and one-half games behind Portland and the month rolls in with the B-Mets hosting Portland in a four-game series. This first Friday in May features happy hour at the park, two-for-one drink specials, and the first of 23 fireworks nights.

Friday night also brings a special treat in that local product, Mike Aguilera, drafted in the 5th round out of Binghamton University (BU) in 2012, takes the mound for the Sea Dogs against Greg Peavey. Spectators from the university are on hand to cheer for Aguilera, as he pursues becoming the second pitcher from BU to pitch in the big leagues. The only pitcher to do this so far is lefty Scott Diamond, who was signed by the Braves as an undrafted free agent in 2007 out of Binghamton. Entering the 2014 season, Diamond had started 58 games in the big leagues, winning 19 and losing 27 with an E.R.A of 4.43. Diamond's best year came in 2012, when he won 12 games for the Twins and was the ace of the staff, leading the team in starts and victories, and posting the lowest E.R.A. of all starters at 3.54.

Diamond attributes his success in professional baseball to many things, but besides playing in an underrated program at Binghamton University, Diamond pointed to two other leading factors. "One, I was able to concentrate 100% on baseball once I signed. At Binghamton, baseball always took a back seat to my engineering studies. Now I can totally focus on baseball, both from a mental and physical view. Second, the wood bats in the pros made it a little easier to pitch. With wood bats, it's tougher to square it up, so I don't have to be quite as fine with my pitches."

Ironically, despite his success in 2012, the start of the 2014 season for Diamond finds him in the same spot as Aguilera—pithing in the minor leagues. 2013 was a disappointing year for Diamond, as he finished with a 6-13 record and a 5.43 E.R.A. Diamond's rough year in 2013 and lackluster spring training performance put him in AAA at the start of the season, and as he tries to pitch himself back to the big leagues, Aguilera tries to pitch himself into the big leagues.

Greg Peavey gets the start against Aguilera as he begins the month of May with his third consecutive start against Portland. He gives up a run on back-to-back doubles to shortstop Deven Marrero and first baseman Travis Shaw in the top of the first.

The Mets counter with a run of their own in the bottom of the third, and it is in the bottom of the fourth inning of the 1-1 game when the contest turned on a couple of miscues by Portland. With one out and Kevin Plawecki on first, Aguilera has Plawecki picked off, but first baseman Travis Shaw fails to catch the throw and Plawecki advances to second. Aguilera then uncharacteristically throws four straight balls to Jayce Boyd, putting runners on first and second. When Lawley hits a routine grounder back to Aguilera, it looks like the start of a 1-6-3 double play, pitcher to short to first. But Aguilera throws the ball into center field to ignite a three-run rally.

The three runs are all the Mets need this night, as Peavey and relievers Jon Velasquez and Cody Satterwhite shut down the Sea Dogs and the Mets win, 5-1.

Matt Reynolds enters the game hitting .373 and is rewarded by holding down the third sport in the lineup. He goes 0 for 4, but eighth place hitter Kyle Johnson goes two for three with two RBIs in support of the win and fifth place hitter Plawecki goes two for four, raising his average to .267. Satterwhite finishes the game by throwing two more scoreless innings, extending his scoreless streak for the season to 14 and two-thirds innings.

Peavey turned in a gritty performance, allowing six hits and walking three batters in six innings. The special treat for him this night was that his wife, Ashley, was in town to see him pitch and accompanying her was their almost two-month-old son, Gaynor, born on St. Patrick's Day. Greg will never forget the day Graydon was born.

"Ashley called me at about 5:30 A.M. and usually I get up at 6:30 A.M., so at first I thought it was a wakeup call. But she told me then that I shouldn't get alarmed, but she thought she was going into labor. I said, 'What do you mean don't get alarmed?' and got my mom on the phone and got her to get me a flight out to see Ashley. She had a pretty quick delivery, so I was able to view it on face time from the airport. Then I got to spend three days with them and that was great."

Ashley, Graydon, and Greg relax at a players' picnic in May.

Being a father for the first time has helped Greg deal with the professional disappointment of being back in Binghamton after having pitched last year in AAA. "I just give it my best and come what may regarding my career," said Greg. "I'm committed to my career but it's just awesome to be able to play baseball and be a husband and father as well!"

Though Peavey's win is a tidy one for the Mets, the sporting event that captures much of the attention of the city occurs seventy miles south, as the Binghamton Senators, the AHL affiliate of Ottawa, gets knocked out of the playoffs at the hands of the Scranton Wilkes-Barre Penguins for the second year in a row, losing Game 4 by a score of five to one. The Senators lose the series, three games to one, and the team's early exit scuttled the plans of the B-Mets front office for a "Senators Night" at the stadium, where the hockey team would autograph team pictures and greet fans before the game. The Senators won the championship of the AHL in 2011, winning the Calder Cup, but have made quick exits from the playoffs in 2013 and 2014.

The next day, the first Saturday in May, the city also gets a chance to hold its 4th annual half marathon, the Bridge Run. The center of activity is the Metro Center mall, located three blocks west of the stadium, as registration for the 2400 runners participating in the *Greater Binghamton Chamber of Commerce Annual Bridge Run* is going full speed from 10 AM to 4 PM. The welcome packets for the runners include water bottles, restaurant coupons, noisemakers and Bridge Run T-shirts. This is the 4th annual race and each year the race has gotten bigger, with whispers about expanding it to a marathon in the not-too-distant future. The early talk has the race starting in Marathon, N.Y., and finishing in Binghamton. It seems like an ideal place to start a marathon, not only because of the name, but because the town of Marathon is 26 miles north of Binghamton as well.

At the Metro Center, various area businesses are hosting tables, including *Confluence Running*, *Tri-cities Runner's club* and the *Binghamton Mets Booster Club*. The center piece however, is the rectangular area in the center of the first floor, where the runners get their racing numbers and packets. Smiling faces fill the room.

Berkshire Farm Center and Services for Youth is the charity partner for the event. The organization has been providing foster care services in the area for more than 30 years. "The bridge run is a wonderful opportunity for us to get the word out about the ever-growing need for foster families within the county," explains Kristina Kuehle, Foster Care and Adoption Homefinder at Berkshire. The farm center supplies purple tee shirts with its logo to all runners and only asks that the runners wear the T-shirts in tomorrow's race. The motto on the tee shirts: "All kids need is a little help, a little hope, and somebody who believes in them."

Part of the handouts at the event are ticket vouchers that can be redeemed at the Mets' ticket offices for two dollars! As the runners pick up their packets in the morning, they can catch a doubleheader in the afternoon. More than one contestant exhorted, "It doesn't get any better than this!"

The first game of the Saturday afternoon doubleheader features a battle of two lefties, Owens for Portland and Gorski for the Mets. The Mets use four hits and a walk in the bottom of the second to plate two runs against Owens and Gorski turns in a superb performance, throwing six innings and giving up two runs on only five hits.

The Sea Dogs load the bases in the top of the ninth on two singles and a walk with only one out against closer Chase Bradford, but Bradford preserves the 3-2 lead by dancing through the danger, getting Mookie Betts to fly to short left for the second out and then on the very next pitch, inducing shortstop Deven Marrero to line out to center.

Portland gets revenge in the nightcap by mauling starter Matt Bowman for nine runs on ten hits as Bowman only registers 13 outs. Abbott and Lopez watch Bowman's performance with disappointment, not only because of the results, but because of the way he goes about his work. Bowman entered the game sporting a 3-0 record, with a sizzling 1.57 E.R.A. But in the second inning he gives up four runs on four hits, working behind throughout the inning, throwing only two first-pitch strikes to the eight hitters he faced. Three of the runs score with two outs, as Bowman cannot execute the big pitch when he needs it.

As bad as the second inning was for Bowman, the fifth was even worse, as he gave up another four runs, this time courtesy of three hits, a hits batsman, and a walk. He got only one out in the fifth inning before handing over the pitching duties to John Church. Once again, Bowman worked behind in the count throughout the inning and, overall, about a third of the pitches he threw this evening were out of the strike zone. Bowman was trying to be too fine with his pitches. Abbott made a note as Bowman went to the showers that he needed to remind Bowman to attack the hitters.

On the other side of the diamond, lefty Brian Johnson made his AA debut for the Sea Dogs and was outstanding, not allowing an earned run in 5.1 innings as the Sea Dogs pound the Mets, 9-3. After the loss, the B-Mets are 14-11, leaving them 1.5 games out of first.

In the get-away game of the series, the Mets get 10 hits, but muster only one run against a trio of Portland pitchers as they leave 10 men on base. Veteran first baseman Matt Clark has a professional day, getting a hit and drawing three walks, as he is one of the few who Lopez felt grinded out each at bat. "I don't think mentally we were all there," explained Lopez about the game. "We constantly tell the guys to grind out each at bat, but for some guys, with the weather giving us so many days off, along with the adjustment to the new league, it just takes a little time."

27-year-old Clark, with his current .346 batting average and prior history of success in the Pacific Coast League (45 HRs in his last two years), is wondering what in the world he is doing in AA. But right now he is a victim of a numbers game as Allan Dykstra, the AA MVP from last year, is manning first base for Las Vegas and Lucas Duda and Ike Davis are blocking anyone's paths to the big leagues. Clark's only choice is to continue to put up numbers that can't be ignored.

Besides Clark's efforts, the bright spot in the team's 4-1 loss is the pitching of Cody Satterwhite, as he throws two more scoreless innings, bringing his shutout streak to sixteen and two-thirds innings. Lopez remarks after the game that Satterwhite has been aggressive in the strike zone and that he and Abbot feel that when the game is on the line, "we will be able to have Cody out there." The loss to Portland puts the Mets two and one-half games out of first. Though they failed to gain ground against the Sea Dogs in this four-game series, they have gained another late inning reliever who can complement the work of Chase Bradford.

After the game the Mets head off to New Hampshire for a three-game series against the Fisher Cats. Pill, Robles, and Peavey get the starting honors but the Mets return home with only one win, as on May 6th they fall to a .500 record. They wait until the last game of the New Hampshire series to get their win, as Peavey throws a two-hit shutout in the final game and Burgamy goes two for five with a homer and three runs batted in to help the team go one game above .500 at 15-14. The 6-7-8 hitters for the Mets in the finale are right fielder Cory Vaughn,

3B Dustin Lawley, and LF Travis Taijeron. They are struggling mightily, batting .176, .191, and .185, respectively, as they head back to Binghamton.

On Thursday, May 8th the team starts a seven-game home stand as they host the Harrisburg Senators, an affiliate of the Washington Nationals, and the Altoona Curve, a farm club of the Pirates. On Friday night Pedro Lopez puts Jayce Boyd into the cleanup spot for the first time all season and gives lefty swinging Matt Clark a night off after his bat cooled to .315 with a 0-for-4 night against New Hampshire the previous night. Boyd rewards Lopez's acumen by going 2-4, with four runs batted in, including a tie-breaking three-run homer to break open the game in the fifth and help propel the Mets to a 12-6 win. After a slow start to the season, Boyd's average is now up to .244.

"I have to stay aggressive at the plate, but at the same time, refine my approach, go after the pitches I want to hit, and lately I've been able to do that," explained Boyd about his recent torrid pace, going 8 for 11 with two homers, two doubles and five runs batted in. Boyd has been alternating at DH and first base for the Mets in the first six weeks of the season, with Clark getting the majority of the time at 1B due to his hot hitting and Boyd's slow start. Regarding his slow start, Boyd said, "Whenever you're struggling a little bit, you try not to let that affect your game, you focus on what you have to do to get going, but it's hard not to look at the numbers when you're not going well."

Boyd is coming back from major shoulder problems last year that caused him to be a designated hitter on a fulltime basis for the last two months of the season. "I still have a ways to go with the shoulder, but it has been getting better, and the rehabilitation is going well," explained Boyd. "As far as DHing goes, it's a whole process you have to learn, not having the field to take your mind off any struggles you're having at the plate."

The next night, despite his hot hitting, Boyd starts the game on the bench, as Lopez reinstates Clark at 1B and in the cleanup slot in the lineup. Finding playing time for everyone continues to be a priority for Lopez. Though Boyd has been spectacular the past three games, he cannot argue with Clark's production. Clark's veteran presence and track record of success at the high levels of the minor leagues set a standard for the rest of the team. Clark himself may not be happy being in AA when he is a proven AAA player, but there is nothing he can do but play well and hope someone, whether in the Mets' organization or not, takes notice.

The Mets lose a tough one to the Senators on this Saturday night, disappointing the over 3800 fans who came out not only to applaud the Mets, but also cheer on the unseasonably game-time temperature of 80 degrees. Closer Chase Bradford gives up a run in the top of the ninth and the Mets fall to the Senators, 4-3. Mat Bowman rebounded from his poor start against Portland to hold Harrisburg to one run in five innings. In the sixth, however, he fell behind top prospect Michael Taylor and gave up a two-run home run. Though the Mets battled back to tie the game in the bottom of the eighth, the Mets fall to 4.5 games out of first.

The team bounces back the next day, May 10th, to beat the Senators, 5-2, behind the two-for-three performance of Lawley, including a home run and three RBIs. After the game, the team's booster club sponsored a spiedies and hamburger picnic dinner for the team in the stadium's picnic area. Rounding out the menu were chips and macaroni salad, with some soda and adult beverages.

The picnic was the club's way of saying thanks to the players for continuing to bring minor league baseball to the area. Just about all of the players attend, and, for some of them, eating this well is a real treat. At home, the players do not get any meal money (on the road it is only $15.00 a day) so for many of them a picnic is something not to be missed. It is a relaxed atmosphere, with the players mingling with the booster club members and stadium crew and everyone enjoying it. Pedro Lopez chatted with the grounds-keeping crew for the better part of an hour while pitching coach Glen Abbot sat with stadium workers and some booster club members.

Abbot is the most notable of the Mets coaches, as he pitched in the major leagues for 11 years, with the Oakland Athletics, Seattle Mariners, and Detroit Tigers from 1973-1984.

Though the Tigers released him in August of 1984, ending his major league career, he logged 44 innings for the World Champions that year and won three games for them, earning a World Series share.

Perhaps his most notable achievement on the diamond was being part of the four-pitcher contingent that threw a no hitter against the California Angels on September 28, 1975, the last day of the season. Abbot threw a scoreless sixth inning in relief of starter Vida Blue before giving way to Paul Lindblad and Rollie Fingers. Abbot worked a 1-2-3 sixth inning, retiring Ike Hampton, Jerry Remy, and Dave Chalk.

Bestselling author and ex-major leaguer Dirk Hayhurst had Abbot as a pitching coach while he was toiling in the minors and in his first book, *The Bullpen Gospels*, Hayhurst discussed how Abbot was affectionately known as "Foghorn Leghorn," due to his body having a similar shape to that of the likeable cartoon character. Abbot went to high school and college in Arkansas and over a half century after his birth, he still exudes the friendly demeanor of a good 'old country boy. He is as easy going as they come and never refuses an autograph request. He is at home at the round picnic table he shares with members of the community.

Jayce Boyd goes out of his way to mingle with the club members and thanks them for the afternoon. When asked what his biggest adjustment had been for AA ball thus far, Boyd does not hesitate, as he smiles and states "The weather!" His listeners evoke a loud laugh, but Boyd isn't kidding.

"Seriously, you come from 70 and 80 degree weather and then you play in such cold here it's an adjustment for sure," he states. Earlier in the game Boyd had a scary moment as he was hit in the head on a 3-2 fastball from right hander Paolo Espino. "On a 3-2 pitch that was the last place I was expecting him to come, high and in," Boyd explains. "I was looking down and away and it just got away from him." Boyd went down as if he were shot, but after Pedro Lopez and trainer Deb Iwanow came out to check on him, Boyd stirred slowly and got to his feet, getting a round of applause from the fans. He stayed in the game, and scored the first run when third baseman Dustin Lawley hit a three-run homer.

Tyler Pill, a soft spoken member of the pitching staff, also visited various tables to thank the club members. He said he enjoyed living in downtown Binghamton in some new apartments that have been built to handle the influx of Binghamton University students as the university continues to grow. "Without a car and all, it makes it easier to live within walking distance of the ballpark," Pill explained. "It's also nice living with Cody (Satterwhite) and a few of the other guys. It definitely works out well." Pill is one of those pitchers low on the Mets radar, what with Syndergaard, Montero, and Matz lurking in the minors. "The hitters are a little more patient up here, looking for their pitch," Pill explained as to the difference between high A and AA ball. Like Boyd, Pill found the competition similar to what he endured in college, as many of his opponents were also his opponents on the college level.

Matt Bowman quickly ate his dinner and then hurried off to another engagement, but not before he explained that his windup similarities to two-time Cy Young Award winner Tim Lincecum were purely coincidental. "We both have kind of the same build, so that may have something to do with us throwing the same," Bowman stated. Indeed, one needs only a quick look at Bowman's delivery and the torque he generates from the rotation of his hip to see the similarities with Lincecum.

"Soup" Debuts

Later this night, at approximately 9:30, Eric "Soup" Campbell becomes the 742nd player from a Binghamton area minor league team to make his debut in the majors. He bats with the N.Y. Mets tied against Phillies, 3-3, with the bases loaded and one out in the bottom of the sixth against hard-throwing lefty Jacob Deekman. In the Citi Field stands watching intently are his parents, Amy and Hugh. His father, interviewed two innings earlier, gave this scouting report of his son, who played for him in high school. "If you're looking for someone to hit home runs, he's not going to be that guy, he's a line drive hitter who can play a variety of positions and who can run well for his size."

As if on cue, Campbell hits an inside 1-0 fastball on a line to right and, for a moment, it looks as if Campbell has his first big league hit, but right fielder Marlon Byrd catches it for the second out. Daniel Murphy tags up from third and scores easily and, as he heads for the dugout he has a wide grin on his face for Campbell. Campbell's seven-year sojourn in the minors is over!

Smiles and high fives greet Campbell as he returns to the dugout. In the stands, his mother photographed his at-bat on her smart phone and gave a fist pump with her right hand when she saw solid contact. After sitting down again next to her husband, she grabbed his knee as he let go a joyful sigh of relief.

Originally the 27-year-old Campbell was in the starting lineup, as first baseman Lucas Duda spent the previous day in a hospital getting treated for food poisoning, but when Duda told Collins in the morning that he felt fine and wanted to play, Campbell's name was scratched from the lineup. "It's a dream come true," Campbell said before the game in describing his call to the big leagues. He told Adam Rubin in his ESPN Blog, "There are a lot of emotions going through my head. This definitely makes it all worth it." Campbell was hitting .355 at Triple-A Las Vegas, and had displayed his versatility by playing every position but center field and catcher. During his stay in Binghamton from 2010-1012, Campbell played the corner infield and outfield positions and hit 19 home runs while knocking in 126 runs in 976 at bats.

Campbell became the sixth player from the 2008 Mets draft to make the big leagues, joining: Ike Davis (first round), Kirk Nieuwenhuis (third), Josh Satin (sixth), Collin McHugh (18th) and Chris Schwinden (22nd). Campbell and his colleagues all passed through Binghamton on their way to the show.

The next day saw a Mother's Day crowd of 2,043 come out to see Tyler Pill oppose one of the Nationals' top pitching prospects, right hander A.J. Cole. Pill deserved to have a better record than his 0-5 slate and he was hoping that the previous day's picnic would provide him with some good luck, as his run support left something to be desired in the early days of the season. Pill brought his 'A' game with him on this sunny afternoon as he shut out Harrisburg in his five innings of work, allowing only four hits while striking out seven. The key for his excellent performance was his ability to command all of his pitches, not only for strikes, but also within the strike zone. Still, after five innings, he only had a 1-0 lead, courtesy of Kevin Plawecki's seventh double of the year in the third inning, which drove in Kyle Johnson from second.

Ironically, as soon as Pill left the game, the Mets scored another run in the bottom of the sixth, as Darrell Ceciliani, batting seventh in the order, knocked in Lawley with a sacrifice fly. The Mets' bullpen closed out the victory, throwing the final four innings and allowing only one run. Without the DH in effect, Jayce Boyd rode the bench and Johnson, Ceciliani, and Vaughn manned the outfield from left to right, leaving Taijeron and his sub-200 average on the bench. Lawley provided a bright spot, as he went 1 for 3 and got his average over .200, to .204. Lopez was encouraged with the way Lawley started to swing the bat against Harrisburg; getting his bat going would be a great sign for the Mets' offense.

Closing as an Art Form

After Harrisburg leaves town, the Altoona Curve comes in for a three-game series. Altoona wears out the Mets in the first game, chasing Hansel Robles from the mound in the third inning, as the team bats around for seven runs and puts a 10-3 drubbing on the Mets. The Mets bounce back to win the second game of the series, 5-3, and it is in this game that Chase Bradford gives a clinic on "The Art of the Closer" as the Mets run their record to 19-16.

Bradford, drafted in the 35th round of the 2011 draft from the University of Central Florida, is primarily a two-pitch pitcher, throwing a sinking fastball in the low 90's and a slider that is 10 miles slower. He relies on changing speeds and location for his success. The lack of a big breaking ball profiles him as a reliever, but even when grouped in the narrow confines of right-handed relief pitchers, he ranks no higher than the seventh-rated prospect in the whole organization. He has, however, produced at every level of the minor leagues. In 2012 he pitched to a 2.47 E.R.A. for Savannah with 3 saves; he followed that with a 6-2 season for St. Lucie with three more saves in 2013. This year he has already saved six of the 18 wins Binghamton has garnered.

"My philosophy is to just attack the hitters and throw strikes," Bradford explains. "Hitters get themselves out a lot of the time. I love pitching out of the bullpen. It's a tough job but I think I fit right in and I have grown comfortable with my role."

Besides having talent, the mental makeup of a closer is vital. Closers are the ones on the mound when the games hang in the balance and no closer is successful 100% of the time. Having the ability to bounce back from a bad outing is essential, as is the ability to also have an arm bounce back with power and precision for two or three days in a row, as closers often need to pitch for consecutive stretches.

With the Mets holding a 5-3 lead, Altoona's leadoff hitter in the top of the ninth is power-hitting Stetson Allie. Figuring Allie is sitting on a first-pitch fastball, Bradford and Plawecki conspire to throw a slider on the first pitch. But Bradford misses with the pitch, a bit high and off the plate. Behind in the count, he comes in with a knee-high fastball, but once again misses off the plate. Now Allie has the count in his favor, 2-0, and he is sitting on the fastball. Bradford, nursing a two-run lead, is ready to attack Allie by going strength against strength. The last thing a closer wants to do is open the final frame with a walk, so Bradford focuses on throwing his fastball for a strike. Allie knows this as well, and when Bradford delivers a letter high fastball, Allie times the pitch perfectly. But he just misses squaring up the ball, catching it only at its bottommost position, and the result is a foul ball straight back against the screen.

Lopez and Abbott wince. The result may have been a strike, but Bradford's first three pitches in the inning are disconcerting. The game is viewed differently when you are watching it from the manager's perch. There is no such thing as a simple ball or a strike. There is always a story behind each pitch. First, there is the pitcher's delivery to dissect, including the release point, then pitch location and selection. Is he being too "cute," trying to trick the hitter too much instead of challenging him? Is he keeping his shoulder closed so he does not open up with his body too quickly, resulting in pitches that are too high?

And if you are watching the batter, the proverbial "good at bat" is what matters, not necessarily the result. Did the hitter make good contact? If not, why not? Did he read the ball out of the pitcher's hand in a timely fashion? Was his swing balanced? He didn't pull off the ball, did he? All these things are the way the game is watched from the dugout, pitch after pitch, and game after game. The smallest of things, missed by the fan in the stands, can find itself into the post-game report compiled after each game by the manager.

Tonight Bradford sees the same thing that Lopez and Abbot do, and he sees that Allie's bat speed is fastball ready. Now the Pitching 101 textbook says it is time to change Allie's bat speed, time for an off-speed offering. But Bradford misses with his offs-peed offering and he is now behind in the count, 3-1. Lopez and Abbot purse their lips. Bradford now has to challenge Allie for the second time, not give him too much credit and come right after him with the "hard stuff." So Bradford delivers his fastball. Allie, however, is once again under it as he sends a popup to second. As Allie heads in frustration to the dugout, Bradford tells himself "One out, two more to go."

Up next is catcher Elias Diaz, who entered the game hitting .333 and already has two hits on the night. He also displayed a rifle arm in gunning down Kyle Johnson trying to steal second in the seventh. Bradford starts him with a 91-mph fastball that is off the plate. Bradford is battling himself right now, as his command of his fastball is elusive. He and Plawecki adjust, throwing nothing but off-speed pitches for the rest of the Diaz at-bat. Bradford attacks the outside corner and gets Diaz to swing and miss at a changeup on a 2-2 count.

Left fielder Justin Howard now steps in the batter's box, and Bradford, once again, throws a first-pitch fastball. This time it is on the black of the plate and home plate umpire John Bacon yells out "One" and raises his hand to indicate a strike. Bradford wastes no time in delivering the next pitch, getting it back from Plawecki and almost immediately throwing another fastball to

Howard, this one belt high and almost down the middle of the plate. This is Bradford at his best, being aggressive in the strike zone and challenging his opponent. Throwing his changeup has helped him fine tune his fastball delivery as the inning progressed. Howard swings and misses and Bradford now is one strike away from notching his seventh save of the season. Ahead in the count, 0-2, Bradford follows the unwritten textbook of pitching that says ahead in the count, you throw off speed, as the hitter has to look for a fastball, to protect himself with two strikes. Bradford misses inside with his 82-mph offering. With the count now one and two, he comes back with a fastball, catching the corner of the plate, but it is a bit high and Howard lays off the challenge from Bradford.

Knowing Howard is looking for the fastball, Plawecki and Bradford again conspire to go off speed. Howard takes Bradford's pitch, thinking it is outside. But Bacon's opinion is the one that counts and the home plate umpire raises his hand and calls the off-speed delivery a strike.

The box score shows the 4-5-6 hitters for the Curve went 2-11 tonight, but it does not show the thinking man's pitcher that Bradford was in the inning as he faced the heart of the order. Battling his control, working behind the hitters, he only threw 8 of his 15 pitches for strikes, but he mixed up the speed and location of his pitches, never giving the hitter a repeat look at the same pitch in the same location. Though Bradford's stuff does not give him a closer's profile for the major leagues, his mental approach, ability to change speeds, and arm resiliency allow him to establish himself as a dark horse candidate to gain a spot on a big league pitching staff someday.

After Bradford's 1-2-3 pitching performance, the B-Mets quickly shower as they have another long trip waiting for them as they head to New Hampshire for the third time in the season and the second time in the month. They have three games under their belt of a stretch of twenty straight days of playing baseball, as their next scheduled off day is not until June 2nd. As with the April road trip, the Mets will follow the New Hampshire series with a trip to Portland. They are playing well, going 6-2 since falling to .500 on May 6th. They head to New England with a 20-16 record.

The Education of Matt Bowman

In the first game of the New Hampshire series, on Friday night, May 16th, Matt Bowman compiles a most bizarre pitching line. He gives up six runs, but all of them are unearned and he strikes out 12 in six innings of work, while walking three. Though the bottom of third inning proves to be disastrous, as he gives up all six runs in this inning, it also provides a lesson for him. The B-Mets had just scored three runs in the top of the third and Bowman entered the bottom of the inning with a four-run lead.

Ninth-place hitter and shortstop Peter Mooney started the inning by reaching safely on an error by first baseman Matt Clark. Bowman then gets two quick strikes on left fielder Jon Berti before getting him to ground into a force out at second. One out, one runner on and a four-run lead puts Bowman in the driver's seat. But Bowman then leaves a pitch up and center fielder Kenny Wilson laces it to center for a triple, scoring Berti. When catcher A.J. Jimenez gets hit with a pitch, it puts runners at the corners with one out.

Then, in an excellent piece of pitching, after falling behind cleanup hitter and second baseman Ryan Schimpf 3-0, Bowman battles back to strike him out. He now has two outs in the inning and after he gets ahead of right fielder Mike Crouse, 0-2, things are looking good for Bowman and the Mets. Abbot and Lopez are impressed with Bowman's determination and grittiness; he is battling well.

But then Bowman implodes.

First he throws a wild pitch, letting Wilson score and moving Jimenez to second. Then nothing but balls to Crouse, as Bowman puts runners on first and second. Then Bowman goes to 3-2 on third baseman Andy Burns before he walks him as well.

Abbot comes to the mound and reminds Bowman that other than Wilson, no one has hit his stuff. An error, two walks and a hit batsmen have created this mess. Bowman needs to regain his rhythm, start throwing strikes again. "Trust your stuff" Abbot tells him. "Just get the next hitter and we're outta here," thinks Abbot.

No sooner than Abbot leaves the mound, and the next hitter, lefty swinging Andy Fermin launches a rocket to right for a grand slam.

Bowman is a heap of frustration on the mound.

But as Fermin rounds the bases, something clicks inside Bowman as he stands alone on the mound. There is no place to hide from the scattering catcalls emanating from the stands. He and the Mets now trail by two runs. Lopez and Abbot, sensing a teaching moment in process, leave Bowman in the game to see how he responds. When first baseman Gabe Jacobo steps in the box, Bowman channels his madness into three straight strikes as Jacobo swings and misses at all three offerings.

Bowman clearly let the third inning get away from him, but only two pitches got squared up—the triple by Wilson and the homer by Fermin. Bowman gave away runs due to his lack of control and when he had a chance to limit the damage, he failed. When Abbot visited him on the mound, trying to build his confidence and no doubt telling him to go right after Fermin, Bowman responded by giving up a grand slam. If this were the big leagues, Bowman would be out of the game. But this is Double A, where player development is essential.

Throughout the early part of the season, Abbot has been working with Bowman, encouraging him to throw his fastball more, to be more aggressive in going after opponents. But Bowman thinks of himself as a finesse pitcher instead of a power pitcher. He looks around at the power pitchers in the organization, including the likes of Noah Syndergaard, Steven Matz, Cory Mazzoni, Jenrry Mejia, and Jeurys Familia and they all have fastballs that make his seem pedestrian.

As Bowman goes out for the fourth inning, the Fisher Cats are taking his first pitches, expecting Bowman to fall behind, but after the disaster of the third inning, Bowman finds his rhythm, commands his pitches and stifles the Fisher Cats. Bowman throws three shutout innings the rest of the way, striking out five and not walking or hitting anyone. As Bowman works ahead in the count, he pitches with more confidence. He has "Etch-a-Sketched" the third inning from his mind, now concentrating on the process of pitching, the execution of each pitch. He pitches with nothing to lose, and the strikeouts just naturally happen, as he keeps his pitches low in the zone.

The Mets come back to win the game, scoring four runs in the top of the eighth, as Burgamy hits a bases-clearing double with one out and the Mets turned what looked like a game they gave away into a hard-earned and confidence-building win. Velasquez, Kolarek, and Bradford throw three scoreless innings to close out the game, allowing only one hit.

Abbot takes Bowman aside before his next start and tells him, "You have to be more aggressive. You're giving the hitters too much credit. Throw your fastball more." Bowman ponders Abbot's words and explains, "Abby's been great, but I have to experience things myself, feel it before I execute."

The B-Mets wind up sweeping New Hampshire to extend their winning streak to five and run their record to 9-2 in their last 11 contests. The next stop on the road trip is Portland, where they have to play six games in four days due to early season rainouts. Heading into Monday night's doubleheader on May 19th, they are in second place, 2.5 games behind Portland and two games in front of third place Reading, which is 4.5 games out of first, in third place with a record of 21-18.

Much of Binghamton's success during the past 11 games is due to the hot hitting of Plawecki, who bats .413 in the first 12 games in May, with 11 R.B.I.s. Portland's outstanding start to the season is fueled by second baseman Mookie Betts, catcher Blake Swihart, and a trio of starting pitchers. Betts entered the game leading the Eastern League with a .383 average and had an unbelievable streak of having reached base at least once for 66 straight games, dating back to 2013. Swihart was hitting at a .289 clip and had thrown out 45 percent of attempted base stealers.

The first game of the doubleheader with Portland matched Owens against Robles and, as expected, a pitcher's duel emerged, as the Mets had a 1-0 lead through four innings. Owens left the game after four innings, having thrown 89 pitches, with four walks and eight strikeouts contributing to his high pitch count. In the top of the fifth, Matt Clark broke the game open for the Mets by hitting a three-run home run off reliever Michael Olmstead, giving him eight homers and a team-leading 27 runs batted in. Plawecki continued his hot hitting with his 9th double in the sixth inning to knock in another run. Hansel Robles was outstanding, throwing six shutout innings, striking out two and not walking anyone. He gave up six hits and dropped his E.R.A. to 4.46. Satterwhite came on in the seventh to close out the 5-0 win that put the Mets within a game-and-a-half of first place. Besides getting the win, the B-Mets also stopped Betts' consecutive game streak for getting on base, as he went 0-3 in the leadoff spot.

Portland, however, came back with a vengeance in the second game, pounding newly activated lefty Angel Cuan for eight runs on 12 hits in four innings. Before the game Cuan's activation was enthusiastically received, as besides the team having to play six games in four days, reliever TJ Chism had been put on the disabled list with a shin contusion and starter Greg Peavey had been promoted to Las Vegas to make a spot start or two.

The third game of the series saw the B-Mets go 0-10 with runners in scoring position as they fell to the Sea Dogs, 2-1. In a battle of southpaws, Brian Johnson bested Darin Gorski, going six innings and allowing only one run on four hits. Gorski was the tough-luck loser, allowing only one earned in five innings. The game turned on a pair of errors in the fourth inning. With Henry Ramos on first, shortstop Heiker Meneses hit a potential double play ball to his counterpart, Matt Reynolds. But Reynolds did not get his glove down and the ball scooted under his legs to put runners on first and third. Then, when Gorski threw over to first to limit the lead of Meneses, Ramos took off for home and

Clark's throw was wild, enabling the run to score. The bullpens then both pitched four shutout innings to keep the final at 2-1.

On Wednesday, 5/21, the B-Mets and Portland played yet another doubleheader, with the pitching matchups being Keith Couch and Luis Cessa in the first game and Robby Scott and Matt Bowman in the second game. Cessa was a fill-in, called up from St. Lucie and he did not make it out of the fourth inning, giving up five runs before he left. Couch meanwhile scattered nine hits and held the Mets to only one run, lowering his E.R.A. to 2.39 while getting his sixth win, 5-1.

In the second game the B-Mets squandered a 5-0 lead as the Sea Dogs took advantage of some control problems from Matt Bowman to rally for six runs in the fifth inning and defeat the B-Mets, 6-5.

Bowman's outing was eerily similar to that of five days earlier. He enters the bottom of the fifth inning with a 5-1 lead, having given up only three hits to go with the one run. He's battling his command a bit, walking two and throwing 69 pitches in his four innings of work. But his pitches have good sink, as he has recorded all of his outs either via strikeout or groundout. In the bottom of the fifth, however, he gives up five runs on three hits and two walks, having thrown 102 pitches.

As in the game against the Fisher Cats, Bowman gives an indication he can get out of the jam before things quickly turn sour. He gives up a leadoff single to Shannon Wilkerson and then allows a double to Mookie Betts. With runners on second and third, he gets shortstop Derrik Gibson to ground out, third to first. Lefty hitter Travis Shaw then grinds out a seven-pitch walk, loading the bases and putting Bowman's pitch count at 89.

Chase Bradford now gets up in the bullpen to warm up.

Abbott pops out of the dugout as cleanup and lefty hitting third baseman Stefan Welch comes to the plate. Abbot reminds Bowman he has a four-run lead and to be aggressive, reminding him his fastball has been working well low in the zone, generating ground ball outs.

Once again, though, as soon as Abbot takes his seat on the bench, bad things happen, as Bowman leaves his fastball up and Welch delivers a two-run single, making the score 5-3 and putting runners at first and second.

    Abbot and Lopez are watching Bowman and his pitch count closely. Bowman gets lefty hitting designated hitter Henry Ramos to take a strike, then ahead in the count 0-2, he gets Ramos to ground out to first baseman Matt Clark, moving Shaw and Welch to second and third. Bradford is ready to come in, but Lopez leaves Bowman to face shortstop Heiker Meneses. Bowman falls behind, 1-0, then Meneses fouls off a pitch before Bowman throws another ball. Meneses eventually grinds out an eight-pitch walk, loading the bases.

    Lopez grimaces in the dugout, Bowman's pitch count is at 102 and he has been up in the zone on all his pitches to Meneses, eventually walking him on a fastball that is high and outside. Lopez goes to the mound, takes the ball from Bowman and asks his closer, Chase Bradford to preserve the lead.

    Bradford is not up to the task tonight, however, as he gives up back-to-back singles to catcher Michael Brenly and left fielder Peter Hissey and the Mets go on to lose to Portland, 6-5.

    As the B-Mets return to their hotel on this night, Bowman has a pattern to ponder. A pattern that he has to break. Two straight starts, two blown four-run leads, two games blowing up for him in one inning, both largely because he worked behind in the count and he couldn't get the big out when he needed it. His record now sits at 3-2, with a 4.46 E.R.A.

    In the final game of the series, with the B-Mets now trailing by 5.5 games and falling from second place, the Sea Dogs rubbed salt in the Mets' wounds. The B-Mets held a 5-4 lead going in to the bottom of the ninth when Satterwhite goes for his first save of the season. But Portland makes quick work of Satterwhite, as Hissey walks, Shannon Wilkerson reaches on a bunt single and then Mookie Betts hits a walk-off double to give the Sea Dogs another 6-5 win. Rainy Lara turned in his worst start of the year, lasting only three innings, giving up three runs on three hits and walking four batters as his E.R.A. rose to 4.40.

    The Mets came to Portland with a six-game winning streak and visions of moving into first. Instead, they leave with a five-game losing streak, in third place, 6.5 games behind

Portland and 1.5 games behind second place Reading. Pitching artistry was lacking for the B-Mets in this series, as Cuan and Cessna turned in disappointing starts in their debuts while Bowman and Lara were ineffective in their regular turns. Gorski was a tough-luck loser and Robles was the only starter to leave Portland with a win.

The Mets limp back to the friendly confines of NYSEG Stadium with a 24-21 record, where they will host New Britain for four games and New Hampshire for three.

Interestingly, the most important game of the home stand occurs in a rain-abbreviated two-inning game on the 27th of May. On this day Matt Bowman makes his first start after the disappointing Portland game and his catcher is Travis d'Arnaud, who is finishing a short rehabilitation stint with the B-Mets. Bowman is delighted to be throwing to a major leaguer, but is surprised by how often the big league backstop is signaling for his fastball. As in his previous two starts, the Mets stake him to a big lead, scoring three runs in both the first and second innings.

Sitting behind the plate is d'Arnaud, and with such a big lead so early, he is signaling fastball after fastball. Bowman is bemused, but tells himself "I'm not going to shake off a big league catcher, clearly I don't know more than what he knows."

So Bowman just looks for the sign, registers it, and throws. "Let me just go with what he puts down, and just concentrate on executing my pitches," reasons Bowman. Though the game is suspended after two innings due to rain, d'Arnaud's two innings with Bowman registers with him. "Maybe I need to shake off the catcher's signals less and just focus on executing my pitches" he concludes.

"You've got a good fastball, use it," d'Arnaud tells him.

This proves to be a turning point in the season for Bowman as he becomes more aggressive with his fastball, delivering quality start after start, lowering his E.R.A. from 4.46 to 3.11.

That final week in May proved to be invaluable for Bowman as he was reminded of some key elements for being an artist on the mound: 1) Don't let any one inning get away from you; 2) Be aggressive with the fastball, pitch off of it; 3) Trust your process, the execution of your pitches, because that is what you can control. If you properly execute your pitches, then good results will follow.

Bowman applied the lessons of May throughout the rest of the season and success followed him. His work for the B-Mets in June earned him a promotion to AAA Las Vegas on July 4th, where he went 3-2 with a 3.47 E.R.A. in 36 innings and he struck out 32 batters while only walking nine. His month of June was outstanding for Binghamton, as he went 3-2, throwing four quality starts in five outings and pitching to a 2.81 E.R.A.

Bowman's Month of June:

Date	Opponent	Won/Lost	IP	H	R (ER)	BB	K
6/6	New Britain	Lost 6-3	5.1	9	4(4)	1	7
6/11	Akron	Won 12-6	7	9	2(2)	3	7
6/17	Richmond	Won 5-1	6	3	0(0)	2	4
6/22	Bowie	Lost 2-0	7	8	2(2)	1	3
6/29	Altoona	Won 7-4	7	6	2(1)	1	9
June Totals		3-2	32.1	35	10(9)	8	30

Bowman's artistry on the mound did not go unnoticed in New York. As he earned his promotion to Las Vegas, some front office personnel were commenting on how Bowman reminded them of another right-handed Ivy League pitcher—Ron Darling, a current broadcaster for the New York Mets who, after graduating from Yale, won 136 big league games and was a star pitcher on the 1986 championship club. Darling achieved success with a good, but not dominant fastball, complementing it with an outstanding curveball early in his career and a superb split-finger later in his career.

Ron Darling as a Tidewater Tide in 1982. He is pitching against Syracuse, in MacArthur Stadium, which has since been torn down.

Chapter 6. "Big Plaw's Gonna Rip a Double… "

The B-Mets entered June with a 30-24 record, in second place in the Eastern Division, seven games behind Portland and only a half-game ahead of the third-place Reading Fightin' Phils. They started the month slowly, going 2-6 in their first eight games and their slow start was attributed, at least in part, to an injury bug that hit the team. Matt Reynolds did not play at all from May 28th through June 2nd due to a strained tendon in his pinky finger that limited his play for a bit when he returned to the lineup, especially in his holding and gripping of the bat. In addition, infielder-outfielder Dustin Lawley, lefty reliever TJ Chism, and second baseman Wilfredo Tovar all started the month on the disabled list.

Add in the fact that half the lineup is still having difficulty getting things going at the plate and the slow start in June is understandable. Cory Vaughn, counted on to be a mainstay in the lineup, is only hitting .190 with three home runs and 10 RBIs in 174 at bats and he is not the only one who struggles.

As the calendar turned to June, Travis Taijeron was sitting at .213, Brian Burgamy was barely hitting his weight at .236 and Lawley was doing the same, stuck at .220. Burgamy also had the burden of filling in at second base while Tovar went on the disabled list with what was originally announced as a sprained thumb.

On the other side of the ledger, the hitters that were carrying the load included Kyle Johnson, who while sharing outfield playing time with Ceciliani, Vaughn, Taijeron, and Lawley, was hitting .331; second baseman Wilfredo Tovar, who was hitting .313; catcher Kevin Plawecki, hitting .321; and shortstop and surprise of the season, Matt Reynolds, who finished May hitting .352. What was the reaction of the manager to the mixed results from his lineup?

Lopez preached patience to his hitters, telling them that they were seasoned hitters whose bats would come around. As for the injury bug, Lopez expounded on the notion that this provided opportunities for others on the roster and it also allowed him to make sure everyone was getting at bats.

The team remained confident throughout the travails of the first two months. When Connor Gates drove starting pitcher Greg Peavey to the airport to meet his wife and Gaynor, his two-month-old child in early May, Peavey explained the team's start with a shrug of the shoulder. "Just wait, this team is going to win. These hitters are proven hitters and are going to come around and when they do, watch out!" Peavey pronounced this opinion in a matter-of-fact manner, without a trace of bravado. For him, it was a simple statement of fact.

Cory Vaughn, coming off an invitation to spring training with the parent club and an impressive 2013 in Binghamton where he hit .281 and had 10 home runs in 174 at bats, knew he just had to work his way out of his slump. "Just gotta keep working hard and the hits will come," he reminded himself day after day.

Vaughn's patience and hard work is rewarded on June 5th, when Las Vegas calls him up to AAA to replace Andrew Brown, who got called up to the big club. Vaughn has started to make better contact, though his numbers are still lacking.

Even when the team lost five of the first six games of the month, the players stayed upbeat. At this point in the season, Lopez told broadcaster Tim Heiman, the key to playing well was being patient and working hard. "The patience of staying positive, knowing we have to continue to work and working out smart will get us through the rough patch," Lopez explained. He was satisfied with the efforts of his players and he felt the team just had to trust its process of preparing to play, that it was only a matter of time before the entire lineup jelled. He acknowledged that injuries were also playing a role, as the team was adjusting to playing different roles.

With Tovar and Reynolds out of the lineup for a five-game stretch from 5/28 through June 2nd, Lopez had to move Burgamy to second and Sandoval to short, leaving him a middle infielder short. When Burgamy got thrown of a game on June 10th, Dustin Lawley had to man 2B for the first time since high school and backup catcher Nelfi Zapata found himself playing third!

    Through the injuries and travails, Lopez encouraged the players to "trust the process, ignore the results." With the right practice habits, the results would come. Even on the morning of June 8th, when things looked bleak, Lopez was upbeat. The team had just found out a few days earlier they would be without the services of Tovar for close to two months, as his thumb required surgery. Explained Lopez, "That puts a big hole in the infield, you are talking about the best defensive player we have being lost for an extended period."

    Entering play on the eighth of June, the Mets had already lost the first two games of their short three-game home stand against the New Britain Rock Cats by scores of 6-3 and 6-4, extending their losing streak to four. This was the third time in the season that the B-Mets had a losing streak of at least four games. On the morning of June 8th, the team was eight games out of first and only a half-game ahead of fourth place Reading. Compounding matters further, they were only two games over .500, which was their lowest point since being at the .500 mark on the sixth of May. Finally, with Tovar out of the lineup, there was no help in sight for the infield. Burgamy had to expect an extended stay at second base.

    The night before they had blown a 4-2 lead they took into the fifth against the Rock Cats, with Jack Leathersich uncharacteristically playing the goat. He relieved Greg Peavey in the fifth after the Rock Cats had tied the game. He got the last out of the inning, then struck out the side in the sixth and quickly recorded two outs in the top of the seventh. But he then walked Kennys Vargas and gave up a single to Reynaldo Rodriguez. Next, New Britain shortstop Brad Boyer worked the count to 3-2 and, after fouling off a tough pitch, Boyer lined a triple to left center to drive in Vargas and Rodriguez, giving New Britain a 6-4 win.

    Coming into the game Leathersich had allowed only one earned run in his previous 13 innings, while striking out 25. In the first game of the series he had come in for an inning and struck out the side. This was his second consecutive outing and his longest one of the season, as he threw 41 pitches, but Leathersich offered no excuses for his failure, never mentioning the word "tired." Rather, he had already shrugged off the loss moment after the game, telling beat reporter Lynn Worthy, "It's already behind me. I'm not too worried about it. I just wish I'd made a better pitch and we could've came out of here with a win."

Lopez did not consider replacing Leathersich with the lefty hitting Boyer coming to the plate. "Leathersich was mixing pitches. The fastball was kept down in the zone. He elevated whenever he wanted to. He just got in trouble with two outs."

While the bad news mounted, Lopez stayed on an even keel. Nowhere was this more evident than on June 8th, the second Sunday in June. As players filed in to get ready for the 1 P.M. start, there was no sulking in the clubhouse. Rather Ryan Sandoval and Darrell Ceciliani were so animated they could have been protagonists in a Disney cartoon. At about 10 in the morning Sandoval and Ceciliani, accompanied by general manager Jim Weed, went up to the press box and chatted with Justin Cohen, the Video Director. Ryan and Darrell were chuckling and pointing to a CD that Darrell held in his hand. Ceciliani handed Justin the CD and told him to play it when Plawecki came to bat. As Sandoval and Ceciliani left the press box area, they had smiles as wide as first graders on Christmas morning.

Tyler Pill was sent to the mound to stop the slide, but in the top of the second he was touched for a run and three hits, and the damage would have been worse, except for Taijeron gunning down a runner at home. The Mets went down meekly in the first, going 1-2-3, leaving cleanup hitter Matt Clark to lead off the second. Clark lined the second pitch he saw to center field for a quick out.

As Plawecki approached the plate, his walk-up music started to play.

Check that, the *walk up CD that Sandoval and Ceciliani had supplied earlier* started to play. The beginning of the tape was the music typically played for Plawecki's song, *Double Bubble Trouble* [by M.I.A. (Mathangi "Maya" Arulpragasam)]. So all was normal at first. He had switched to this song from *Ghosts N Stuff* (by Deadmau5) once his bat had heated up in May and he was spraying doubles all over the field.

Ballplayers are often a superstitious lot, and maybe *Double Bubble Trouble* had nothing to do with his rising batting average, but as Plawecki kept hitting doubles, Ceciliani and Sandoval had noticed. Indeed, during the past few weeks, whenever Plawecki was at bat, Ceciliani would break into song in the dugout, saying "Big Plaw's gonna rip a double." The starting pitchers were also impressed with Plawecki's performance, as charting pitches behind home plate gave them a close up view of Plawecki's prowess. "Every time we look up, we expect to see Plawecki at second, he's living right now" noted Darin Gorski as his eyes grew wide and a smile lit his face as he spoke of his catcher.

As Plawecki settled into the batter's box this afternoon, however, he lost focus. Expecting to hear the song's opening lyrics, *"Uh oh, you're in trouble, I step up in the game and I burst that bubble,"* Plawecki had to step out of the batter's box as he instead heard—

"Uh oh, you're in trouble, Big Plaw's in the box and he's gonna rip a double."

"Say what?" he thought.

He stepped out of the box, chuckling to himself as he saw Ceciliani guffawing in the dugout. He shook his head from side to side as he waited for the lyrics to finish. He looked at Ceciliani and uttered a good-natured profanity, wearing a big smile on his face. Plawecki did not want to hold up the game or draw too much attention to Ceciliani's antics, though. He quickly stepped back into the box. As he took the first pitch for a ball, the entire dugout was full of wide eyes, laughter, and slapping hands.

After Plawecki took a strike, the dugout animation started to fade. With the count 1-1 and the prank complete, Plawecki settled down to business by lining a single to right. As he stood on first, he looked into the dugout and had a huge smile on his face, but his smile was not as wide as the one Ceciliani had as he popped out of the dugout to head to the on-deck circle in preparation for his first at bat. Meanwhile, Jayce Boyd, the next hitter, gingerly walked to the plate, glancing over his shoulder, wondering if the pranksters had doctored his walk-up song too.

Never again would walking up to the plate be taken for granted among the B-Mets.

Though the change in lyrics provided an interlude of laughter, it did nothing for the immediate needs of the bats of the B-Mets. Boyd flied out to right and Ceciliani grounded back to the pitcher to end the inning.

In the bottom of the third, the B-Mets got a helping hand from the Rock Cats. The Mets jumped out to a 2-1 lead, courtesy of a throwing error by New Britain's second baseman Eddie Rosario, who turned a potential double play grounder to short off the bat of Matt Reynolds into a two-base throwing error. If Rosario had turned the double play, the Rock Cats would have gotten out of a bases loaded, one out jam.

After Pill gets opposing catcher Kyle Knudson to ground out to third to end the top of the fourth, Plawecki hurries off the field just a little faster than normal, as he is due to lead off the bottom of the inning and he has to shed his catching gear first. Intern Joe Campione, manning his usual station in the press box on this day, now picks up the story.

"When Plawecki came up, we played the Ceciliani/Sandoval tape again. I mean, he got a hit the first time up so it was working. But as Plawecki came up this time, he actually sped up his routine once he heard Ceciliani's voice."

"Hey, look, he's not smiling this time," a voice called out in the press box.

"Yeah, he actually looks annoyed," commented another.

Plawecki takes the first pitch for a ball. He then takes a strike. He is all over the next pitch, hitting a line drive to right center, and does not stop running until he reaches second. He is now two-for-two with his new walk-up song! Both the press box and dugout are full of laughter and smiles, with animated discussions taking place in both places. "At that point," mentioned Campione, we're thinking "We need to play that new walk-up song as long as possible, as it was creating good mojo!"

The Mets, however, waste Plawecki's lead-off double, as Boyd and Ceciliani fly out and Lawley goes down swinging.

As the Mets head out to the field for the top of the fifth, Pedro has heard enough of Ceciliani's voice. He calls the press box and succinctly commands, "Go back to the usual song."

When Plawecki comes up in the bottom of the sixth, with the Mets nursing a 3-2 lead, he takes a called strike, then swings and barely makes contact, tipping the ball off the catcher's glove. Then he swings and misses on the third pitch.

"Looks like his bubble has burst," yells out someone in the press box, mimicking the standard lyrics. The press box resembles a Seinfeld audience, complete with smiles, laughter, and shaking heads, and of course wondering what might have happened if Pedro's order had been ignored. Without the aid of the new words, there is no double for "Big Plaw" during this at bat. But the Mets hold on and break their four-game losing streak, sealing the game with a four-run inning in the bottom of the eighth, bunching 4 hits, a walk, and a wild pitch for a 7-3 win. In his final at bat during the 8th, Plawecki keeps the line moving with a four-pitch walk.

So Plawecki goes 2-2 with his new walk up song, then strikes out and walks after reverting back to his usual song. More than one player tells Plawecki, "Plaw, man, you gotta go with that new walk-up song the boys did for you," as they embark on their longest road trip of the season, visiting Akron, Erie, and Richmond.

As they sit in the bus on the way to Ohio, the players try to catch some sleep. The four-game losing streak and the flirting with .500 seem an eternity ago. The team is loose and confident, despite Portland being in the driver's seat.

Four Games, 41 Runs

Though the Mets lose the first game of the series in Akron, 10-2, the score is not indicative of how well they played.

Hansel Robles turned in a superlative start, allowing only three hits in six innings and striking out six. His undoing came at the hands of Tyler Naquin, who hit a two-run homer in the fifth. Heading into the bottom of the seventh, the Mets were down by only one run, 3-2. Akron broke the game open in the bottom of the seventh by reaching reliever Chase Huchingson for six runs on four hits, as Huchingson battled his command, walking two and giving up a two-run homer to catcher Tony Walters.

It was Huchingson's first outing of the year, and his inactivity showed, as he was coming back from a 50-game suspension to start the year. A roster spot opened for Huchingson because Chase Bradford received a promotion to Las Vegas. Though Bradford has been outstanding, the team does not plan to miss a beat, as Lopez simply announces that Cody Satterwhite will be the new closer. Satterwhite earned the promotion with a 3-1 record and a 1.65 E.R.A in 24 appearances.

The next night the Mets get to play against Nick Swisher, who has been sent to Akron for a two-day rehabilitation assignment. Swisher starts the first game of the doubleheader, hits third and plays first. On this day, though, it is Binghamton's leadoff hitter, Kyle Johnson, who sets the tone early. Ahead in the count 2-0, he hits a home run to center off of RubberDucks' right hander Cody Anderson in the first inning.

Before Swisher gets a plate appearance, the Mets are ahead 6-0, as they string together five consecutive hits, highlighted by Ceciliani's two-run homer that plates the fifth and sixth runs of the inning. As Ceciliani gets high fives from his mates, the only one in the dugout not smiling from ear to ear is Burgamy, who, after being called out on strikes on a 2-2 pitch, gets thrown out of the game arguing the call. The Mets are short infielders already, with Reynolds still nursing his injured pinky finger, so Lawley has to play the rest of the game at second and third-string catcher Nelfi Zapata gets unexpected time at third!

With a six-run lead, though, Angel Cuan pitches aggressively and with confidence, facing only three batters in the first and ending the inning by striking out Swisher. The Mets are never challenged in the game and cruise to an 8-1 win.

Between games the Mets are relaxed and confident and once again, the clubhouse is full of laughter. They've now won two of three since Ceciliani and Sandoval played their prank on Plawecki and it seems as if the laughter has not stopped since that Sunday afternoon. They are busy now chiding Burgamy for getting thrown out and kidding Lawley about playing second base for the first time in his professional career. Plawecki can be forgiven if he thought he got "pranked" beyond measure when his walk-up lyrics went missing, but imagine Lawley's initial reaction when Lopez tells him he's moving over to second—the last time Lawley played there was when he was 13!

Fortunately for Lawley, the six-run cushion eased his nerves a bit, but when Francisco Lindor hit a hard grounder toward him with a runner on first and no one out in the bottom of the first, half the dugout must have wondered if Ceciliani and Sandoval conspired with Lindor to smoke a shot at Lawley. Lawley smiled as he recounted the play. "That rocket hit at me, me and Sandy were able to turn it, and that kind of got me comfortable with it (playing second)."

Four of the B-Mets get two hits in the first game, as Plawecki, Clark, Boyd, and Ceciliani combine for eight hits, two homers and four RBIs while Lawley knocks in three. Ceciliani is the hitting star, hitting two homers and knocking in three.

In the second game of the doubleheader it's time for Hamilton Bennett to feel as if he is getting pranked, as the righty reliever winds up starting the second game. He starts off almost as poorly as Anderson did in the first game, as the first five batters reach safely with a single, single, walk, single, and double. By the time Abbot visits him on the mound, the B-Mets are 3-0 and the RubberDucks still have runners on second and third with no one out. But the quick chat Bennett and Abbot have settles him down and he gets a strikeout and two quick groundouts to limit the damage. Hamilton only allows one more hit in his three-inning stint and by the time TJ Chism relieves him in the bottom of the 4th, the game is tied at 3.

Ceciliani is in the middle of a two-run second inning for the B-Mets, as he triples in a run and then scores on a wild pitch by Matt Packer. When Ceciliani slides into home his head hits

Packer's knee hard, but he shakes it off and stays in the game. The Mets break open the game with seven runs in the fifth, using five hits and two walks to do the damage. Backup catcher Xorge Carrillo gets the big hit of the inning, a two-run homer off of Adam Miller, once a top prospect who is trying to make a comeback. The final score is 10-5.

By the end of the doubleheader, the B-Mets have scored 18 runs on 22 hits. The only disappointing thing to come out of the doubleheader is the next day Ceciliani is out of the lineup, as he is feeling a little under the weather due to his close encounter with Packer's knee.

The following night it is Burgamy's time to shine and gain atonement for his getting thrown out of the first game of the doubleheader. He goes 3-4, with 2 home runs and 7 RBIs, outperforming Nick Swisher, who once again plays 1B and bats third for Akron. Though Swisher also goes 3-4 and has two doubles and two RBI, Burgamy bests him on this night.

It's a "B&B" night at the park, as Bowman supports Burgamy's blasts with seven solid innings, giving up two runs and striking out seven. The poor performance of the pen, which gave up four runs in the final two innings is an afterthought, as the Mets roll to a 12-6 win.

In the final game, the Mets are once again on cruise control, routing Akron, 11-3, behind the stout pitching of Peavey (four hits and two runs in six innings) and the three-hit games from Kyle Johnson, Xorge Carrillo, and Ryan Sandoval.

In the final four games of the series, the B-Mets score 41 runs! This will turn out to be their best four-game stretch of the year and they do it largely without the services of Matt Reynolds, whose .360 batting average only got one at bat in the series, as his pinky is still bothering him. Ryan Sandoval stepped in for Reynolds and went 6 for 17 in the series, hitting at a .353 clip. And when Ceciliani had to sit out the final two games of the series, Xorge Carrillo got two starts as the designated hitter, going 6 for 14, with a home run and three runs batted in.

As the Mets head back to NYSEG Stadium, taking 4 of 5 from first-place Akron proves to be a turning point in the month and the season, as they never look back, going 13-3 the rest of the month. "Stepping Up" starts to make its presence felt as a subplot of the season, as players like Sandoval and Carrillo produce when called upon and Satterwhite seamlessly replaces Bradford as the closer.

A Visitor from Flushing

When the Mets return home, a surprise awaits them when they see Eric Young Jr. in town from the big club. Young is fresh off a two-game rehabilitation assignment in St. Lucie and despite threatening weather, he arrives in Binghamton at around 5:30 on Friday, June 13th.

His debut in Binghamton has to wait a day, as the game is rained out. But on Saturday, June 14th, Young plays left field and bats leadoff in the first game of a doubleheader against Erie. Lopez juggles his lineup, as Young pushes Kyle Johnson to the ninth position in the order, despite his .310 average. Matt Clark takes a seat on the bench, despite his .312 average and team-leading 41 runs batted in. But Young's presence sparks the Mets to a doubleheader sweep, as they win the first game, 4-2, and take the nightcap by a 6-0 margin.

In the first inning of the opener Young displays what the big club has been missing all season, as he draws a five-pitch walk from starting pitcher Kyle Ryan. Young did not swing at a pitch even though Ryan's deliveries were around the plate. By taking all five pitches, Young set an example for his temporary teammates, as his patience gave his mates a look at the assortment of pitches Ryan had in his repertoire.

The entire Mets organization preaches patience at the plate, encouraging players to look for a pitch that they can drive at the risk of taking a strike or two. The players are taught to have a plan for each at bat and to focus on getting a pitch that plays to their respective strengths. Throughout the organization, players are taught to be *patiently aggressive* at the plate. That is, look for a pitch you can handle and when you get it, swing at it, no matter the count. But if you don't get the pitch you're waiting for, be patient. Throughout the young season, Pedro and his coaches have echoed this philosophy, encouraging batters to "grind out the at bats." Now, in just a single at bat, Young demonstrated the value of patience at the plate to the Binghamtonians watching his every move.

The New York Mets have struggled since Young went on the disabled list and many observers feel part of the reason for their struggles has been the lack of a true leadoff hitter. Young's greatest assets as a leadoff hitter are that he has patience and also displays great speed, which is reflected in his leading the NL in stolen bases in 2013. With Eric Young working his way back, the other "Young" in New York, Chris Young, has not performed up to expectations in left field. Though Chris Young signed a $7.5 million free-agent contract in the off season and has taken at bats away from Eric, so far he has been a huge disappointment. Eric Young, to his credit, just focuses on getting healthy and getting at bats so he can help the big club. When asked about his playing status, Eric repeatedly says "I'll be happy to do whatever the team asks me to do."

With Burgamy hitting second in the order, Young takes a long lead off first and, before the fans fully settle into their seats, Young is running full speed for second. He slides into second well ahead of the throw from catcher Ramon Cabrera. "That was part of the plan, to test it early," remarked Young after the game, referring to his hamstring. "It felt fine."

Burgamy followed with a line drive single to right and Young had to stop at third because the ball was hit so hard. Matt Reynolds then displayed an excellent case of situational hitting as he lofted a long fly to right and Young tagged up and scored easily.

Just as the Mets have been lacking a leadoff man with Young's limited playing time, the big league Mets have also been notorious for lacking skills in situational hitting this year. Too often those on the big league team have struck out with runners in scoring position. The N.Y. Mets are in the top five in strikeouts in the majors, with 583. Add in a .231 team batting average, which is only ahead of the .216 mark posted by the Padres and you have a lethal combination. The Mets 47 home runs don't help either, as the team's total puts them 27th in the majors in that category.

In the second game of the doubleheader, it is Young's turn to DH as Matt Clark returns to the lineup at his regular 1B position. Clark picks up where he left off, hitting a two-run homer to give him 10 homers for the season, tying him with Burgamy for the team lead, who also homers in the second game, as does Reynolds. Right now hitting is contagious; it seems as if the warm weather of June has put life in all the bats. Though Young goes 0-4 in the nightcap, he is feeling healthy and the Mets are feeling even better as they shut out Erie, 6-0, in the second game behind the three-hit pitching performance of Hansel Robles.

For the players, the most enjoyable part of Young's visit was when he treats the whole team to dinner from a neighboring Outback Steakhouse. Whenever rehabbers play in minor league games, it is an unwritten rule they treat the team to a nice meal as a token of appreciation for letting them take some innings away from those striving to get a shot in the big leagues.

In Young's final appearance for the B-Mets, he goes 0-3 with a walk as the Mets lose to Erie, 5-3. He completes his rehab assignment going hitless in nine at bats, with two walks, showing that although his batting eye was back, his timing was not.

Celebrity Watch at the Park

As the Mets say goodbye to Young, they say hello to the top finishers of the most recent American Idol competition. On *American Idol Night* at NYSEG Stadium on June 17th, eight of the top ten finishers were on hand to throw out the first pitches, meet and greet the fans, and sign autographs.

American Idol contestants being introduced to fans on June 17, from left to right, with their standings in parenthesis [CJ Harris (6), Jena Irene (2), Majesty Rose (9) and Jessica Meuse (4)].

    On the field, Burgamy stole the show from the Idol contestants, as he went two for four with a grand slam and a double, knocking in four runs. Greatly assisting Burgamy in the winning effort was starting pitcher Matt Bowman, who threw six scoreless innings, surrendering two hits while striking out four and walking only one.
    The key point in this game came in the top of the sixth when, with Bowman nursing a 1-0 lead, Richmond's Devon Harris, entering the game hitting .270 with six homers, came to the plate with the bases loaded with two outs. Bowman had entered the sixth inning with a one-hit shutout, having given up a single up the middle to opposing pitcher Ty Blach in the third inning. (Ironically it was Blach's first AA hit.)
    But the Flying Squirrels now staged a two-out rally, with Kolby Tomlinson starting it with a single to left. Then Matt Duffy hit a hard grounder to the left of third baseman Burgamy and when Burgamy bobbled the ball, Tomlinson alertly ran all the way to third as both Reynolds and Bowman were caught just looking at the play, with neither covering the vacated third base.

When Burgamy picked up the ball he raced Tomlinson to third, but as he did so, Duffy also raced to second.

After Bowman missed with back-to-back breaking pitches to Jarret Parker, Lopez ordered him to intentionally walk Parker to load the bases for Harris. Lopez did not want Bowman to work to Parker being behind in the count, as Bowman had a tendency to get hurt when pitching from behind. In explaining his earlier struggles to *Press & Sun Bulletin* report Lynn Worthy, Bowman reasoned "I had a bad streak in there where I was not being very aggressive with how I was pitching guys and I'd get behind and then make them better hitters. They'd punish me for it."

Bowman was determined not to work from behind with Harris and when he started him with a fastball, Harris was on it, fouling it straight back. Bowman's aggressiveness had gotten him ahead now as Harris, hitting with the bases loaded, had to be expecting a first-pitch fastball, but Bowman just challenged him, in effect saying, "Here it is, come and get it!"

It was with the next pitch that Bowman displayed his pitching artistry. He followed his heater up with a changeup that was 7 mph slower and had late movement down as it approached the plate. Harris, out in front, rolled a weak groundball to Bowman. Harris's bat was timing the fastball just right, so Bowman changed the speed of his bat by spotting a changeup.

After Bowman fielded the weakly hit grounder, he took half a dozen steps to first and flipped an underhand toss to Boyd to end the inning. After the game, Lopez told Heiman, it was the best performance of the year for Bowman. "We saw a guy pithing off his fastball and utilizing all his pitches instead of just throwing off-speed stuff," Lopez beamed.

In the bottom of the sixth, Burgamy iced the game with his grand slam. After the game, Burgamy explained the "game within the game" that goes on between the lines. In the third inning he had come up with the bases loaded against Blach. He narrated, "Blach threw a fastball middle-in and I kind of balked on it and I took it and it put me in a bad position." The best Burgamy could manage was a weak fly to right as he left three runners stranded. "That (fastball) was the pitch I wanted to hit, and I don't know why I didn't."

So when Burgamy came up in the sixth, he was not about to make the same mistake again. As he watched lefty reliever Jake Osich take his warm-up pitches, he was thinking only one thing: hunt the fastball. As Burgamy uncorked his swing, he hit a long home run to left. That homer was icing on the cake for him and the team, as he celebrated being named Eastern League Player of the Week from 6/9 through 6/15, where hit .500 in 24 at bats, with three homers and nine RBIs.

The American Idol members were not the only celebrities in attendance on this 17th of June. Mookie Wilson was sitting in the stands taking in the game. He was in town this weekend to work with the minor leaguers and, before the game, tossed batting practice. Wilson graciously signed autographs and posed for pictures for the two dozen or so fans who recognized him in the stands.

"I enjoy coming to Binghamton," Mookie said. And when he was told by a few fans that they wished they could still see him coaching first base for the New York Mets, he said "Thanks for that, but that's ok, that's just the way baseball is."

Second Half Changes

On June 19th, the Binghamton Mets made history, as for the first time in their 23-year existence, they called up three position players from St. Lucie and put all three in the starting lineup on their arrival day: Brandon Nimmo, batting fifth and playing center field; TJ Rivera, batting 7th and playing shortstop; and Dilson Herrera, batting 8th and playing second base. All three had played in the Florida State League All-Star game, sporting respective batting averages of .322, .341, and .307. In addition to the three players aforementioned, the team also called up lefty starter Steven Matz and righty reliever Randy Fontanez, who were also members of the Florida State League All-Star team for the Southern Division.

With the influx of so much talent and the B-Mets eight games over .500 (39-31), Lopez knew the challenge facing him as he stated, "First and foremost, the challenge will be getting everybody in." But Lopez was not complaining. "It is never a bad thing when you get position guys like Nimmo, Herrera, and Rivera and pitchers like Fontanez and Matz. They should spark what we already have."

On this same day they said goodbye to shortstop Matt Reynolds, who left the team hitting .355 with a phenomenal .430 on base percentage. Reynolds had surpassed all expectations, as he not only played a sound defensive shortstop, but during the course of his ten-week stay in AA, he moved from # 8 in the order to # 3. During his stay in Binghamton, Reynolds had made a strong case for re-entering the organization's list of top prospects.

Entering the 2013 season, Reynolds had been listed as consensus top 30 prospect by various organizations, and Baseball America had him ranked as the 23rd best prospect in the Mets' system. But a disappointing inaugural season in 2012, where he hit only .259 for Savannah, followed by an even more disappointing .226 season for St. Lucie in 2013, found him off all prospect lists starting the 2014 season.

As Reynolds said goodbye to his teammates, he looked forward to continuing his breakthrough season in Las Vegas. With Wilmer Flores in the big leagues, the shortstop position was going to be his in Vegas. The promotion of Reynolds to Vegas did not surprise Lopez. "He earned it," he stated. "His going to Vegas provides an opportunity for someone else to step up, in this case, Rivera." Reynolds's teammates treated his leaving with bittersweet emotions; they were all happy to see good performance rewarded, but also sad to be missing his daily presence in the clubhouse and the lineup.

As the team took its 40-31 record against the Richmond Flying Squirrels on the 19th of June, it was in second place, five and one-half games out of first and three games ahead of the third place New Britain Rock Cats.

In the bottom of the third, starting pitcher Tyler Pill took matters into his own hands, hitting a home run off of the Giants' top prospect, right hander Kyle Crick. Pill pulled a 95 mph fastball over the right field fence, giving his team a 1-0 lead. As Pill rounded the bases, the handful of scouts charting Crick's pitches behind the plate looked at each other in befuddled amusement.

"That was off his heater!"

"And 95 miles an hour at that…who saw that coming?"

Pill, who pitched and played the outfield at Cal State Fullerton, showed his hitting prowess was no fluke in the bottom of the sixth when he came up with the bases loaded and one out and hit a three-run triple down the right-field line off of righty reliever Andrew Carignan. Pill and the Mets never looked back from this 5-0 lead as Pill threw eight innings, striking out nine, allowing only four hits and not walking a batter. Pill kept the Richmond hitters off balance, showing a sharp breaking curve that he kept down all evening. He did not break 90 miles per hour on the radar gun, showing that location and movement are just as important as velocity in getting professional hitters out. Throughout the night, Pill mixed in pitchers ranging from a tops of 89 mph to a 74 mph curveball.

His opponent, Crick, won the velocity battle, as he showcased a fastball that touched 97 mph and sat at 94-95 mph throughout his 4.2 innings. Crick got a lot of swings and misses throughout the night and had the Mets chasing his fastball when it was up in the zone. His final line included seven strikeouts, four hits and two runs, with four walks as well.

2011 first-round pick Brandon Nimmo had a quiet debut, as he grounded out twice and drew two walks. Herrera went 2-4 and Rivera went 1-3 and a walk. It was a long but satisfying day for the trio. Nimmo told Lynn Worthy, "It's been a long day with a lot of packing involved, but one that you'd rather do than not!" Nimmo explained that after packing they got up at about 3:30 in the morning to catch a 6:20 flight out of Florida. After a layover in Philadelphia they got to the park in the early afternoon. "Fortunately, we had some help in getting a place to live, so we're set for now," explained Nimmo to inquiring fans as he, Herrera, and Rivera all signed autographs before the game.

In his four trips to the plate, Nimmo showed why he led the Florida State League in on-base percentage as he displayed a discerning eye. In the second inning he drew a four-pitch walk and in the fourth he worked a two-out walk from Crick, fouling off two 3-2 fastballs that were low and on the outside corner. Nimmo scored the first run of the game when Lawley followed with a run-scoring double.

Among those in attendance were two notable members of the big league club's organization. New York Mets Chief Operating Officer, Jeff Wilpon, watched the game from one of the stadium's skyboxes and ex-Met Mookie Wilson again watched the game from the stands.

As the Mets boarded the team bus for a three-game set against Bowie, all sets of eyes were on Plawecki, who even after going 0-4 in the third spot in the lineup, was hitting .326 with six homers and 41 RBIs, with an on-base percentage a tick under .380. The players boarding the bus knew it was only a matter of time before Plawecki got the call to AAA. The only thing keeping him in Binghamton was that Travis d'Arnaud, touted to be the Mets catcher of the future, was playing in Vegas, having been sent down on June 8th as he was struggling mightily in the big leagues, hitting under .200. Since returning to Vegas, d'Arnaud had gone on a batting rampage, hitting .432. Once d'Arnaud got the call back to Flushing, Plawecki would be on his way to Vegas.

In the first game against Bowie, when Plawecki was not in the lineup and Carrillo was catching, the first thought of many B-Mets' fans tuning into Heiman that night was that the call came for Plawecki on the bus trip south. But it turned out to be just a spot start for Carrillo.

Spot start or not, Carrillo made a statement as he went 2-5 with a home run and four runs batted in, bringing his average to .304. Dilson Herrera went 3-5 with two RBIs, as the Mets took the first game of the series, 12-4.

The big league triumvirate of Sandy Alderson, John Riccardi, and Paul Depodtesta, along with the New York Mets' owners, the Wilpons, have been under intense scrutiny from the media in the last few years, as 2014 sees the big league team in the midst of its sixth-straight losing season. One thing the front office had done, though, was stockpile minor league talent. Besides the young pitching prospects that were drawing raves, the number of catching prospects the Mets now had also was being noted. Behind d'Arnaud were not only Plawecki, but Cam Maron, who was having an all-star year in St. Lucie and Carrillo as well. And Juan Centeno, in AAA, was considered the best defensive catcher in the organization. Under the preceding regime of Omar Minaya, the catching position had been devoid of big league potential.

The next night Plawecki was back behind the plate and in the cleanup spot in the lineup. He did not miss a beat, going 2-4 with two more RBIs, as the Mets beat Bowie 7-6, for their fifth win in a row and their tenth in the last 11 games. Herrera had another two hits, raising his average to .583 for his first three games in AA. The game marked the return of Darrell Ceciliani from the disabled list from his concussion that he suffered on June 11th and the AA debut of Steven Matz.

"Actually, I thought Matz threw well," Lopez explained, ignoring the statistics that showed Matz gave up five runs in five innings on seven hits. "Just watching him go out there, he has a great fastball and a really good changeup. He just pitched a little too high in strike zone tonight."

The outfield was becoming crowded for Lopez, with Nimmo, Ceciliani, Johnson, and Taijeron vying for time. In the infield, Clark and Boyd were largely sharing 1B and DH duties, with Rivera and Herrera playing short and second, respectively. This left Burgamy to rotate among DH, 1B, 3B to get his at bats while Lawley was getting most of the starts at third. Ryan Sandoval, despite his positive clubhouse presence and solid overall play, was the odd man out, ultimately getting his release from the B-Mets on August 3rd.

On June 25th the inevitable happened, as Plawecki got the call to report to Vegas. Indeed, d'Arnaud was also called up to the big club, after tearing it up in Vegas, where he hit .436, with six home runs and 16 runs batted in only 15 games. Summing up how he fixed things at Vegas, d'Arnaud stated "It wasn't the swing. It's kind of funny," he told the *Colorado Springs Gazette*. "It was just all in my head."

Colorado Sky Sox manager Glenallen Hill said he could relate to the struggles d'Arnaud was going through at the big league level. "I think it's very beneficial to be in a position where you're not putting a lot of pressure on yourself as a player because you want to help the team win," Hill told the *Gazette*. "Not being able to make the mental adjustments you need to make at that level can snowball on you, so having a break is good."

The New York Mets were eager not only to see if d'Arnaud could translate the dominance he had in AAA to success at the big league level, but they were also interested to see if Plawecki could replicate his AA performance at Vegas as well. Members of the New York media were already speculating that if d'Arnaud continued to falter in the big leagues, Plawecki could see time in New York by September.

Lopez, of course, was happy for Plawecki. "He did a great job, not only offensively, but he took the bull by the horns behind the plate in handling the pitching staff," explained Lopez. "Our main goal here is to get guys better, get them promoted. Now it is Carrillo's time to step up."

With Plawecki's promotion, Kai Gronauer was sent to Binghamton to back up Carrillo. Also on June 25th, the Mets gave Matt Clark his release so that he could work out a deal with the Milwaukee Brewers, who were eager to sign him for their AAA club. (Getting picked up by the Brewers was fortuitous for Clark, as the big club called him to the majors in September.)

Lopez was unruffled by the loss of 89 RBIs from the middle of his lineup, as Clark was leading the team in runs batted in with 46 and Plawecki was second with 43. "We lost two big bats in Plawecki and Clark, but I'm confident we have guys in the clubhouse who will step in," stated Lopez. Looking for the silver lining with the loss of Plawecki and Clark, he knew it would make his job easier in getting everyone at bats. Ideally, Lopez foresaw Burgamy and Boyd sharing the 1B and DH duties and Lawley holding down third on a permanent basis. This only left him to juggle playing time among Nimmo, Ceciliani, Taijeron, and Johnson in the outfield.

The B-Mets finished June the way they opened it, with a game against the New Britain Rock Cats but, unlike June 1st, when they lost to the Rock Cats 6-1, they beat them, 8-3, behind the 3 for 5 and 4-RBI performance of Dustin Lawley.

Since the St. Lucie quintet of Nimmo, Herrera, Rivera, Matz, and Fontanez arrived on 6/19, the team's record is 9-2. Though Rivera went on the disabled list on June 23rd with a strained hamstring and Nimmo has had trouble getting started, Herrera has sparked the team with his bat and glove, hitting at a .345 clip and playing solid defense in the middle of the diamond. Herrera's presence has offset the loss of EL leading hitter Matt Reynolds. Meanwhile, Lawley and Burgamy have had an excellent month of June, showing they want to be considered as solutions to the problems at Citi Field.

At a cursory glance, team observers were tempted to attribute the outstanding June record to the reinforcements that arrived on June 19th, but on closer reflection, the team started to turn it around 11 days earlier. From 6/8 through 6/18, the team had also gone 9-2, making up for a 1-5 start to the month. The professionals following the team and the players would only call it coincidental, but from the moment Plawecki's walk-up music changed, the team improved its play. The simple prank pulled by Sandoval and Ceciliani served as a reminder that baseball needed to be enjoyed, allowing the players to be intense on the field, without playing tense.

The Mets had established a trend, continuing to get better each month, as the team finished the month of June with a record of 18-9, bettering their April record of 12-10 and their May record of 18-14.

Entering July, despite owning a 49-33 record and a .598 winning percentage, the Mets still found themselves five games behind Portland, which had one of the best records in all of minor league baseball at 54-28, for a .659 winning percentage! The Mets were firmly in second, seven games ahead of New Britain, which sported a record 41-39.

Photo Gallery

Matt Clark (far left) and Ryan Sandoval (middle) get a kick out of Ceciliani's antics at the Welcome Home Dinner in April 2014.

The B-Mets listen to the National Anthem before hosting the Akron RubberDucks on Opening Night in 2014.

Matt Bowman displays his Lincecum-like delivery, with its long stride and roll of the hips in April.

Aaron Sanchez shows his changeup grip against the B-Mets in April.

No double in this swing for "Big Plaw"!

Greg Peavey, Binghamton Mets' Pitcher of the Year, releases his fastball in an early season start.

Blake Swihart takes a cut with Kevin Plawecki doing the catching. Swihart and Plawecki are two of the best catching prospects in baseball.

Henry Owens, one of Boston's top pitching prospects, delivers a pitch against the B-Mets in May 2014.

Tyler Pill is all smiles as warm weather arrives in Binghamton.

Kyle Johnson, Darrell Ceciliani and Cory Vaughn line up with Field of Dreams participants moments before the National Anthem.

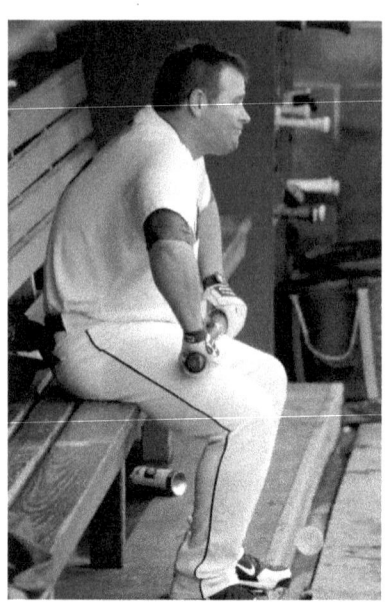

Brian Burgamy sports a smile as he stays ready as a designated hitter. "Have bat, will smile" could be his motto!

Eric Young steals second during his rehab assignment.

In this view from the press box, Wilfredo Tovar is safe at home against Akron.

Hansel Robles shows his low release point in this delivery.

A packed house at NYSEG Stadium watches the B-Mets in action.

Chase Huchingson relaxes by making like a quarterback during a post-game picnic. Two months later, he would get the biggest double play of the year.

Wilfredo Tovar and Darrell Ceciliani (a.k.a. the "prankster") perform their pre-game handshake ritual.

Dilson's first day in Binghamton.

Dilson goes to the opposite field.

The "kid with the red shoes" poses on his first day in Binghamton!

The first pitch Nimmo sees in AA is a ball, off the plate.

Left to Right: Xorge Carrillo, Dilson Herrera, Rainy Lara, and Juan Centeno dining at the *Little Venice* restaurant during a community fund-raising event.

The B-Mets celebrate the first-round playoff win in Portland!

Cody Satterwhite and Xorge Carrillo embrace before they are engulfed in the celebratory pileup!

One of John Bernhardt's signs cheers on the B-Mets, as on September 12th, the B-Mets get that One More Win….

Thanks in large part to the great pitching performance by Steven Matz.

Jayce Boyd is in the middle of the pile, having just sealed the Eastern League Championship!

Pedro Lopez and Kyle Johnson share a special moment.

2014 Eastern League Champions!

P-Lo, We did it!

The historic starting lineups on September 12th. Note that Johnson AND Nimmo are listed in CF. For the record, Nimmo played center.

The Town shows its pride for its team!

Chapter 7. Hunting the Sea Dogs

The first week in July was dominated with some sluggish play, as the Mets got off to a 2-4 start, with the team looking ahead to a series with Portland at NYSEG Stadium from 7/7 through 7/10. The Mets opened the month by splitting a two-game series in New Britain and then losing 3 of 4 games to Erie at home. The Erie series proved to be taxing from both a mental and physical point of view, as the Mets lost a 16-inning game on Friday, the Fourth of July, 9-6. Though the game ended right around 12:30 A.M, both clubs had to be on the field again at 1 the next afternoon to play a doubleheader!

Matz and Robles saved the day on the Fifth of July by turning in stellar performances to give the bullpen some rest. Though Matz lost a heartbreaker in the first game, 2-0, his long outing saved the pen. Then Robles, Huchingson, and Satterwhite returned the shutout favor in the second game, shutting out Erie, 4-0. Portland, however, started July playing superbly, opening with a 5-1 record and by the time the "showdown" series started, the Sea Dogs had increased their lead by three games since the month began. Portland and the Mets, having already played each other 11 times, would not play one another after July 23rd, when the Mets would finish a three-game series against Portland. Because these teams would not meet in the final seven weeks of the season and because both had control of the division, the seven head-to-head games they had listed for July were critical.

Right before the first game of the series the B-Mets received news that four players were selected for the Eastern League All-Star game on July 16th. Brian Burgamy and Kyle Johnson were the two position players selected while relievers Cody Satterwhite and Jon Velasquez were the pitching selections. Burgamy, the seasoned veteran and quiet leader of the team at 33-years-old, had 14 homers and 51 RBIs at the time of his selection. Johnson's .288 average and 34 RBIs, along with his speed and defense were his calling credentials for selection. Satterwhite's All-Star nod was in recognition of his 1.60 E.R.A.

and 42 strikeouts, while Velasquez, as the setup man in the bullpen, recorded a 3.05 E.R.A. The promotions of Plawecki and Reynolds in the prior month precluded their selection to the team; Matt Clark would have also been a selection, but his release prevented his selection as well.

The Mets, like the Sea Dogs, were weathering promotions well, as player development did not impact the won-loss totals for each team. As the Mets and Portland squared off, Portland had a dominant lead at eight games.

The Mets needed to make a statement.

Playoff Preview

The first game of the series on 7/7 pitted lefthander Brian Johnson against righty Cory Mazzoni. Mazzoni was making his first start for Binghamton, as he was recovering from a lateral muscle strain he suffered during the final days of spring training with the parent club. This was Mazzoni's third rehab start, as he had made a start in the rookie Gulf Coast League and one start in the Florida State League for Port St. Lucie. "It was tough getting hurt the last day of spring training what with everything being packed and being ready to go north with your teammates," Mazzoni explained to Gabe Altieri, B-Mets broadcasting intern, before the opener of the four-game series against Portland. "But you just have to stay positive, you can't try to rush back, you have to take it slow and make sure everything heals when you return."

The Mets jumped out early in the game, scoring three runs in the first off Johnson. The southpaw struggled with his command and he only got seven outs, giving up seven runs on eight hits and walking two. Mazzoni explained that the early lead helped. "It's always nice to get some runs working for you early, I was just trying to execute my pitches, pitching to contact and being aggressive in the zone." Mazzoni showcased a fastball that topped out at 96 mph, and he also mixed in a slider and occasional curveball, giving up three runs and five hits in five innings. Overall, Mazzoni was pleased with his performance, telling Lynn Worthy "My slider didn't really come around until the later innings, but my fastball felt good. I made a big mistake there with two out, second and third. I threw the wrong pitch. I threw a fastball down the middle and got hit. Other than that, I felt good, felt like I attacked the hitters."

    The mistake that Mazzoni mentioned was the fastball he threw to Michael Brenly in the 4th inning. Brenly turned on the pitch and hit a double to left, driving in two runs. Ironically, Mazzoni had gotten away with a hanging breaking ball to Brenly in the second inning with runners on second and third. Brenly couldn't capitalize, hitting a routine fly to left. As Mazzoni left the mound after the top of the second, he slapped his fist against his mitt, knowing that he had gotten away with a bad pitch. Luck, however, was not on his shoulder with his second mistake to Brenly.

    With the 9-6 win in the opener of the series, the B-Mets knocked Portland's lead to seven games.

    The following night was a washout, calling for a doubleheader to be played on July 9th. Before the doubleheader Satterwhite commented on his all-star selection and his ability to come back from shoulder injuries that limited him to only eight games from 2010-2012. "It has been a long journey, but it's been satisfying to be able to come back and throw in this league—put in the hard work and see it be paid off. The Mets gave me the opportunity to be out here and throw."

    Satterwhite also recognized that one of the good things in being sidelined for so long was that he now was no longer just a thrower. "Before the injuries, I was a power pitcher, just a hard thrower, see if you can hit it. Now it is mental, throw the pitches where you want them to go." One of the bonuses of his rehabilitation work was an added pitch. "I had trouble developing a changeup, but during the rehab process, the more I threw a split finger, the more depth I got. So that gives me another pitch with the same arm speed to go along with my slider, that's helped a lot."

    Ironically, in the doubleheader that unfolded, the Mets did not need to call on Satterwhite. Starting pitchers Angel Cuan and Gabriel Ynoa provided outstanding pitching as the Mets swept the doubleheader, 6-1, and 1-0. Cuan threw five shutout innings in the first game, striking out five and not walking anyone. Velasquez followed with a scoreless sixth and Ryan Fraser finished it by giving up a single run in the seventh. The Mets broke open the game with four runs in the bottom of the fifth inning, as Brian Burgamy and Dustin Lawley hit home runs against Mike Aguilera, who gave up all six runs in his complete game effort. Burgamy's shot was a real moon blast, as it cleared the video scoreboard in right field, resulting in one of the longest home runs ever hit at NYSEG Stadium.

Explained the humble Burgamy: "I was able to get extended on a fastball over the plate."

In the nightcap it was all Ynoa, as he threw a four-hit shutout, striking out nine and not walking anyone. The lone run of the game came when Ryan Sandoval, playing third base, came up with a two-out single in the bottom of the second, scoring TJ Rivera.

The Mets, having knocked the lead down to a manageable five games, looked for a sweep of the four-game series on Thursday evening, as left hander Steve Matz headed to the mound. Opposing him was 22-year-old righty Luis Diaz, who had recently been called up from the Carolina League, and since making his debut on June 18th, had pitched in outstanding fashion, carving a 3-1 record with a 2.00 E.R.A. in 35 innings. Diaz was signed out of Venezuela as a 16-year-old in 2008 and though he had a string of good years in the minors, he failed to appear on any prospect lists for the Red Sox. Matz, meanwhile, was the prized lefthander in the Mets organization.

In the bottom of the second Diaz helped the Mets score four runs by walking a batter, hitting another and committing a two-base error on a pickoff attempt as the Mets also added two singles and a double. Matz preserved the 4-0 lead until the fifth, when he gave up a double to Sean Coyle and a run-scoring single to left fielder Keury De La Cruz, making the score 4-1. The Sea Dogs continued to show their mettle in the top of the sixth as top prospect Blake Swihart followed a single by Hector Meneses and a walk by Peter Hissey with a two-run double to left. His hit knocked Matz from the mound, but lefty fireballer Jack

Leathersich restored order by getting Sean Coyle to ground out and Michael Almanzar to fly out to preserve the 4-3 lead.

The Mets broke open the game with a four-run seventh; their efforts were abetted by an error by Meneses on a potential double play ball. Instead of having two outs and one on, lefty reliever Robby Scott had to face a bases loaded, no out situation. Lawley followed with a sacrifice fly and then Ceciliani capitalized with a triple and Taijeron followed with a double, plating the four runs.

Travis Taijeron put the proverbial "icing on the cake" in the eighth with a three-run homer, giving the Mets their final three runs in their 13-3 rout. As the Mets gathered in the clubhouse to get ready for their final road trip of the first half of the season to Erie, it was hard to tell who was happier, them or the 5,906 fans who had turned out to cheer for the Mets.

After the series was over, Lopez was bold in his comments as he echoed the thoughts of many fans. "I think it will be a preview of the playoffs. It was good for us to play Portland that well at home. We have to play fundamentally sound to beat Portland and we did that." Lopez was even nonchalant about having lost his three best bats for the first half of the season in Matt Reynolds, Matt Clark, and Kevin Plawecki. "We lost three big bats, but the three guys we got from St Lucie (Herrera, Rivera, and Nimmo) are younger, hungry, and have made a big impact. The guys are playing hard, the right way. The intensity of the younger guys has really rubbed off on the older guys," he noted.

The Mets kept the pedal to the floor on their playoff-bound bus at Erie, as they took 3 out of 4. Darrell Ceciliani led the way against the SeaWolves, hitting .500 in 16 at bats, with a double, two homers and 5 RBIs, raising his first half average to .279. Though the All-Star break came when he was red hot, he was looking forward to the two-day break and was bullish about his team's chances in the second half. He told Tim Heiman, "I think team chemistry is big. We all seem to have a lot of fun together, staying loose, pulling pranks, everything else will take care of itself." Regarding his season, Ceciliani attributed his recent hot streak to feeling more comfortable at the plate. "I widened my stance earlier in the year, so I could have less movement and see the ball better. This is my sixth year and it was just another adjustment I made. It wasn't comfortable at first, but I've stayed with it and the results are coming."

    No matter how much Ceciliani's bat heated up, it could not match the intensity that he brought to the Mets clubhouse on a daily basis, as he was clearly the team leader in pranks and energy. When he wasn't changing someone's walk up music, he kept the team lose in a variety of ways, whether it was through his excitement over seeing chocolate chip cookies on the team bus or in the affectionate moniker he had supplied for Binghamton Mets' employee Eddie Saunders, who always seemed to be running errands for him. "Hey bitch," Ceciliani would blurt out when he wanted Eddie to run another errand. And Ceciliani had taught just about everyone on the team his ritualistic pre-game handshake that included elbows, fists, wide smiles and constant movement. At the age of 25, Ceciliani was a poster child for hyperactivity. But with a player like him in the clubhouse, Lopez knew the team would never get too down.

    Between the lines, Ceciliani's match was Dilson Herrera. Though Herrera was still learning the English language, he needed no lessons for effervescent play on the diamond. Herrera was a sparkplug for the offense, constantly running hard whenever he hit the ball and being a 5'9" package of energy. He played the game with an "edge" that sent energy throughout the team. He was a fountain of youth and exuberance on the diamond, reminding fans of Jose Reyes. Herrera's presence in the lineup had not only replaced the bat of Matt Reynolds, but his speed added a new dimension to the Mets' offense, as he would finish the season with 23 stolen bases. In the 25 games since Herrera joined the team, he had helped spark it to an 18-7 record, as he hit at a .326 clip, with three homers and 20 runs batted in. Herrera had systematically moved from the eighth position in the batting order on June 19th to the second spot in the final game of the first half of the season.

    While Herrera had plenty of help in the lineup, no player matched his energy. He treated the season as if it were a sprint. His keystone partner, T.J. Rivera, finished the All-Star break hitting .309 and provided steady defense at short. Rivera was the perfect complement to Herrera, as Dilson provided the constant energy, whether it was clapping his hands after a close play on the bases, or busting it down the line on a play at first. Rivera provided understated excellence, happy to play the role of the everyday grinder. If Herrera and Rivera were comic strip heroes, Herrera would be Batman or the Green Hornet, while Rivera would be an understated sidekick, like Robin or Kato.

Portland, meanwhile, shook off its sweep at the hands of the Mets by taking four out of five from New Hampshire. Blake Swihart, entrenched in the #3 spot in the lineup, went four for thirteen, with two doubles and a home run as he finished off his first half with a .296 average. Sean Coyle, the Red Sox 30th-rated prospect entering the season, finished the half at .336 and Brian Johnson, who won his eighth game in the New Hampshire series, ended the half season at 8-2 with a 2.51 E.R.A.

Manager Lopez, though happy with the team's 58-38 mark at the All-Star break, also set the tone for the second half with his comments before the final game against Erie on July 14th. The night before the B-Mets had beaten Erie 5-4, but had made five errors, and Lopez was not content to let the team rest on its first-half record.

"As Abby says, 'a win is a win,' " remarked Lopez, but he thought the team lost its focus for a game. "Second half will be challenging, everyone is always getting better. We just have to keep doing our thing, pay attention to the little details and not expecting to win just because we show up," exhorted Pedro.

Though the All-Star break found the Mets 20 games over .500, the Mets somehow found themselves 4.5 games behind Portland, as the Sea Dogs had an unbelievable record of 65-34 at the close of play on July 14th.

Meanwhile, at Citi Field…

The parent New York Mets finished the first half of the year with 13 fewer wins than the B-Mets, with a record of 45-50 and in doing so, the team was well on its way to its sixth consecutive losing season. Binghamtonians took consolation in the fact that of the twelve New York Mets to suit up to beat the Marlins, 9-1, in the final game of the first half of the season, no fewer than nine of the players had toiled the diamond for the Binghamton Mets during the past few seasons.

Of the Mets' starting lineup, only leadoff man and right fielder Curtis Granderson and catcher Anthony Recker had never put on Binghamton's uniform. On this day, Jake deGrom, Jeurys Familia and Buddy Carlyle combined to five hit the Marlins and of that trio, only Carlyle failed to wear the Binghamton uniform.

Jake deGrom was superb this day, throwing eight innings and allowing one run on five hits while striking out 8. He even contributed at the plate, going 1 for 3 with a run batted in. Having 75% of its players in a game coming from Binghamton was nothing new for the New York Mets. Just the day before, during the Mets' 5-4 win over the Marlins, seven of the eight starters had played for Binghamton, leaving only Granderson off the list. Granderson, however, had played at NYSEG Stadium as a member of the Erie SeaWolves in 2004, when he put together a banner season, hitting .303 with 21 HRs and 93 RBIs.

Two former B-Mets, Eric Campbell and Ruben Tejeda, turn two against the Marlins to help close out the first half of the season on July 13th.

Striking Distance

The highlight of the second half of July was the Mets' series against Portland from July 21st though the 23rd. The Mets entered the series coming off a split of its four-game home series against Trenton while Portland had lost three of four to New Hampshire, dropping its lead over the B-Mets to 3.5 games and opening the door for the Mets to gain some ground. The pitching matchups for the three games were Gabriel Ynoa against Wilfredo Boscan; Rainy Lara against Luis Diaz; and for the finale, Steven Matz against Mike Aguilera. The Mets were catching an unasked-for break, missing lefties Henry Owens and Brian Johnson (#2 and #14 rated prospects).

Both lineups had a combination of youth and veterans. The Sea Dogs had veteran minor leaguers that included the likes of Derrik Gibson, Ryan Lavarnway, and Shannon Wilkerson. Blake Swihart and second baseman Sean Coyle provided the youth in the lineup. The Mets, meanwhile, had veterans Burgamy, Ceciliani and Carrillo complement Nimmo, Herrera, Lawley, and Boyd, who were rated the respective number 8, 11, 26, and 30th prospects in the Mets' organization.

6, 152 fans packed Hadlock Field to see the Friday night opener and the temperature was an ideal 73 degrees for the game's first pitch. Portland was the first to score, netting two runs in the bottom of the third, helped along with some sloppy play by the Mets.

Meneses started the inning with a single and Lara made matters worse when he hit Ryan Dent with a pitch. Leadoff hitter and center fielder Derrik Gibson then put down a sacrifice bunt and when Burgamy tried to get the lead runner at third, he threw the ball into left field, allowing Meneses to score and putting runners on second and third. Lara then settled down, getting two groundouts and a fly out, but Dent came home on the second groundout, giving Portland a 2-0 lead.

Herrera doubled in a run in the top of the fifth, momentarily cutting the lead to 2-1. But Lara gave a run back in the bottom of the inning, as the Sea Dogs bunched three singles to make the score 3-1. Mike McCarthy relieved Boscon in the sixth, but couldn't protect the lead as he gave up a two-run home run to Nimmo in the top of the seventh.

The Sea Dogs showed their resiliency in the bottom of the seventh, however, while the Mets exhibited some more sloppy play. With Ryan Fraser still on the mound, after having gotten the final out of the sixth inning, Derick Gibson singled to right for his fourth hit of the game. He then promptly stole second. Fraser then walked Swihart, with ball four getting by Carrillo for a passed ball. Manager Billy McMillan kept the pressure on by having Swihart steal second. Two batters up, runners now on second and third, courtesy of a single and a walk, and two stolen bases and a passed ball!

Randy Fontanez now replaced Fraser and though he got Coyle to ground out, the out brought in Gibson with the lead run. With Swihart on third, Fontanez struck out David Chester on a wild pitch, letting Swihart score the second run of the inning. Fontanez got out of the inning without further damage, but Portland held on to win the game, 6-4.

The sloppy defense did not surprise Lopez, though it did disappoint him. "Right now we are not playing good defense, this can really hurt us. We need to play better defense. We had some problems in the Trenton series catching the ball and that's unfortunate," he explained after the game.

The next day Lopez stressed to his players that they needed to play solid baseball and play within themselves. He told the team it was important to remain focused. "It's as if every game is a playoff game for us, not just these games against Portland," reasoned Lopez, who preached that the key to playing the game was to play *intense* every game, without being *tense*.

One of the bright spots in the loss was the play of shortstop T.J. Rivera, who went 4-4 and raised his batting average 40 points to .348. Rivera spoke for the whole team when he explained his mindset during this series. "This is a huge series right now. They're the top dog and we're chasing them."

A Bronx Grinder

Rivera provides a New York City flavor to this team as he was raised in the Bronx. At Herbert H. Lehman High School, Rivera played varsity ball for three years, hitting .618 and .609 in his junior and senior years, respectively. Signed as an undrafted free agent in 2011, he has carried this ability to "rake" into his minor league career. His .289 average for the first half of this season at St. Lucie is lowest he has hit in any of his minor league seasons. Though he has excelled with his bat every year in the minors, he has failed to crack any prospect lists. A lack of speed and power prevents him from ranking high on the proverbial "five-tools list" that talent evaluators use as a measuring stick, but his work ethic and respect for the game are a source of admiration from his teammates.

Jack Leathersich loves the way Rivera plays the game. "He's the real deal. I've never been around a kid who prepares as well as he does. He just really loves the game and it seems like every time I see him he's out on the field working on something. Rivera plays hard and is completely balls to the wall—he'll do anything to make sure we win. He's a great teammate and obviously a great player and everybody should be real excited about him."

Despite being a Florida State League All-Star in 2013, Rivera found himself starting the 2014 season again at St. Lucie, as Mets' brass rated middle infielders Matt Reynolds and Wilfredo Tovar ahead of him at AA. For his part, Rivera is happy to be known as a grinder and was delighted to get the belated call to AA. "I was really excited when I got the call-up, I was waiting a little while for it. The players here have accepted me real well. I look at every game as a new day. "The big leagues are the big picture, to be with a hometown team would be great. My dad grew up a Met fan. If I could that for him it would be great."

Rivera does not have a great arm. He does not possess great speed. He does not have home run power. Rather, he makes contact, gets on base, and plays with passion. His offseason from

2013-2014 was spent in the Binghamton area, and it included an intense workout regimen at *The Edge*, a multi-sport indoor training facility.

Willem Rathgeber is a ten-year-old boy who loves baseball. A student at Homer Brink Elementary School, in the summer Willem is a Maine-Endwell baseball all-star. Looking to improve his performance on the diamond, Willem signed up to receive hitting instruction last winter (2013) at *The Edge*.

With snow covering the ground and the Binghamton area staggering through multiple sub-zero temperatures, Rivera "raked" in the indoor cages and took note of the "little man" working hard to improve his game. A social guy by nature, it wasn't long before Rivera introduced himself to Willem and offered the baseball novice some batting tips. And, it wasn't long before a friendship built around baseball took root.

"T.J. was incredible with Willem," the young lad's mom explained to John Bernhardt, a diehard Binghamton Mets fan, who has season tickets even though he lives almost two hours away. "He's a great guy and was so patient and encouraging, helping Willem with his batting. We just loved him."

During the summer, NYSEG Stadium became a home away from home for Willem. And, in 2014, Willem signed up to attend the B-Mets Youth Baseball Camp, which was run by manager Pedro Lopez and included many B-Mets as instructors. When Rivera worked as an instructor at the camp, it didn't take long for T.J. to spot Willem. T.J. took Willem under his wing, encouraging his protégé to become an infielder and sharing some of the infield basics with his eager student.

"T.J. plays shortstop and second base, so he taught me the basics," Willem remembered when speaking about his time at the B-Met baseball camp. "He showed me that you have to take some baby steps before you're trying to do the fancy stuff." And, Rivera emphasized to Willem the fact that if he wants to be a baseball player he has to put in the time. He has to play more. Willem got the message. "T.J. plays second base and he got here. I'm going to play second base and play and train and practice as much as I possibly can, so I can get here, too," explained Wilhelm.

Whenever Rivera took the field at NYSEG Stadium this summer he had vocal and passionate support from the Rathgebers. They called him "Bronx" and shouted their encouragement loudly and with prodigious pride. T.J. didn't disappoint the Rathgebers or any B-Mets fans, as he played second base, short, and third as situations dictated during the season, and was a hitting machine. Rivera finished his regular season B-Met campaign hitting .358, which led the team. Seeing Willem Rathgeber's eyes light up when T.J. Rivera stepped to the plate during the year, it's hard to minimize the positive impact a professional athlete can have on a young person.

Lara and Matz and a Split

The second game of the series saw Lopez go with the same starting eight he used in game one, with the exception of catcher, where he gave Xorge Carrillo the night off and gave a start to veteran minor leaguer catcher Kai Gronauer.

Player	Pos
Kyle Johnson	RF
Dilson Herrera	2B
Brian Burgamy	1B
Dustin Lawley	3B
Darrell Ceciliani	LF
T.J. Rivera	SS
Brandon Nimmo	CF
Travis Taijeron	DH
Xorge Carrillo	C

Portland made two changes from the lineup of the previous day, giving Lavarnway the nod at DH instead of David Chester and also starting Michael Almanzar at third over Ryan Dent. Hadlock Field was again packed, as 5,578 fans showed up, proving that New Englanders loved pennant races, major or minor league.

Player	Pos
Derick Gibson	CF
Blake Swihart	C
Ryan Lavarnway	DH
Sean Coyle	2B
Michael Almanzar	3B
Stefan Welch	1B
Shannon Wilkerson	RF
Peter Hissey	LF
Heiker Meneses	SS

  Luis Diaz gave the Mets a gift run in the top of the third when, right before he struck out Lawley to end the inning, he uncorked a wild pitch to score Taijeron, who had started the inning with a single to right. In the bottom of the fourth, however, the B-Mets' weakness with the leather played a key role in seeing Portland jump out to a 3-1 lead against Rainy Lara. After Ryan Lavarnway hit a homer to tie the score, the Sea Dogs had Sean Coyle on first with two out with Stefan Welch at bat. On a 1-2 pitch Welch singled sharply to right field and Taijeron got to the ball quickly and unleashed a throw to third that was in time to nab Coyle. Third baseman Lawley could not handle the throw, however, so instead of being out of the inning, the Sea Dogs had another chance to score with Shannon Wilkerson coming to bat with runners at second and third. After taking a strike, Wilkerson made the Mets pay, lining a single to left to plate two more runs.

  As in a tight boxing match, the Mets came right back, trading a blow for a blow. In the top of the fifth, both Taijeron and Herrera homered, tying the score. The game remained even going into the bottom of the ninth. The inning started innocently enough, with Velasquez getting Derrik Gibson to ground out to second. Then Swihart, with a 1-2 count, singled into the hole between first and second, stimulating animated chatter and some loud clapping in the Portland dugout. Velasquez eyed Swihart closely at first, knowing he might be running. Gronauer was on the alert, putting down the signs to Velasquez and also eyeing Swihart. But Jonathan Roof had his own idea of how to end the game, as he hit a long double to left, scoring Swihart with the running win.

Two showdown games with the Sea Dogs, two losses by a total of three runs, with the B-Mets chipping in with four errors to fall 5.5 games out of first. Definitely not the way that Lopez wanted to start the series.

He turned to Matz in the final game, while also giving Boyd a start at DH and giving Kyle Johnson the night off. Binghamton University graduate Mike Augliera took the mound for Portland, looking for the sweep. As the Mets took part in the pre-game workout, Lopez was hoping the beautiful summer day that brought temperatures of 85 degrees and blue skies would also bring some good fortune for the Mets and help improve their 1-7 record at Hadlock Field. He also had a hunch that moving Taijeron to the cleanup slot would help, as Lopez liked the way Taijeron had recently been swinging the bat. Travis was feeding off the increased playing time resulting from seeing the earlier release of Clark, as well as seeing Lawley being moved out of the outfield rotation as Lawley was now manning third base on an everyday basis. The beautiful day brought a packed house to Hadlock Field, with 7,368 fans filling the seats.

Taijeron was unfazed hitting cleanup. "I'm still looking for the same pitch that I always look for, looking to drive the ball. I can only worry about things that I can control." Taijeron was also looking forward to see Matz take the hill. "We have Matz on the mound tonight, and he's gonna have a great start."

Cleanup hitter and sparkplug Sean Coyle led off the bottom of the second with a home run, after Matz retired the Sea Dogs in order in the first. Coyle was a fan favorite at Hadlock Field and the fifteen thousand eyes watching him this night could be forgiven if, just for a moment, they thought they were watching Boston's beloved Dustin Pedroia. Coyle not only plays the same position as Pedroia, but at 5' 8" and 175 pounds, Coyle is built very similar to Pedroia and plays the game as if his hair were on fire. Both athletes' backgrounds are eerily similar, with Pedroia being a second-round pick of the Red Sox in 2004, and Coyle a third-round pick in the 2010 draft (out of Fort Washington High School in Pennsylvania).

In 2005, when Pedroia played at Hadlock Field, he .326 with eight homers and 40 runs batted in and stole seven bases in 256 at bats. By the end of the 2014 season, Coyle's numbers would be even better: .296 average, 16 HRs, 61 runs batted in and 13 stolen bases in 336 at bats.

Matz shook off Coyle's shot and retired the next three hitters in order. Ryan Sandoval, who was getting a rare start at third, immediately got the Mets even when he led off the third on a 1-0 pitch with a home run. The Mets chipped away with another run in the fourth, giving them a 2-1 lead entering the fifth. Taijeron rewarded Lopez's faith in him as a cleanup hitter as he doubled to left on a 3-1 pitch with runners on first and third and one out. When the Mets were done hitting at the end of the half inning, they held a 4-1 lead. Matz remained in command throughout his seven-inning stint, throwing 67 of his 97 pitches for strikes, walking only one while allowing two runs on seven hits and striking out four. Randy Fontanez and Cody Satterwhite threw the final two innings, with Satterwhite notching his ninth save to preserve the 4-2 win.

As the Mets left Portland and headed to Trenton, Portland was in command in the division, holding a four-and-one-half game lead, as well as a 7-2 record at Hadlock Field. It was clearly a two-team battle in the division. The Mets, meanwhile, had left the third place team in the dust in the division, holding an 8-game lead.

The Mets stumbled a bit in their last eight games of the month, going 4-4, while the Sea Dogs, perhaps also suffering from a bit of a letdown after their head-to-head play against the Mets, finished the month winning five out of their final nine games, giving them a five-game cushion over the Mets as the dog days of August beckoned.

Chapter 8. A Team, a Town, and a Rebound

The total population of the Greater Binghamton Area is approximately 250,000, and with the B-Mets drawing close to 200,000 fans practically every season, the ratio of baseball supporters to community members is a ratio that instills pride in Binghamton baseball fans. (In comparison, the N.Y. Mets drew 2.2 million fans in 2014 from a New York City population base of eight million.)

Support from the business community has also been unquestionably strong, allowing the Binghamton Mets to hold numerous special events throughout the season. One glance at the signage in the stadium–from the concourse walls, to the fences behind the seats, to the outfield–shows the business support. There are over 60 advertising signs lining the outfield fence, ranging from local pubs and restaurants with names such as "The Relief Pitcher" and "The Ale House," to industry stalwarts such as NYSEG and Lockheed Martin. Another dozen or more signs line the concourse walls as well.

In turn, the team supports the community, as in 2013 the team was recognized with the Binghamton Chamber of Commerce's "Business of the Year" award, due to its community endeavors. Throughout the year the team partners with local and national charitable and not-for-profit organizations for numerous fundraising activities, as well as sponsoring student achievement nights and "Field of Dreams" events, where local youth teams get to take the field with the Binghamton Mets.

NYSEG Stadium hosts local community nights, provides a home for high school baseball games, and serves as the finish line for the Binghamton Bridge Run–a half-marathon and 5K event that draws over 2,000 runners to downtown Binghamton every May. Every season the team also conducts a handful of autographed jersey raffle nights, where the players wear the jerseys of a designated local charity/non-profit organization and the team auctions the jerseys after the game, with all proceeds going to the local charity.

"Running a minor league team is all about being interwoven with the community as much as possible," points out Binghamton Mets General Manager, Jim Weed. "Being a good community citizen is a large part of what we are all about," adds Weed. "Not only do we want to put a good product on the field and put on a good show between innings for our fans, but we want to be a foundation for the community as well."

Denis Wickham, a season-ticket holder since 1992, was instrumental in forming a booster club in support of the team in 2012. "We're proud of the area's historic relationship with baseball and being so close to Cooperstown is an added attraction of living in Binghamton and rooting for the hometown team," exhorts Wickham. "The booster club supports the players and community in various ways, including providing meals for the players and discount tickets for the fans. When players get to Citi Field, we want them to remember their days in Binghamton with pride."

Jeff Smith, another founding member of the booster club, sees the success of the baseball team as a fundamental part of the revitalization of the Greater Binghamton Area. "As with many cities in New York State, we have lost our share of manufacturing jobs in the past three decades or so, but the capability to retain community assets is the first step of economic growth," notes Smith. A smile fills his face as he expands on the topics of baseball and Binghamton. "During the 2014 season we celebrated the 100th anniversary of minor league baseball in our community through a series of events, including the writing of a book and the production of special 100-year anniversary bats. Minor league baseball was in Binghamton as early as 1877, the year before the National League was even formed!"

First the Team…

Since 1992, the Binghamton franchise has won the Eastern League Championship three times: in 1992, led by right hander Bobby Jones and catcher Brook Fordyce; in 1994, led by the "Generation K" pitching duo of Bill Pulsipher and Jason

Isringhausen; and of course, in 2014, when the team was led by Pedro Lopez's "Six More Wins" theme. Until 2013, when the team finished first in the Eastern League, the franchise had only one winning season since 2005.

From 2011 through 2014, a number of elite prospects passed through Binghamton, including Matt Harvey, Dilson Herrera, Steven Matz, Rafael Montero, Kevin Plawecki, Noah Syndergaard, and Zack Wheeler. These players have enabled the Binghamton franchise to turn the corner and become an envied team in the Eastern League.

Outside the foul lines, the B-Mets front office has proven to be a consistent winner, providing a high level of entertainment for its fans, as a theme night is held practically every night of the year. Of the 71 home dates in 2014, 65 of them had a special event associated with them, including:

- *Magic Mondays* – Fans get special ticket pricing by repeating what they hear on FM radio station *Magic 101.7*
- *Two for Tuesday* – Every Tuesday at the park adult beverages and fountain drinks are two for the price of one!
- *Thirsty Thursday* – Every Thursday is *Thirsty Thursday*, with more two-for-one pricing for adult beverages and fountain drinks
- *Friday Fireworks Nights* – 10 of the 11 Friday night home games include a fireworks display after the game
- *Card Strip Give Away Saturday* – Every Saturday included a card strip giveaway, as a way to commemorate 100 years of minor league baseball in the Greater Binghamton area. In addition, local TV station Fox 40 sponsored four tickets, four hot dogs, four sodas and a souvenir program— all for only $40.00 – every Saturday home game during the season!

Today the local ownership is a quartet, with the four members – brothers David and William Maines and George

Scherer and Michael Urda – all part of the group that purchased the team in '94. Though not brothers through blood, Scherer and Urda are "brothers in action," as they have been lifelong friends and Binghamton schoolmates all along the way.

Michael Urda is the team's president and spokesman and feels owning a minor league baseball team is all about community involvement. "The team is here for the community and youth is the future of our community," explains Urda and a smile lights up his face as he outlines the *B-Mets' Birthday Bash* Program. "A parent can book children's birthday parties for only $10.00 per child and everyone at the party gets a ticket to game, a hot dog, a soda, an ice cream, and unlimited use of our park's fun zone."

In 2014 the team also added to its "Fun Zone" area across from right field, adding an inflatable slide to the other attractions that the younger fans can enjoy while the game holds the attention of their parents. Also, a new picnic pavilion was built along the left-field line, as entertaining large groups with such traditional menu items as hamburgers, hot dogs, and various salads complement servings of the area's noted "spiedie" sandwiches (marinated chunks of meat on a roll).

Though Urda loves talking about the present, his face lights up like a little leaguer when he talks of his days attending games at Johnson Field. "I saw Bobby Bonds, Barry's dad, play here when he was playing for the Waterbury Giants," beams Urda.

To honor the area's baseball heritage, two large banners depicting the names of all the players who have played for Binghamton's teams and gone on to play in the big leagues were hung in the stadium concourse behind home at the start of the 2014 season. "Your face lights up when you realize the number of great players who have called Binghamton their home," notes Urda.

Indeed, the avid baseball fan will be able to pick out such Hall of Famers on this honor roll as "Wee" Willie Keeler, Whitey Ford, and Lefty Gomez.

Now the Town...

Stated succinctly, the Greater Binghamton Area, like the New York Mets, has seen better times. In the early 1900's the area was home to corporations that would soon become international giants—the International Business Machines (IBM) Corporation and the Endicott-Johnson (EJ) Shoe Company. The two giants ensconced the community in a corporate cocoon, insulating the community from economic adversity. During the 1930's, when the rest of America suffered from the Great Depression, the "Valley of Opportunity" (one of the monikers for Binghamton and its surrounding area) thrived as both IBM and EJ prospered. The prosperity of the 30's continued Binghamton's growth, which started almost immediately after its inception.

The city of Binghamton was incorporated in 1867, after undergoing expansion that could be traced to the opening of the Chenango Canal in 1837 and the arrival of the *New York and Erie Railroad* in 1848. The Chenango Canal connected to the Erie Canal in Utica, allowing goods to be transported to Western New York. The railroad paved the way for train service to New York City in 1849 and then to the western end of the state as well, in 1851.

The railroad established Binghamton as a crossroads of travel across the state of New York. Today, the city still exists as a crossroads of travel, as its surrounding highway system connects it with Syracuse and beyond to the north, Scranton to the south, Buffalo to the west, and New York City to the east.

The growing city proved to be an excellent home for the cigar industry, owing to its geographical area, excellent transportation system, and labor force. By 1900 there were over five thousand workers that produced over one million cigars each year, placing Binghamton second only to New York City in cigar manufacturing.

At the end of the 1800's, more than 200 products were being produced in Broome County at hundreds of factories. The success of those firms led to the growth of Lester Brothers Shoe

Company, which became Endicott Johnson, and the opening of Bundy Time Recording Company, which became IBM.

Endicott Johnson started to fade not long after its longtime chairman, George F. Johnson, passed away in 1948. With his dynamic nature no longer leading the way, coupled with the corporation's failure to enter the lucrative sneaker market, the shoe company started to decline. By the time the New York Mets were born in 1962, the shoe company's glory days had faded.

Meanwhile, IBM continued to flourish in the 1960's. With the advent of its System 360 computing system, the computer giant's presence – along with many satellite firms – brought the Greater Binghamton Area economic health through the next three decades. During the 1960's the number of IBM employees nearly tripled, expanding from 104,241 in 1960 to 269,291 in 1970.

The Endicott History and Heritage Center shows an IBM System 360 Computer, which revolutionized the computer industry and led IBM to almost triple its number of employees.

The advent of the open computing environment and increased competition in the 1980's adversely affected IBM, especially in the Southern Tier, and IBM used mass layoffs in the area starting in 1994 to help its overall recovery. The community, however, is still in recovery stage from the IBM decline, for as IBM downsized, so too did neighboring businesses, many of which saw contracts with IBM dry up. Today, there are around 800 employees based in Endicott, down from a peak of around 14,000 to 15,000 people in the 1980's.

In 1992, when the Binghamton Mets came to town, though Endicott-Johnson was withering, IBM was still flourishing, Binghamton University was solidifying its reputation as an elite public university, and SUNY (State University of New York) Broome was establishing itself as an affordable way to complete an Associate's degree. Its two-year technical degrees also provided an excellent talent pool for area firms.

Juanita Crabb, then the mayor of Binghamton, was relentless in her pursuit of a baseball team for the city, which had gone without baseball since the Triplets played their final season in 1968. She saw professional baseball not only as a way of improving the quality of life in the area so neighboring businesses could attract employees, but also as a vehicle for economic stimulus. Almost a quarter-century later the economic and aesthetic impacts are obvious. Gone are an empty railroad yard and seedy taverns on the city's northwestern border. Instead, the stadium, modern restaurants like *Amici's* and *Tranquil,* and a beautiful building housing the Broome County Library populate the area and bring in thousands of people to the area on an annual basis.

These improvements, along with the $2.5 million in enhancements to the *Floyd L. Maines Veteran's Memorial Arena*, and the increasing presence of Binghamton University downtown have "bookended" the city's revitalization in recent years.

And Now a Rebound...

Jeff Smith, a pleasant-faced man of average height and graying hair, who has the energy of a high school kid on his first date, gets effusive as he discusses the potential of the Binghamton area and the start of a rebound that he sees taking place. "We are blessed with many sports and cultural attractions for a city area of our size," he emphasizes. Among booster club circles he is affectionately called the "Mayor," as he constantly promotes the city of Binghamton and its surroundings.

"Our booster club and our book are two small ways we can contribute to the development of a bright future for the next 100 years for our area and our team. Our ongoing theme of 'Our Team, Our Town, Our Pride,' says a lot about the way the way the B-Mets Boosters view their community," Smith states with the pride of a man who has been happy to make a lifetime home here for his wife and his four children. As president of the Endwell Rotary Club, Smith rarely misses an opportunity to remind listeners of the area's past glory and present potential.

With civic pride Smith continues, "We have some great role models. One chapter of our book is devoted to George F. Johnson and should be read by all students. Mr. Johnson set the standard for community service and is directly responsible for many of our accomplishments in baseball, community development, and the arts here in Binghamton."

After more than two decades of steady decline, there are signs the worst is over for the "Valley of Opportunity." Economic revitalization is taking place and, just as the New York Mets hope to use the talents of such Binghamton-bred prospects as Wheeler, Syndergaard, Plawecki, Nimmo, and Herrera to return to post-season play, the Greater Binghamton area is looking to extend its rebound as well. The players who have passed through the playing fields of NYSEG Stadium and are arriving at Citi Field serve as a metaphor for brighter days for Greater Binghamton.

Sandy Alderson assumed the reigns of general manager of the New York Mets in October 2010 and interestingly, his strategy for restoring the competitiveness of the franchise echoes that of Frank Cashen, who became the New York Mets General Manager in January of 1980 and took a full six years to produce a World Series Champion. Briefly looking at the strategy Sandy Alderson has employed shows that he can be considered a Cashen acolyte, as he has concurrently:

- Embraced the past.
- Capitalized on the selection of players through baseball's annual amateur draft.
- Maximized returns from player trades.
- Promoted homegrown talent through the system.

Cashen felt an essential ingredient for a championship was to have an excellent pitching staff and marveled at the historic staff of the 1969 Mets team that had Tom Seaver and Jerry Koosman leading the way. During Cashen's first few years, knowing the Mets were not contenders, he largely eschewed the free-agent market and though his trades were few, when he made a trade, he made it count. On April Fool's Day in 1982 he made a fool of the Texas Rangers organization by trading Lee Mazzilli for starting pitchers Ron Darling and Walt Terrell. In November of 1985 he traded for starting lefty Bob Ojeda.

He built the core of the 1986 team through the baseball draft, selecting such players as Lenny Dykstra, Dwight Gooden, Kevin Mitchell, and Darryl Strawberry. He capped off his moves by trading four prospects for Gary Carter in time for the 1985 season, putting in the final piece needed to win the 1986 World Championship.

Similarly, Alderson has relied on stockpiling pitching as a key part of his strategy. He also has largely eschewed the free agent market and has traded veterans such as Carlo Beltran and R.A. Dickey for a core of young talent in the form of Wheeler, Syndergaard, and d'Arnaud. He too has built through the amateur draft, selecting Brandon Nimmo, Gavin Cecchini, Domonic Smith, and Michael Conforto. Finally, Alderson has relied on homegrown talent, as much of the current New York roster reflect promotions from the farm system. Only time will tell if Alderson's embrace of Cashen's history will provide a championship team, but clearly he has embraced the strategy that Cashen used to build a contending team in the second half of the 1980's.

Ironically, the road for the revitalization of the Greater Binghamton Area has also followed the pattern of Cashen and

Alderson. The challenging road for Binghamton's revitalization has begun and it too can be broken down into four very similar concurrent steps:

- Embrace the past
- Capitalize on private and state initiatives
- Maximize the benefits of higher educational growth
- Encourage and promote Grassroots (homegrown) efforts.

Step 1. Embrace the Past

While Binghamton's Triplets have been gone for years, the Binghamton Senators, Binghamton Mets, the *Dick's Sporting Goods Open*, and the *Levene, Gouldin, & Thompson Tennis Challenger Tournament* provide an eclectic menu of sporting events that are unprecedented for an area of Greater Binghamton's population.

Numerous athletes from the area have also left their mark in their respective sports – a small sample includes: the Super Bowl Champion Jones brothers, Arthur (with the Ravens) and Chandler (Patriots); Isaiah Kacyvenski, who played in the NFL for eight years and played in the 2006 Super Bowl; Jon Jones, brother of Arthur and Chandler, who is the UFC's Light Heavyweight Champion; and baseball all-stars Jimmy Johnson, "Wild Bill" Hallahan, and Johnny Logan.

In addition to its sports heritage, Binghamton also has a Southern Tier Broadcaster's Hall of Fame (stbahall.com), in the historical Bundy Museum on Main Street, which boasts over 50 members. The city also has a Walk of Fame, whose 45 members are depicted with a star on the walls of the Forum Theater, which is located in Downtown Binghamton.

Sports and entertainment are not the only areas with rich legacies that Binghamton proudly touts. The Greater Binghamton Area not only provided a place of steady work for waves of European immigrants in the early 1920's but also provided engineering brain power for the dawn of the computer age after World War II. The *Endicott History and Heritage Center* takes pride in preserving and displaying the history of Endicott and provides numerous displays on the history of IBM and Endicott-Johnson, with tours provided by many former employees from these firms. Meanwhile, the Broome County Historical Society features numerous documents and photographs outlining the history of the area, including videos produced by the local public radio station WSKG, that highlight the area's rich accomplishments in the fields of transportation and the arts.

The number of Binghamton residents who have gone on to achieve great fame in their respective careers is high, and it is impossible to mention everyone here. A brief sampling includes: creator of the *Twilight Zone,* Rod Serling; actor Richard Deacon; comedian and actor Paul Reiser, who graduated from Binghamton University in 1978; author John Gardner, who taught at Binghamton University in the 70's; film director Nicholas Ray, who also taught at Binghamton in the 70's; and of course, BU graduate and current Hollywood screenwriter and director, Marc Lawrence, whose recent film, *The Rewrite*, was partially shot on the Binghamton University campus and downtown Binghamton.

On Sunday, February 8th, 2015, Binghamton University hosted the national premiere of Lawrence's movie, with Lawrence and Hugh Grant, its star, in attendance. After the premiere, Lawrence and Grant answered questions from the filled theater audience for an hour.

Ironically, the story of Keith Michaels in *The Rewrite* draws parallels to the real life story of Nicholas Ray, only set 40 years later. From 1971 to 1973 Ray, the director of such classic films as *Rebel without a Cause*, and *The True Story of Jesse James,* found himself teaching at Binghamton after his Hollywood work dried up.

The Rewrite was the area's third national movie premiere, with *Lieberstraum* (starring Kim Novak and Kevin Anderson) and *Twilight Zone: The Movie* (starring Kevin McCarthy), also having the distinction of premiering in Binghamton.

Marc Lawrence (left) and Hugh Grant share a laugh at BU's U.S. premiere of "The Rewrite" on February 8 2014. (Photo courtesy of Eileen Plunkett.)

By tipping its hat to its past, the Greater Binghamton Area not only pays tribute to its previous leaders, but also provides models for tomorrow's successes. The area may well never again have two industrial giants exist side-by-side as it did in the middle of the 20th century when Endicott-Johnson and IBM thrived, but the principles that built those two corporate giants are in evidence today as the Greater Binghamton Area transitions itself to a revitalized and vibrant community.

It can be said the first step in economic recovery is to retain the assets a region has and to take pride in these assets; pride starts with the tipping of the hat to the passion and perseverance of prior generations.

Step 2. Capitalize on Private and State Initiatives

As part of the "*New* New York Works" campaign, one of the major initiatives in New York State is the development of Economic Regional Councils which serve as a link between areas of New York State and funding initiatives from the governor's office. The state is divided into ten regional councils, with the Greater Binghamton Area being part of the Southern Tier Regional Economic Development Council.

In 2014, New York State awarded $81 million in state grants, tax credits and bonds to the Southern Tier Regional Economic Council, which has been diligent in using the funds, forming alliances where necessary with other groups to help ensure the money is put to use in a timely and efficient manner.

For example, in December 2014, the council awarded a $3 million grant to the Broome County Land Bank to develop a decaying property on 50 Front Street, part of the city's river bank area. Land banks are not-for-profit, public benefit corporations authorized to take control of and redevelop vacant or abandoned properties to serve the public interest. They were authorized in New York State under legislation signed by Governor Andrew Cuomo in 2011.

The 50 Front Street Property that will the Broome County Land Bank will develop.

Stacy Duncan, executive director of the Broome County Land Bank, was excited about being able to work with the property on Front Street. "This will stabilize the gateway to the city and transform that eyesore to a very vibrant new space." She goes on to explain that properties like 50 Front Street present problems with development that land banks are uniquely positioned to solve: "It has millions of dollars of environmental work that it needs, so it's not an attractive project to developers. You have county governments that are strapped financially. So you bring in an organization like a land bank, and you have a way to address these problems with large properties, to get them back on the tax rolls and return them to usefulness for the community."

Binghamton's mayor, Richard David, also praised the collaborative work of the land bank and the Regional Economic Council, "I look forward to working with our partners to transform this property, which has been vacant and blighted, into a dynamic mixed-use housing development on Binghamton's riverfront."

Duncan feels that the redevelopment of the 50 Front Street property is just the beginning, and hopes to take up projects in other parts of Broome County. It was awarded $805,000 from the state in response to a $2.9 million application that had sought to fund the acquisition, rehabilitation, or demolition of up to 26 county-owned properties across Broome County, with most being in the city of Binghamton and the Village of Endicott.

Another major initiative in the state is the *Start-Up New York* program, which was created in 2013 and seeks to accelerate entrepreneurialism and job creation across the state on a large scale, with a particular focus on Upstate New York. Under the program, businesses can operate tax-free for 10 years on eligible land and space. Businesses partner with the higher education institutions, enabling them to access industry experts and advanced research laboratories. Once a college or university is admitted to *Start-Up NY*, interested businesses may begin to apply to the program through the sponsoring school. Binghamton University and SUNY Broome are the backbone of *Start-Up NY* in the Greater Binghamton area.

A private initiative that has gained traction in upstate New York is the *Upstate Venture Connect* (UVC) program, which is a 501c3 non-profit organization set up to create an entrepreneur-led ecosystem for upstate New York. UVC is set up to follow the best practices guidelines as outlined in *StartUp Communities: Building an Entrepreneurial Ecosystem in Your*

City, by Brad Feld. Martin Babinec, the founder of *Upstate Venture Connect*, sums up why he started the venture its web page:

> "If you're a parent in Upstate NY, understanding the big picture motivator is a no brainer. We have world class education and quality of life communities here, and all of us that put kids through college come to accept the reality that after they graduate – our children will move on to other areas where the opportunities are more in line with their aspirations since there are so few jobs here that are in tomorrow's business model or industry. As families disperse, our own quality life goes down. What parent looks forward to their child moving across the country so that future contact is only on an infrequent basis?"

Babinec feels strongly that besides state initiatives hosted by governments and institutions, there needs to be support for entrepreneurs to engage, and nurture their creative energies with the community.

Binghamton's own *Entrepreneur Alliance*, established in 2014, is a local extension of the *Upstate Venture Connect* project. The same Jeff Smith who is a founding member of the B-Mets boosters is also a founding member of this alliance.

The alliance has a three-fold mission, Smith explains. "First we want to continue to map the companies that are using the Upstate Venture Connect program by being a liaison between them and the Upstate Venture Connect program. Second, we are here to provide mentoring services to start-up companies, and finally, over time, we will be a source of investment funding." The alliance currently has 19 members, with many members having already successfully established new companies.

Step 3. Maximize the Benefits from Higher Educational Growth

The combination of the growth of Binghamton University and SUNY Broome, coupled with various community efforts, state funding initiatives, and efforts by local businesses, have dramatically increased Binghamton's reputation as a college town. It is currently rated as the 28th best college town in America by Best College Reviews (http://www.bestcollegereviews.org/50-best-college-towns-america/), which uses five criteria to rank the towns:

- Cultural Offerings
- Large Employers
- Livability
- School Presence
- Student-to-resident ratio.

The American Institute for Economic Research (AIER) rated Binghamton even higher. Its ranking had the city listed as the 18th Best College Town in the nation in a survey it published at the beginning of 2015.

"These cities offer opportunity and a high quality of life not just for students, but for residents as well," said Luke Delorme, a Research Fellow at AIER responsible for the study. "People considering a new place to live or open a business would do well to consider these locations."

Less than a mile away from the NYSEG Stadium, signs of a better Binghamton and one that is proud to be called a college town are on clear display. Across from the *Floyd L. Maines Veteran's Memorial Arena,* which was built in 1971 and today hosts the AHL hockey team, the Binghamton Senators, a four-block area on Washington Street serves as a model of resurgence. Binghamton University opened its University Downtown Center in August 2007. Springing up around this educational complex have been multiple housing developments, catering to the Binghamton students. Accompanying the housing developments have been small businesses that focus on catering to the leisure-time activities of the students, including additional housing, restaurants, brewing companies, and gyms.

Binghamton's University Center is in the background, with the student housing development, Twin River Commons, in the foreground.

Mark Reisinger, an associate professor of Geography at Binghamton University who has been studying the economic impact of the University Center on Binghamton, told reporter Megan Brockett of the *Binghamton & Press Sun-Bulletin* in October 2014: "Certainly, when a university makes its presence in a downtown area ... where it typically hasn't been located, we see this kind of boom occur with the population, and it kind of has a spillover effect into the retail sector in particular.".

In July 2014, Kai Gronauer, a backup catcher for the B-Mets for a portion of the 2014 season, returned to the city for the third consecutive season. He was impressed with the changes he'd seen. "There are a lot more apartments downtown now and the area really seems more alive, I live downtown with some of the guys and it's really convenient getting to the park," Gronauer said. B-Mets pitchers Tyler Pill and Greg Peavey also lived downtown and appreciated the convenience of being able to walk to the park, as well as having a variety of eating options as well.

The city of Binghamton is not the only part of the area to benefit from the growth of the University. In August 2014, Governor Cuomo visited the neighboring village of Johnson

City, home of the Binghamton Triplets from 1913 to 1968, to participate in a press conference to announce the university would build its pharmacy school on Corliss Avenue, about two tenths of a mile from downtown Johnson City. The $60 million facility is expected to open in 2018 and because the site will be part of Binghamton University, any start-up companies that open within a mile of the school will be eligible for the benefits of the state's Start-Up New York zone, which includes relief from paying any New York State taxes for ten years.

The first classes in the pharmacy school are scheduled to be offered in the fall of 2017, with enrollment reaching 400 when it reaches full capacity.

Julie Deemie, president of the Johnson City Partners, a non-profit organization aimed at increasing economic opportunity and attracting new business, told the *Binghamton Press & Sun-Bulletin* in October 2014 that she expects the multi-million dollar project to spark a lot of interest in the area, starting a cycle that will lead to further investment.

The building of the Southern Tier High Technology Incubator in downtown Binghamton is another project that has Binghamton University's footprint on it. A ground-breaking ceremony was held on October 2, 2014 for the $19 million, 350,000 square-foot facility that will sit on the corner of Hawley and Carrol Streets, a half mile from NYSEG Stadium. Scheduled for completion in the fall of October 2016, the building will serve as an incubator for those companies that are part of the *Start-Up New York* program. Katie Ellis, in her October 2014 article for *Inside Binghamton* notes that "The facility will also include 18 laboratories and a shared high bay space dedicated to research in health sciences, energy-efficient technologies, and systems integration and packaging."

The Binghamton Incubator will replace the brownfield shown here under a bed of snow in downtown Binghamton, less than a mile from NYSEG Stadium.

The incubator is an example of work collaboration, as it is a partnership among Binghamton University, the Binghamton University Foundation, New York State, SUNY Broome, the city of Binghamton, Broome County, as well as sectors of private industry.

SUNY Broome has also undergone some recent expansion, with the opening of its Student Village for the fall class of students in 2014. The village, the first on-campus housing facility for the college, houses 350 students. The 18,000 square foot housing complex is one of the reasons the full-time enrollment increased by two percent for the start of fall 2014 semester.

Also, in 2014 the community college's plan for the *Start-Up NY* economic development initiative was approved as well. Explained SUNY Broome President Kevin Drumm, "We have identified key markets for development in areas such as basic and advanced manufacturing, agricultural manufacturing, hardware and software development, and other vital areas of business growth."

The ongoing growth of Binghamton University and SUNY Broome has led to the creation of the *SUNY Business and Education Cooperative of the Southern Tier* (SUNY BEST) initiative, which is looking to increase the revitalization of the area by turning it into a full-fledged college town, using the town of Ithaca, only 60 miles northwest – and home to Cornell University and Ithaca College – as an inspiration.

The theme of the SUNY BEST initiative is to capitalize on the symbiotic nature of a college and its community, which can create an ongoing cycle of development. Its theory is that good transportation and good business start-up practices can entice graduates to stay in the urban areas where they went to college. Having a community that attracts college students and fosters an environment where those same students are interested in residing can greatly help long-term economic health.

Interestingly, by recognizing that its community members are its most important asset, the Greater Binghamton Area is practicing the same principle that George F. Johnson and Thomas Watson used to build their respective companies of Endicott Johnson and IBM.

Step 4. Encourage and Promote Homegrown (Grassroots) Efforts

The revitalization of a community occurs in many places and forms, and in various shapes and sizes, with the key being dedicated people making it happen. One of the smaller but most visible projects in the revitalization of downtown Binghamton is the work of the Department Of Public Art (DPA), which is a group of local artists and volunteers committed to painting murals around the city that reflect its history and culture. The DPA was an offshoot from the city's Commission on Downtown Development, which started in 2011 and whose primary goal was revitalizing the downtown of Binghamton, seeking input from its residents. When residents were asked what they wanted to see, the answers often touched on "vibrancy" and "color within the city," instead of the gray and dull presence that dominated the city through its colorless concrete structures. The DPA commissioned itself to respond to this feedback by targeting areas of the city for bright and historic murals.

Cars entering the Water Street ramp are now met with this vibrant painting, touting the area's birthplace of IBM and other high technology endeavors.

In 2014 the parking ramp on Water Street in downtown Binghamton was chosen as a site. This structure has five ramps for vehicles to park and is a dark, dirty gray and foreboding facility. That is, it was a foreboding facility until the DPA started to get to work. The site of the ramp is an historic one, the building that once stood at 183-185 Water Street housed the Bundy Time Recording Company (TRC), which later became IBM, from 1893 to 1907, before the company relocated to neighboring Endicott for its expansion. After TRC left, the building housed the Automatic Music Company, which manufactured player pianos. Later, it became the site where the idea for the Link Flight Simulator was launched, and a flying school was housed here. The building was destroyed by flooding in the 1930s and eventually a parking ramp was built on the site.

Kady Perry, a resident of the city and a founding member of the DPA, is bullish on the group's efforts. She told the *Binghamton Press and Sun-Bulletin* in October 2014: "Public art strengthens communities. It enhances the aesthetics of the community and affects the psyche of residents." She feels strongly about its potential for achieving tangible results as well. "It also develops the economy. When people see things happening downtown, they're more likely to invest, they're more likely to stay. They're more likely to engage."

Peg Johnston, a DPA member and overall project manager at the ramp is also excited. "To me, public art is a sign that we're alive and hopeful," she said in a fall 2014 interview with the local paper.

Besides murals adding color and distinction to the gray facades of downtown Binghamton, residents have also seen mosaic tiles dressing up the city's infrastructure. *Susan Jablon Mosaics,* a company on the East Side of Binghamton that specializes in creating custom-made mosaics, has partnered with the *Southern Tier Celebrates* organization to get permission from Binghamton's Commission on Architecture and Urban Design to create visual art along the city streets in the form of mosaic tiles.

Emily Jablon, the creative director for *Jablon Mosaics*, explains the excitement in creating the mosaic art: "You get to stand back, it's all shiny, it's all pretty, and you know the city is forever changed. It's just like, little by little, reclaiming and re-owning these forgotten pocket parks and these forgotten planters, and giving our downtown these spaces that will bring our community back to life. What's really exciting for me is to really feel like I'm part of a movement."

Mosaics fill the decorative wall that highlights a public area off of the Court Street Bridge in downtown Binghamton.

As the Greater Binghamton Area relies on Binghamton University and SUNY Broome to be key institutions that allow it to benefit from various state initiatives, leaders in the area also recognize the value in fostering an entrepreneurial culture that can not only complement the state's Start-Up campaign, but can also provide job growth outside the governmental and university paths. The area's sports teams, fine arts attractions, and cultural vibrancy all contribute significantly to the overall quality of life in the area today and retaining these assets and facilitating their growth are also an essential element of economic resurgence for the Greater Binghamton Area.

The similarities between revitalizing a baseball franchise and a city cannot be ignored. In both cases, embracing the past provides motivation to turn potential into reality, as well as a path for learning life's lessons. In baseball, a key part of the rebuilding process is to take advantage of the sport's infrastructure, which means capitalizing on the amateur draft. In Binghamton's revitalization, an essential ingredient has been to capitalize on the state's initiatives – which has meant rebuilding through the Regional Economic Development Council and *Start-Up NY*. And just as Alderson has succeeded in getting maximum return on the trade market for such veterans as Carlos Beltran, Marlon Byrd, and R.A. Dickey, the Greater Binghamton area has focused on getting maximum benefit from the presence of its institutions of higher education. Finally, just as Flushing's hierarchy has relied on its farm system to populate the big league roster, Binghamton has come to rely on its local residents to populate downtown with positive reminders of the potential of a picturesque and vibrant downtown community.

Interestingly, even Sandy Alderson recognizes the comeback trail that Binghamton is on. In early January of 2015 he wrote to the Binghamton Mets Booster Club, thanking them for sending him a championship calendar that the booster club had produced in commemoration of the team's championship season in 2014:

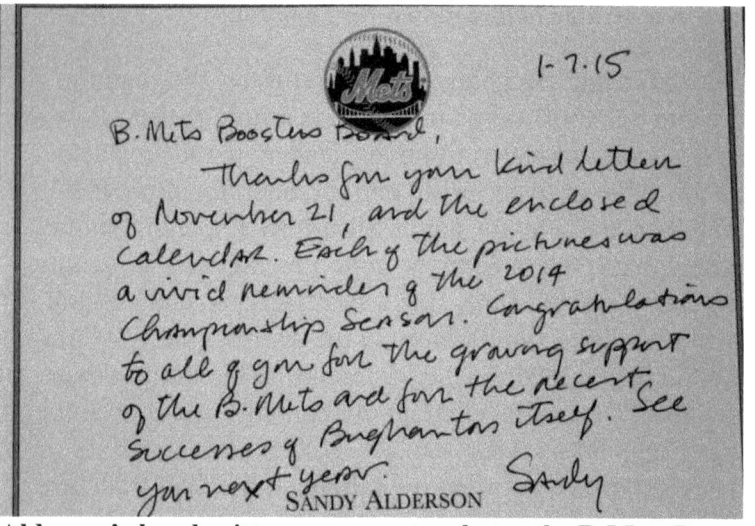

Alderson's handwritten response to a letter the B-Mets Booster Club wrote him when it sent him a commemorative calendar, along with an outline of some recent successes on the city's comeback trail.

Chapter 9. A View from the Press Box

Author's Note: In this chapter we take a break from the day-to-day happenings on the diamond to focus on the minute-by-minute happenings in the press box during an August game.

    Did you ever wonder how many video messages are flashed on the video board during the course of a game and who decides what is displayed? Well, if you are Justin Cohen, Director of Video Operations for the Binghamton Mets in 2014, these are the things you ponder every day. In 2014, Justin was in charge of the frenetic "game day" activity in the press box, where the between innings video events get scripted down to 30-second sound and video bytes, and are coordinated to blend in with the on-field entertainment between innings.

    Justin's crew shares the cozy press box with the team's beat reporter for the *Binghamton Press & Sun-Bulletin,* Lynn Worthy, and the team's official scorer, Steve Kraly. The video crew includes all those tasks involved with communicating with the crowd via the electronic scoreboard in left field and the video board in right-center field. These roles include the public address announcer, as well as those in charge of video replays; cameras within the stadium; music, video, and audio selections; statistics, MILB *GameDay* operation, and graphics. It is when the action stops on the field that the real action begins for those in the press box.

    These same dozen or so workers become a family during the season, meeting for a three-to-four hour spell during every game to share some laughs, do their job, and most importantly, provide memories for the fans and enhance the overall experience.

An idyllic view from NYSEG Stadium's press box.

On Sunday, August 24th, while the Binghamton Mets were doing their stretching and warming up, and Steven Matz was warming in the bullpen to face the Akron RubberDucks, the game for Justin's video team had already begun. They were posting their 19th item on the video board. Scores of stadium occupants were listening intently as the PA announcer read off the starting lineups. *"Leading off for your B-Mets, left fielder Brandon Nimmo, batting second and playing second base, Dilson Herrera..."*

"Generally, we try to get the lineups announced the same time before each game, right around a half hour before the first pitch or so," Justin explained. "A fair amount of people get here early and like to settle in with their scorecards."

On this day, the PA announcer, Chris Schmidt, finished his lineup right on cue, at 12:36:45, just in time for the *Pizza Hit Man of the Game* to be announced; for this promotion a member of the Mets starting lineup is announced and if he gets a hit during the game, everyone goes home with a coupon from Pizza Hut for a discounted pizza.

The day's game script called for no fewer than 113 selections, starting approximately 40 minutes before the first pitch, right up until the final signoff. While the game takes place on the field, the comments in the press box fly just as they do in the stands.

Matz starts the game by throwing a fastball for a called strike to 24-year-old center fielder Ollie Linton, who entered the game hitting .275 with one homer and 10 RBIs. Matz is finishing his second month for the B-Mets and has been impressive, establishing himself as the ace of the staff in just a handful of starts.

"O.K, that's the way to start it, keep it crisp," barks a voice behind Cohen. On a 2-1 pitch Linton hits a routine grounder to short and Wilfredo Tovar fields it and throws him out easily. Six pitches later the half-inning is over, with Matz displaying a live fastball and excellent command.

Now is when the game for Cohen and his staff really gets started, there is so much to do and so little time to do it! The first task at hand is to run the Stop DWI 15-second video spot, and while that runs Cohen makes sure the stadium cameras can pick out some of the groups attending the game as the DWI video is followed by a 30-second "spot" listing the groups in attendance at the game and a quick shot of two of the groups.

At the 45-second mark, first baseman Jayce Boyd's face appears on the video screen as he explains he was drafted in the sixth round of the 2012 amateur baseball draft and his segment closes with the words "This draft pick brought to you by the Galaxy Brewing Company on Court Street in Binghamton." As the promotion for the brewing company is in its final seconds, Cohen directs the stadium cameras to follow Ballwinkle, one of the two mascots for the team, as Ballwinkle delivers a free pizza to a lucky fan in the stands.

105 seconds and four video events have passed when lefty hitter Bandon Nimmo steps into the box for the Mets in the bottom of the first.

Nimmo looks at two strikes and a ball before he uses his bat, fouling off the fourth pitch down the left field line. On the fifth pitch he sees he hits a soft line drive down the left field line and runs hard right out of the box, never stopping until he slides into second with a double. That brings up second baseman Dilson Herrera, who enters the game hitting over .340.

"This kid Herrera looks like the real deal," says Matt Ferraro, the MILB GameDay operator.

"Yeah, and he's only twenty," states intern Joe Campione.

In August 2013 Herrera and Vic Black came over to the Mets in a trade for outfielder Marlon Byrd. The Pirate general manager, Neal Huntington, explained the trade by stating "Today we gave up a small part of our future for a big part of our present," as the veteran power-hitting Byrd was acquired to help the Pirates down the stretch drive of the season. The trade worked out for the Pirates, as Byrd hit .318, with three homers and 17 RBIs, helping the Bucs secure their first playoff berth since 1992. The Mets, meanwhile, were also delighted with their return in the trade.

Herrera hits a hard line drive single to right, and Nimmo has to stop at third because the ball is hit so hard. Switch hitting Brian Burgamy now steps to the plate and catcher Alex Lavitsky jogs out to have a quick chat with his pitcher, Will Roberts.

"A good hit here might be all that Matz needs, with the way he's been pitching," states John Reid, the statistics operator.

"Yeah, but remember, the front office has him limited to only pitch a certain amount of innings, so this game will be in the hands of the bullpen," states Cohen.

"Oh, don't bring up pitch counts," barks Ferraro "I hate them, just let the pitchers pitch!"

Steve Kraly, the regular official scorer, is off today. But if he were in the press box, he would be smiling from ear to ear. A member of the 1953 World Champion New York Yankees' pitching staff, he has no tolerance for pitch counts, as is the case with the overwhelming majority of his generation. Kraly is a local legend and has been the scorekeeper at Binghamton since baseball returned in 1992, after he retired from a 30-year career at IBM. His history in Binghamton is a long one, as he was a star pitcher for the Triplets in the '50s before and after he got his stint with the Yankees.

Steve estimates he is asked to speak publically five or six times a year in the local area and is honored to do so. He still gets fan mail asking for his autograph, and he responds to every letter with a beautifully written signature. "I don't understand the players of today who sign their names so you can't read the signature," he says. "I write my name so people can read it!"

Burgamy is now in the box as Nimmo and Herrera lead off the bases. Five pitches later Burgamy draws a walk and Lavitsky fidgets behind the plate. Bases loaded.

Two singles and a sacrifice fly later, the Mets have a 3-0 lead when Xorge Carrillo, manning the eighth spot in the lineup, despite entering the game with a .291 batting average, approaches the plate.

"Carrillo is due. I feel Xorge is gonna get a knock now," barks the left-field scoreboard operator as catcher Carrillo gets into the batter's box.

"Yeah, playing part-time has been an adjustment for him this year, Centeno's really good too, so there's not much he can do," barks out another voice as Carrillo enters the batter's box with two runners on and two outs and three runs already in.

"Heck, it's been almost a week since he last got into a game…"

Cohen never gets to finish his sentence, as Carrillo swings at the first pitch and grounds out to second baseman Joe Wendle for the third out. Before first baseman Ronnie Rodriguez catches the throw from Wendle, Cohen barks out "Zona, then the Dash," making sure the PA announcer is ready to go with his 30-second promo for the local eatery, *Zona and Company Grille*, and that the cameras are focused on the field for the "Dental Dash" that follows the promo. In the Dental Dash, a young member of the audience races against the clock to clean all three bases with a gigantic toothbrush—talk about a great photo opportunity for the parents!

Buddy the Bee and Ballwinkle tell the young contestant to start cleaning the bases! That's Brian Burgamy (#7) in the background.

"Ok, go to the promo," barks out Cohen.

"If you're hungry, *Zona and Company Grille* is the place for you to…" begins the PA announcer. While he barks out his promo, Cohen is barking out instructions to the cameras, "Ok, get on the first base bag, the toothbrush is about to come out."

With impeccable timing, as Schmidt finishes his promo, the graphic for the *Zona Grille* disappears from the video scoreboard and a live shot captures the activity at the first base bag. Within seconds, the camera is following the young entrant around the bases, holding a toothbrush that towers over him as he races to second. With aplomb that makes an umpire proud, the contestant cleans the second base bag with the bristles of his brush within seconds and dashes to third.

"Stay on the kid, stay on the kid," Cohen yells out, encouraging the cameraman to hold the shot as long as he can.

RubberDucks and Spiedie Races

After the dash, control is handed down to the field, where Connor Gates, the overall coordinator for the on-field entertainment, is standing on the first-base dugout roof to introduce those celebrating their birthdays today. Gates leads the crowd in singing "Happy Birthday" to the celebrants. After he finishes the "Happy Birthday" serenade, he turns control back to Schmidt for the start of the second. Schmidt barks out, *Now batting for the RubberDucks, catcher Alex Lavitsky.*

It is only the top of the second, but the video crew has finished 44 spots, with another 70 or so still scheduled.

"When did Akron start calling themselves the RubberDucks?"

"This is the first year," explains Cohen as Matz strikes out Jordan Smith to start the second inning.

"How'd they come up with that name?"

"I think it was to honor all the tire companies out there, Goodyear, Firestone, and a couple of other tire companies started out there," remarks Cohen.

"Yeah, and they wanted to appeal to the kids, so they put a 'ducks' at the end."

"Yeah, selecting nicknames is a sensitive thing," remarks Cohen. "You want to appeal to as many fans you can."

Ferraro can't resist the opening, painfully thinking of the losing seasons of the New York Mets. "Well, heck, we call our team the 'Mets,' and don't worry about all the fans that stay away because of that!"

The press box erupts in self-deprecating laughter and Cohen barks out a 'Touché!'"

Matz goes on to get Bryson Myles to fly out to right for a quick 1-2-3 inning. In the bottom of the second, after a leadoff single by Tovar, the Mets go down in 1-2-3 fashion. The highlight of the between innings video work is the "Great Spiedie Race," which shows three staff members adorned in costumes replicating a spiedie sandwich, a chef, and a bottle of marinade. As the three enter the field through the centerfield gate, the on-field master of ceremonies, TeJay Schwartz announces the action as the contestants race one another from the outfield fence to the finish line along the first-base foul area.

In this race the sandwich pulls away at the halfway point and wins by a wide margin. Fans sitting in Section 212, which the sandwich represented, all win a coupon for a free sandwich at a neighboring *Lupo's Spiedie* restaurant.

The next two innings go by quickly as Matz is mixing in his breaking pitches with his overpowering fastball and Roberts has also settled into a rhythmic groove.

Between the fourth and fifth innings it is all on-the-field entertainment, as Gates enters the field from the right-field picnic area regaled in his *Hickory the Hotdog Horse* costume. As he jogs down the first base foul area, his assistant, dressed as a hot dog named *Frankie*, hands him a hot dog to throw into the stands. "Who wants a hot dog?" exclaims Gates in rhetorical fashion. He will point to the stands, imploring for more cheers and from time to time he will cup his left hand to his ear, letting the fans know they are not loud enough. He then throws hot dogs into the stands with his right hand and he admits he takes devilish delight when a hot dog escapes its wrapper during his throw. "It's interesting to watch the reaction when one of the dogs gets separated from its bun," he points out. "They get all squeamish on me."

It's time to stretch a bit as hot dogs get tossed to the crowd. Lynn Worthy stands in the first row, with Justin Cohen to his left.

It's always an event to see if Gates can throw a hot dog over the high netting behind home plate. More often than not, it takes him multiple tries to get it over the huge net. Gates has to be quick, for he only has about 90 seconds to make his way around the ballpark and get rid of his half dozen or so hot dogs. He exits down the left field line, and does a quick change to be ready for his next on field adventure, whether it is leading the Kids Dash run across the outfield grass between the innings, or making sure everything is lined up to announce the winner of the day's 50/50 raffle.

As Gates gets out of his costume, the game enters the top of the fifth and the press box inhabitants become animated. Matz has started the inning by striking out the first two hitters for his fifth and sixth strikeouts of the game. And when Matz gets two strikes on the third batter, Ronnie Rodriguez, Cohen yells, "Two strikes on Rodriguez, Matz has a chance to strike out the side!"

Groans erupt in unison, however, as Rodriguez lines out to shortstop. If Matz had struck out the side, a lucky fan would have won over $150.00 as part of a local restaurant's "Strike out the Side" promotion.

"Oh man, Cohen, you really jinxed that one!" echoes more than one voice.

Just Get Started

One of the few people in the press box who was not outwardly rooting for Matz to strike out Rodriguez was the B-Mets beat reporter for the *Binghamton Press & Sun-Bulletin*, Lynn Worthy. Before joining the Binghamton paper in October 2010, Worthy was a sports reporter for the *Lowell Sun*, where he covered high school, college, and professional sports, including the Boston Celtics and the NY-PENN League baseball team, the Lowell Spinners. Before joining the *Sun*, Worthy worked as a correspondent for the *Varsity New England Magazine*, where he wrote biographies and features on high school athletes.

As the beat writer for the team, Lynn gets to the park around 3 p.m. for every home night game. This gives him time to get background material for his stories. In 2014 and 2013, those pre-game interview sessions proved invaluable for Worthy, given the team's winning ways. "Because the team has been doing so well, there is more newsworthy material concerning baseball that I've written about," Worthy explained.

As a reporter, Worthy roots for a good story, though he admits that because he gets to know the players he covers, he "quietly" wishes they do well. "Their success on the field means I have more news to write about," explains Worthy.

During any home game, you can find Worthy sitting in the first row of the press box, bent over his laptop. Typically he gives himself a half hour after the game to get in some post-game interviews so that he can file his story, which means he's at the park, right until 11 PM most nights.

The success of the B-Mets during the past two seasons, along with the disappointing seasons of the major league team, has seen Adam Rubin, writer for ESPN Blog for the New York Mets, refer to Worthy's work fairly frequently as the Mets fans from the Big Apple want to know everything they can about the pipeline of prospects in Binghamton. This national attention, however fleeting, is part of what keeps Worthy excited about his job. As for those wanting to break into sports writing, Worthy has two words of advice—"Get started."

As a youngster in high school Worthy aspired to be a sports journalist and he was given the same advice, to "Get Started" writing—whether it was the high school newspaper, local weekly paper or something for the internet. "That's what I would also tell people today," Worthy said as he explained the advice still works. "Just start writing, whether it is a blog, a high school or newspaper publication, whatever, just get started and develop your craft."

Regarding Binghamton's crop of players, Worthy has been impressed with the overall attitude of the team. "There is a good vibe in the clubhouse, they are used to winning and they expect to win." Worthy was quick to praise the work of manager Pedro Lopez—"He has managed to keep everybody fresh, everyone has gotten enough at bats to contribute and feel a part of the team and that is one of the reasons the team has done so well this year," explained Worthy.

From the Kiss Cam to a Spot Start for deGrom

At the end of the fifth inning, the video selections start with a one-minute update on the Las Vegas 51s game from the night before. Then the popular *Kiss Cam* camera focuses on selected couples while the video scoreboard frames them in a heart. The on-field emcee, TeJay, implores the couple to smooch. Before all the smooching is done, however, Cohen barks out "New pitcher" as he sees a pitcher jogging in from right field.
"Anyone got a number?" immediately becomes the question of the moment. Within seconds, "Number 27" is shouted out and, as the *Kiss Cam* promotion fades from the video board, Schmidt announces, *Now pitching for the Mets, Number 27, Randy Fontanez.*
While Fontanez takes his warmups Cohen barks, "Now go to the deal of the day," where a one-minute video highlights the items on sale in the "On Deck Circle" gift shop, and as the video ends with the words, "located in the concourse area behind home plate," Fontanez is ready to go.
The final stat line on Matz is impressive: five innings pitched, 71 pitches thrown, with an astonishing 53 for strikes! He gave up only three hits, did not walk a hitter and finished with six strikeouts.
"A few more performances like that and he might finish the season in Flushing," remarks Worthy to the person next to him.
As Fontanez gets ready to throw his first pitch, Reid barks "Five innings in a little over an hour, what a fast-moving game!"
Immediately, everyone's head turns toward the voice and groans emanate from all the throats. Reid has just broken an unwritten rule of the press box, where fast-paced games are always hoped for, but never acknowledged. The denizens of the press box are just as respectful of the "quick game jinx" as

players are of not audibly acknowledging a no-hitter that is in progress. Too many times the press box inhabitants have seen a short game turn into a long one, so the rule of thumb is "the less said the better," concerning fast moving games.

When Ollie Linton leads off with a ground ball single to right, frowns fill the press box. But Fontanez gives Reid a reprieve for the moment by getting third baseman Justin Toole to hit into a double play. Then Fontanez uses five pitches to get shortstop Jaime Pedroza to ground out, third to first. Five and one-half innings in the books and the game is not yet ninety minutes old!

At the end of the sixth, Justin turns the in-between innings entertainment over to Tejay, who is sanding on top of the home team dugout and becomes master of ceremonies for the 45-second "Almost Impossible Question" sponsored by local radio station Magic 101.7. Schwartz's contestant stands alongside him as he barks out to the stadium, "What Year was it when the following occurred?" as the scoreboard displays the following: 1) Michael Jackson wins eight Grammy awards; 2) The Edmonton Oilers defeat the New York Islanders to win their first Stanley Cup; 3) Astronaut Kathryn Sullivan becomes the first American woman to perform a spacewalk.

Then Tejay reads from the choices displayed on the scoreboard: A) 1980; B) 1984; C) 1978; D) 1994

Fans in the seats call out their thoughts to help the contestant; after about ten seconds, the contestant responds in a tone that mimics a question more than a statement: "B?" But luck fills the air today and 1984 is indeed the year!

In the top of the seventh Fontanez gives up a home run to DH Anthony Gallas, but then retires the side in order and the B-Mets hold a 5-1 lead. During the seventh-inning stretch, all activity is directed to the on-field "Buzz Brigade" trio of workers who entertain the fans by throwing out T-shirts for approximately two minutes. Fans are screaming and jumping at the thought of getting a free T-shirt! The final two innings of the game fly by, with the game finishing in two and one-half hours.

Cohen's two-year stint with the B-Met has provided him with a fair share of funny stories. In 2013, his two interns, Trevor

Levine and Mark Talley, shred a house about five miles from the stadium, in the town of Port Crane, with some players from the B-Mets. One of those players was Jacob deGrom. After an early season game, deGrom popped his head in the apartment and told his apartment mates that he had to go to Vegas to make a spot start and he would be back in a day or two. With a record of 2-5 and an E.R.A. of 4.80 and only 44 strikeouts in 60 innings, deGrom had no delusions. He was being called up only because it was his turn to pitch and Vegas needed some innings. He'd be back in Port Crane before anyone missed him.

DeGrom had an excellent first start with Las Vegas, so that first start was followed with a second one and when the second start was a good one too, a third start followed. DeGrom finished the season at Vegas, making 14 starts and getting 4 wins.

He had to send his father three weeks later to pick up his truck, but when his dad tried to start the vehicle, it failed to start!

Port Crane is still waiting for deGrom's return.

Chapter 10. "Etch-A-Sketching" to the Playoffs

July 31st is a line of demarcation in professional baseball, as it's the deadline to make trades without having to pass a player through waivers. There is usually a flurry of major league trades occurring on July 31, and scores of transactions as well. The minor leagues are also heavily affected, as prospects are traded and/or moved up the ladder to replace those players changing addresses. In 2014, there were 54 transactions by major league teams on 7/31 and an astonishing 75 moves on 8/1, according to Major League baseball's web site. (http://mlb.mlb.com).

In this flurry of activity, the Boston Red Sox traded:

- Lefty ace Jon Lester and reserve outfielder Johnny Gomes to the Oakland Athletics for outfielder Yoenis Cespedes.
- Righty John Lackey and lefty Corey Littrell to the Cardinals for right fielder Allen Craig and righty pitcher Joe Kelly.
- Infielder Stephen Drew to the Yankees for third baseman Kelly Johnson.
- Lefty setup man Andrew Miller to the Baltimore Orioles for lefty prospect Eduardo Rodriguez.

These moves had a trickle-down effect on their top minor league teams, as the Sox called up pitchers Tommy Layne and Alex Wilson from Pawtucket. Then Pawtucket tapped Portland for its ace lefty Henry Owens and catcher Blake Swihart. Portland's fans were left to mull over that what was good for the Fenway faithful in Kenmore Square was bad for the Hadlock habitants. As the dog days of August loomed, Portland had lost its star battery.

The New York Mets, however, made only one small move over this two-day stretch, demoting backup catcher Taylor

Teagarden to Las Vegas, opting to carry only two catchers, Travis d'Arnaud and Anthony Recker. Sandy Alderson realized the Mets were out of the pennant race and saw no need to acquire veteran talent. The front office was content to see how its experiment of playing Wilmer Flores at short played out for the rest of the year, as well as seeing how such youngsters as Jenrry Mejia, Jeurys Familia, and Zack Wheeler would fare for a complete season in the big leagues. With a record under .500, Alderson had resigned himself that the Mets were in the fourth year of their rebuilding plan and he was hoping that his youngsters would instill enough confidence in the fans to view 2015 as the year the big club could compete for a playoff spot.

For Binghamton's fans, though, Teagarden's ill fortune bodes well for their hometown team. Las Vegas turned around and sent Juan Centeno back to Binghamton as the logjam of Plawecki and Teagarden at AAA meant Centeno had to return to AA. In 2013, Centeno had played in Binghamton and Las Vegas and even had a brief stay with the N.Y. Mets. Though Xorge Carrillo had done well as the starting catcher during the past six weeks, gaining Centeno was a plus for Binghamton, as he was generally regarded as the best defensive catcher in the organization.

"They just sent me here to play more," Centeno told the *Binghamton Press & Sun-Bulletin* upon arriving in Binghamton. "It's good for me. I just take that the right way, and do my best here with the team."

In addition, Wilfredo Tovar joined the B-Mets, recovered from his surgery, so the B-Mets had gotten stronger up the middle with the calendar flipping to August.

"With Tovar coming back, it is an upgrade at short, because T.J. is not a true shortstop," reasoned Lopez. "We are now stronger up the middle. Centeno has some Triple A and big league experience too, so it is good to have Tovar and Centeno back." With Tovar's return to the lineup and Herrera entrenched at second, Rivera now had to move over to third. Rivera downplayed his move and took it in stride. "It's a reaction position so it is really about that first step and being in a good position," he explained.

With Rivera's move to third, it also meant that Lawley would be seeing more time in left field, competing with Ceciliani, Johnson, and Taijeron for playing time. With Nimmo being the first draft pick of the organization in 2011, no one was going to be taking playing time from him. The addition of Tovar and Centeno made the team stronger, but also made the manager's job more difficult. Somehow Lopez had to put his best team out there every night, distribute the playing time, and ensure everyone was thinking of the team just as much as their individual careers.

On a warm summer evening in Binghamton, under a partly cloudy sky, the B-Mets opened August with a Friday evening matchup against the Bowie Baysox, with Gabriel Ynoa taking the mound against lefty Jake Petit. Both Petit and Ynoa lasted only four innings, however, giving up nine runs on fifteen hits between them. Entering the sixth inning the game was tied. But the bullpen had some mound difficulties, and the Mets trailed, 8-7, entering the bottom of the ninth.

Bowie's righty closer Oliver Drake started the inning by getting ninth-place hitter Wilfredo Tovar to ground out to short. Drake had shoulder surgery in 2012 and bounced back to garner eight saves in 19 appearances for Bowie in 2013 with a 1.74 E.R.A. Now, 27, he was too old to be considered a prospect, but he lent a veteran presence to the Bowie staff and was enjoying a solid year as Bowie's closer. He relied on a low 90's fastball and a split-finger fastball that resembled a fastball until it broke sharply down as it approached the plate. Primarily a two-pitch pitcher, having his splitter break low in the zone was a key ingredient to his success as he relied on groundouts and strikeouts for registering outs. He was in the tail end of an outstanding season that would see him convert 31 of 35 save opportunities.

Tonight, though, would be one of his four failures.

With Nimmo in the batter's box, Drake got ahead in the count, 1-2. When he tried to finish him off with a splitter, he left the pitch up, and Nimmo hammered it to right field for a double. Dilson Herrera then lined a 1-1 pitch over the head of right fielder Ron Bermudez to score Nimmo with the tying run.

Herrera broke hard out of the batter's box, sensing a triple all the way and, as he came up from his slide into third, Herrera bounced up, clapped his hands and smiled broadly, looking into the Mets dugout with glee. Lopez was all smiles as he greeted him from the third base coach's box and the crowd was as excited as it had been all night, feeding off their second baseman's energy.

Since Herrera joined the team, he had brought an edge to it, playing the game with unrestrained energy. While Ceciliani, with his mischievous grin, animated handshakes, and prankish nature had the biggest personality in the clubhouse, Herrera, a native of Colombia, had the biggest personality on the field. He had no inhibitions, whereas off the field he was a bit self-conscious about his ability to speak English.

Herrera's eagerness to learn the nuances of the English language impressed his teammates and also provided them with some light-hearted moments.

On a recent rainy day, Nimmo had darted from some water that was dripping from the edge of the dugout roof. When he used the word "drip," Herrera looked at him in a quizzical nature.

"Drip? What is drip?" Herrera asked.

Nimmo's face broke out in a big smile, and his first inclination to point toward the roof of the dugout, but he realized that Herrera would think he was pointing to the sky. As Herrera's face contorted into a puzzle, Nimmo found himself thinking "How the heck do I pantomime a drip?"

Through a series of hand gestures and some slow talking, Nimmo added the word "drip" to Herrera's vocabulary. Now, as Herrera led off third, the B-Mets' dugout was dripping with anticipation of a win.

Just ten pitches into the inning and the Mets had a run home with one out and third place hitter Brian Burgamy at the plate. Burgamy knew Drake was primarily a two-pitch pitcher, and he had a hunch Drake would start him off with a splitter. "I was looking for something to go up the middle with, I knew he had a good splitter, and laying off that pitch is difficult, so I expected him to throw that pitch," explained Burgamy.

Drake did come in with the splitter, but his release point was a bit early and he missed the strike zone and his catcher's glove, throwing a wild pitch, enabling Herrera to score the winning run!

"Winning games like this just increases our overall confidence" said a smiling Burgamy after the game, as the B-Mets came back from deficits of 4-0, 6-3, and 8-7. "I like the approach of this team, everybody kept their heads in the game and we ended up scratching away and coming away with a win."

Though Burgamy went two-for-four, hitting his 19th home run and getting two RBIs to up his team-leading total to 62, he also was humbled by leaving five men on base. Burgamy's 12 seasons of playing baseball have taught him to never get too high or too low.

In explaining his baseball philosophy, Burgamy loves to refer to a toy of his youth. "You have to have an Etch-a-Sketch® approach to this game. Shake the board clean and start new. This is the way you have to look at every at bat, every game!"

Rivera, who had been given the night off with Tovar's return to the lineup, discussed how good play can be contagious. "Good at bats like Herrera had in the bottom of the ninth will motivate you even more to bring that run in," he reasoned. As for the team, he liked the vibe in the clubhouse and the results on the field. "We just kept battling and we were able to come out in the end. Dilson had an awesome at bat with that triple and scoring that run."

Lopez Passes Tamargo while Tovar and Centeno Shine

The B-Mets, getting a lift from the steadying presence of Tovar and Centeno in the lineup, along with their excellent play in the field, were applying pressure to the Sea Dogs during the first two weeks of August, going 9-4 while the Sea Dogs, perhaps adjusting to life without Owens and Swihart, stumbled out of the gate to go 6-7.

With a 3-0 win against the Harrisburg Senators on August 10th, the B-Mets presented Pedro Lopez with the record for most career wins by a Binghamton Mets' manager. The win gave Lopez 226 wins, passing John Tamargo on the all-time winning list.

Centeno and Tovar showed they were more than just defensive stalwarts in the August 14th game against the Erie SeaWolves. On that Thursday evening, they led the B-Mets past Erie, 9-4, pulling even with the Sea Dogs in the loss column and only trailing the Sea Dogs because of two fewer wins, attaining a record of 73-50. Centeno, batting eighth, went three for four and knocked in three runs while Tovar went two for three and drove in two runs. Burgamy chipped in with his 22nd home run and Jayce Boyd matched Centeno's output, also going three for four with three RBIs. The team was in great spirits as it headed to Reading to start a five-game road trip.

On Friday, August 15th, the big news in the Greater Binghamton Area was the first round of the *Dick's Sporting Goods Open* that was taking place at the En-Joie Golf Course in Endicott, which is a village about 13 miles to the west of Binghamton. The tournament is a stop on the *Champions Tour* for golfers 50 and over. In addition to the opening round of golf that was taking place on this day, the evening events at En-Joie included a performance of the *Zac Brown Band.* Well over 25,000 people attended the concert that was held just off the 18th green.

The field of golfers during the day included such luminaries of the links as Bernhard Langer, Collin Montgomerie, Fred Couples, Fred Funk, and Brad Faxon.

Though many of the fans of the B-Mets were roaming outside the ropes of En-Joie's tight fairways and undulating greens, the team was also providing excitement for those listening on the radio. While Zac Brown had his fans literally dancing on the 18th fairway with hits such as "Chicken Fried," "Colder Weather," and "Toes," the B-Mets were putting the finishing touches on an 8-7 win over the Reading Fightin Phils.

Though Rainy Lara did not get out of the fourth inning, surrendering five runs, the B-Mets shook off his subpar performance by hitting three home runs, with Herrera getting his eighth, Nimmo his sixth and Burgamy his 23rd. Randy Fontanez and Cody Satterwhite threw a scoreless eighth and ninth inning, respectively, to preserve the win, with Satterwhite notching his 14th save.

As fine as a night Friday night turned out to be for the Binghamton-area denizens, Saturday dwarfed the events of Friday. At En-Joie, Kevin Sutherland shot the first-ever 59 recorded on the *Champions Tour* and then rehabbing N.Y. Met starter Daisuke Matsuzaka beat Reading in the first game of a doubleheader at FirstEnergy Stadium *t*o bring the B-Mets within a half-game of first.

Matsuzaka was outstanding, throwing six innings and allowing only one run on three hits. Forty three of his 69 pitches were strikes and he had not walked a batter when he turned the game and a 2-1 lead over to Jon Velasquez, who retired the Senators in order in the seventh to gain his first save of the year. The Mets only had six hits, but Reading starter Jessie Biddle walked three and hit a batter in the fourth inning, allowing the B-Mets to score two runs on only one hit.

Though Portland won its game that night, besting Richmond 1-0, in ten innings, the Mets kept the pressure on, beating Reading in the nightcap. Tovar was the hitting star of the game as he went two for three, lifting his average over .300 for the season at .303, as well as hitting a homer and knocking in three runs.

With the doubleheader sweep, the Mets were feeling good about their chances of finishing first. One of the Mets who was feeling particularly good was outfielder Brandon Nimmo who had raised his average 67 points since July 1st, when he was barely hitting his weight at .179. "I feel good at the plate now, the confidence is definitely there now," explained Nimmo.

The Kid with the Red Shoes

Though Nimmo is only 21, the Mets' first pick and 13th overall in the 2011 draft carries himself as a seasoned veteran. This is even more remarkable when you realize that Nimmo never played high school baseball. Cheyenne East High School was where Nimmo received his high school diploma, but the school did not have a high school baseball team. So Nimmo has the unusual distinction of being a first-round pick who never played high school ball. In Wyoming, the weather is so cold that the state does not carry baseball as a sport.

That first round of that 2011 draft was filled with talent. Players drafted ahead of Nimmo included Gerrit Cole, Anthony Rendon, Francisco Lindor, and Javier Baez. Those drafted behind Nimmo included Jose Fernandez, Sonny Gray, Kolton Wong, and Joe Panik.

"I had incredible support from my parents," explained Nimmo. "In our barn they built a heated batting cage for me and my brother. My older brother taught me a lot about the game and he got to play in the College World Series."

Without a high school team to showcase his talent, Nimmo got noticed on the diamonds of American Legion ball. He gained the attention of the scouts through his outstanding summer performances for his legion team, where he played approximately 80 games each summer. Nimmo's status as a prospect increased dramatically with his standout accomplishments in all-star play. "In one of the first all-star tournaments I played in, no one even knew my name," explained Nimmo. "I was known as the 'kid with the red shoes' because I wore red cleats to match our legion team's red colors."

The Mets negotiated with Nimmo right down to the deadline.

"I had my bags packed and either I was going to play professional ball or I was heading to the University of Arkansas; I was packed either way," Nimmo explained. Only ten minutes before the midnight deadline did Nimmo autograph the Mets' contract.

Nimmo is thankful he can play a kid's game for a living. His approach each day is "work as hard as you can and have no regrets." Concerning his success in 2014, Nimmo attributes it to working hard and making some adjustments at the plate. "You have to make adjustments when you fail and you have to draw on those experiences in difficult times. I had a little hitch earlier and the movement of my hands has stopped a bit," he explained as he recounted how he has a tendency to wrap the bat a bit behind his head before unleashing his swing.

Nimmo shows his tendency to "wrap his bat" as he awaits a pitch with the bat logo behind his head.

As Nimmo now enjoyed success, he knew the pitchers would make adjustments. "The ball now is in the pitcher's court to make adjustments, the game is just a chess game, with adjustments on either side," reasoned Nimmo. "When I first came up they were pitching me all outside, so I was just going with the pitch, being sure to not fall into the trap of trying to pull everything."

Regarding Binghamton's chances of finishing first, Nimmo, who was part of Savannah's championship team in 2013, focused on the importance of working hard and letting the hard work speak for itself. "We would love to finish first, but we'll let that take care of itself, see where the chips fall. Last year I was part of a championship with Savannah. You don't forget that, it stays with you for the rest of your life. (It's an)

Amazing accomplishment to win a championship in professional baseball, no matter the level."

Though the bus rides in AA can be taxing, Nimmo does not complain. He is appreciative of everything about his life, as he knows he is living a dream that most of America can only dream about. He focuses on the positive, being sure to point out the little things that make the road trips pleasant. He even is quick to give a shout out to the person from the booster club that does most of the cooking for the road trip snacks for the players. "The cupcakes and cookies on the road trips are great and the dinners that the booster club sponsor are great too. This is a beautiful city, I love it, the hills and trees remind me of my hometown, and the fans are just great!"

Portland Goes on a Winning Streak

One of Nimmo's teammates on that championship Savannah team, Steven Matz, headed out to the mound on Sunday, August 17th to try to pitch the Mets into first. As he took the mound against Reading, three hours to the north, at En-Joie, Kevin Sutherland took his one-stroke lead out to the links, teeing off right around 1 p.m. He had a large gallery of fans following him, after his round of 59 the day before. If the B-Mets had been in town last night, he might very well have celebrated by taking in a ball game, as he is a big baseball fan, though the Oakland A's are his favorite team.

Matz pitched brilliantly this day, throwing seven innings and giving up only one run on six hits while striking out four. His only blemish was a run-scoring single by first baseman Jake Fox in the fourth. 23-year-old righty Holby Milner bested Matz on this day, however, as the 6' 2" righty threw 71 of his 99 pitches for strikes and shut out the B-Mets on only three hits. In stark contrast to Biddle's efforts the night before, Milner did not walk a batter. Explained T.J. Rivera, concerning Milner's effectiveness: "He threw inside effectively, coming in really hard and then going with the changeup, using both parts of the plate. He had us off balance the whole game."

The loss dropped the B-Mets to 11-5 for the month and, coupled with Portland's 7-1 defeat of Richmond, dropped the B-Mets to 1.5 games from first. Portland rode a five-run second inning to coast to victory as Richmond's starter, Kyle Crick walked four batters in less than two innings and gave up all five runs.

Meanwhile Hall-of-Fame golfer Bernhard Langer was overcoming a four-stroke deficit to overtake Kevin Sutherland and capture the *Dick's Sporting Goods Open* with a round of 66. Sutherland faded badly, following his scorching hot 59 with a 71 to finish in a tie for seventh place. (Diehard N.Y. Mets fans lamented at how Sutherland's fade reminded them of the Mets' dramatic fades in 2007 and 2008, when the team blew large September leads to the Phillies.)

On Monday, August 18th, the B-Mets traveled to Erie and pounded its pitching for 11 runs and 15 hits as Peavey notched his tenth win, 11-4. Portland was idle; The B-Mets, with a record of 77-51 were now one game behind Portland!

On Tuesday, August 19th, the Mets gave the ball to Michael Fulmer in his AA debut. Fulmer was the Mets' first-round supplemental pick in the 2011 draft (44th overall). That 2011 draft was rich in pitching prospects and part of the reason they Mets went with Nimmo so high was that they felt they could get first-round pitching talent in the second round. They passed on righty Jose Fernandez, who was taken by the Marlins immediately after the Mets drafted Nimmo.

The Mets were excited about drafting Fulmer and saw potential in his 93-95 mph fastball and developing slider.

Fulmer's first full minor league season was an outstanding one, as he won seven games for Savannah, posting an E.R.A of 2.74 while averaging almost a strikeout an inning. His 2013 season, however, was marred by injury, including a torn meniscus to his right knee. He dropped from being the # seven prospect in the organization to holding the 14th slot at the beginning of 2014. At St. Lucie, Fulmer was having a mediocre season, posting a 6-10 record with a 3.97 E.R.A. Adding to his disappointing won-lost record was that his strikeout-to-walk ratio had declined from Savannah to St. Lucie. So as Fulmer prepared to make his AA debut for the B-Mets, he also realized it could be the first step in reclaiming his elite prospect status.

But Fulmer battled his control on this night and Erie's Wilson Palacious was dominant, throwing seven shutout innings and striking out nine as Erie blasted Binghamton, 7-0. Three scoreless innings in relief by Hansel Robles were wasted.

At Harrisburg, Portland spotted Harrisburg four runs in the first, but came back to win, 5-4, behind home runs by catcher Carson Blair, left fielder Keury De La Cruz and first baseman Stefan Welch. Reliever Noe Ramirez notched his 14th save with an inning of hitless relief.

Binghamton's deficit now stretched to two games.

Wednesday, August 20th, saw the Mets beat Erie as Dilson Herrera hit his ninth homer and Gabriel Ynoa threw seven innings of one-run baseball. Randy Fontanez and Cody Satterwhite made the game interesting as each of them gave up two runs in their respective inning of work, but the Mets held on to win, 8-5. Meanwhile, on the other side of Pennsylvania, Carson Blair hit a three-run homer in the top of the seventh, giving Portland a come-from-behind win over Harrisburg, 5-3. Blair raised his average to .313 by going two for four.

Thursday was an off day for the B-Mets, but Portland kept the pressure on by beating Harrisburg, 1-0, as third baseman Mike Miller accounted for the game's only run with a homer. Hard throwing lefty Eduardo Rodriguez threw seven scoreless innings and Mike McCarthy finished the game with two scoreless frames. Portland was now riding a six-game winning streak and the Mets, though they took two out of three from Erie, saw themselves fall to two and one-half games out of first.

All was not lost, however, as the Mets officially clinched a spot in the playoffs on their off day due to a loss by New Britain.

The Mets returned home on Friday, August 22nd, and Juan Centeno and Wilfredo Tovar combined for five hits, but as impressive as that was, their offensive output was almost negligible in the Mets' 12-3 win over the RubberDucks before 5,189 fans. The meaningful output was generated by Dilson Herrera, who went three for three and knocked in four runs, raising his average to .346; Darrell Ceciliani, who went three for five with a home run and three RBIs; and Jayce Boyd, who drew three walks, went one for two and hit a three-run homer in the first.

Portland, however, again won another one-run game, 4-3, this one over New Hampshire. Stefan Welch hit another home run and Keith Couch, following in the footsteps of Henry Owens and Brian Johnson, raised his record to 8-1 by allowing only two earned runs in seven innings, dropping his E.R.A. to 2.69. Pennant fever was prevalent in Portland, as 7,012 fans packed Hadlock Field to cheer the Sea Dogs on to victory as the team preserved its two and one-half game lead.

Centeno was unfazed that his offensive production went unnoticed on Friday, as on Saturday he improved on his output from the night before, going four for four, with two RBIs. The Mets again defeated Akron 5-1, behind the two-hit pitching of Greg Peavey over five innings. Peavey only lasted five innings due to his uneven five-walk and nine-strikeout performance. The Binghamton faithful again came out in support of its team as 3,728 fans were on hand for the Saturday fireworks night.

Portland and its fans just sneezed at Binghamton's efforts, as 7,538 fans showed up at Hadlock to see Portland win, 7-1, behind Brian Johnson's ten strikeouts and one-hit performance over seven innings. The lone hit Johnson gave up was a home run to first baseman Andy Burns in the bottom of the sixth.

On Sunday, the Mets kept the pressure on Portland, beating Akron, 5-2, behind the three-hit and shutout performance of Steven Matz over five innings. The Mets scored three runs in the first and cruised to victory. Matz attributed his success in this game and to his overall season to the improvement with his curveball. "I felt really comfortable with the curveball. I had two gears with it, throw it for a first pitch strike and later on when I was ahead in the count as well. It makes pitching so much easier when you can throw a secondary pitch for a strike. For me the curveball is definitely a feel pitch. This year it has gotten better. The key for me has been feeling comfortable with it and throwing it early."

Portland, meanwhile, battled the Fisher Cats to a scoreless tie through six innings as Luis Diaz stifled the New Hampshire bats. Portland broke open the game in the eighth inning by scoring four runs. Mike Aguilera, making a rare relief appearance got the win as 6, 902 fans showed up to see Portland sweep New Hampshire and keep its two and one-half game lead over Binghamton intact.

The Mets had gone 7-2 only to see Portland win nine in a row! Portland was unfazed with the winning ways of Binghamton; like a heavyweight champion Portland just traded blows with the Mets, landing a couple of extra ones for good measure.

If the B-Mets were to take the title from Portland, the Sea Dogs would make them earn it.

On Monday, August 25th, the New Britain Rock Cats came to Binghamton and this time it was the Mets' turn to play in a nail-biting game, as the game was tied at one apiece going into the bottom of the eighth. Rainy Lara was brilliant, pitching into the eighth, allowing only one run on five hits. The Mets scored three runs in the bottom of the eighth, to win by a score of 4-1. Once again, however, Portland responded with a win, making it ten in a row, as the Sea Dogs beat Reading, 3-0, behind the pitching of righty Justin Haley. Carson Blair, Stefan Welch, and Mike Miller each knocked in a run.

Finally, on Tuesday, August 26th, the Sea Dogs lost a game, ending a ten-game winning streak that started on August 16th. Reading righty Ryan O'Sullivan tamed the bats of the Sea Dogs, throwing seven shutout innings and striking out six batters. Eduardo Rodriguez lost a heartbreaker, as he too pitched seven innings, giving up only one run on seven hits while striking out seven. Reading added three runs in the final two innings to make the final score 4-1. The Mets meanwhile, split a twi-night doubleheader against New Britain, losing the first game, 5-1, but coming back to win the second game, 3-2.

The deficit now stood at two games.

Get Out the Etch-A-Sketch®

The Mets had six games left to overtake the Sea Dogs. In addition, with 83 wins under their belts, the B-Mets players could set an all-time record for wins in a season if they could win four out of the final six games. This would break the record that the team had set just the year before. As the evening of August 27th approached, the Mets carried a record of 18-7 for the month of August.

Throughout the month of August, the Mets had little need for Burgamy's "Etch-A-Sketch®" to come out; the only thing that kept them in second place was the sizzling play of Portland, as the Sea Dogs were doing everything they could to give New England baseball fans a reason to ignore the plight of the last place Boston Red Sox. From mid-June to now, the Mets had gone from a team a few games over 500 to a team that now sat with a record of 83-53. The only problem was Portland was 85-51.

The Mets treated their rival's August performance with respect. Travis Taijeron, in his soft-spoken voice, summed up his teammates' feelings as he spoke of both teams' performances and the upcoming playoffs. "You know, that's just the way it goes. They're going to be hot, we're going to be hot. We're excited—they're a good team, we're a good team, too."

Taijeron, however, unwittingly showed how confident he was about advancing to the final round of the playoffs when he talked about the need to stay fresh with playing time being split among five outfielders. "In the playoffs anything can happen. You're going to be playing those National League teams and you have to be ready to come off the bench whenever you're called."

2,189 fans came out to NYSEG Stadium on Wednesday night, August 27th, the second-to-last home game of the season for the Mets. The B-Mets were almost unbeatable at home the whole year, sporting the Eastern League's best record by being 20 games over .500.

After New Britain, the Mets would go on the long ride to Richmond, where they would take on the Flying Squirrels in a four-game series to close the season. Portland meanwhile, was looking to start another winning streak as it hosted Reading for two more games before the Harrisburg Senators came in to close the regular season at Hadlock Field.

The Mets put the pressure on New Britain early, jumping out to a 5-2 lead after three innings. They started with a two-out rally in the bottom of the first to score two, riding back-to-back doubles by Jayce Boyd and Travis Taijeron, the 4th and 5th hitters in the lineup. In the bottom of third, the team strung together four hits to score three more runs. Tyler Pill held the Rock Cats to two runs in five innings and Lopez went to the bullpen in the top of the sixth due to an innings/pitch count being imposed on Pill.

Randy Fontanez followed with three innings of relief, but was touched for two runs, so when he turned the game over to Satterwhite in the top of the ninth, the Mets nursed a 6-4 lead, having added a run in the bottom of the sixth on a double by Nimmo to knock in Tovar, who had singled.

With Satterwhite on the mound, the Binghamton faithful were already putting a mark in the win column, and with Portland trailing Reading, 5-2, in the seventh, many were thinking about first place.

"Three more outs and it'll be one game and five left to go!" murmured more than one spectator in the stands.

As New Britain's second baseman and seventh hitter, Tony Thomas settled into the batter's box, another fan talking loud enough for those sitting three rows away to hear stated, "This win will give us 84, only two away from last year!" As Satterwhite looked in for the sign, Thomas was a picture of concentration, anxious to improve on his frustrating hitless night, with two strikeouts. Thomas had come into the game hitting .241. Satterwhite started him with a fastball.

Thomas wasted no time sending a jolt through the stadium.

He drove the ball high over the left-center field fence. The fans flinched in their seats as he rounded the bases. Satterwhite rubbed up a new baseball.

Even after the homer, Cody was thinking this game was his. But three straight balls to the right fielder Mike Kvasnicka put him in a bad spot, and Kvasnicka did not have to take the bat off his shoulder, walking on five pitches. Satterwhite was wild high and outside to the lefty hitting outfielder, an indication he was flying open with his front shoulder. As catcher Kyle Knudson stepped to the plate, Satterwhite focused on throwing strikes. But, struggling with his release point and overcompensating for his being wild high, Satterwhite threw the first pitch to Knudson in the dirt. The next pitch was eye high for another ball as Knudson squared to bunt. Lopez and Abbot exchanged glances in the dugout.

    Satterwhite's next pitch was down the middle of the plate and Knudson put down a sacrifice bunt, putting the tying run at second with the top of the order coming up. Left fielder Corey Wimberly quickly got ahead in the count, 2-0, and sat on a fastball. When he got it, though, he could only foul it off. Satterwhite, working from behind again, threw another ball. On a 3-1 pitch, Wimberly got an infield single to the right side of the diamond. Now runners were at the corners with one out and top prospect Eddie Rosario approaching the plate. Abbot and Lopez remained in the dugout and the bullpen remained still. This was Satterwhite's game to save.

    "No need to change what has worked all year," thought Lopez.

    Satterwhite threw a first-pitch strike to Rosario and the crowd let out a breath of relief. But Rosario was up to the task on this night and on the next pitch he got the run home on a force out from third to second. Nate Burgamy then finally ended the inning, grounding out short to second. As Satterwhite walked off the mound, the stadium crowd was stunned.

    The Mets came storming back in the bottom of the ninth, loading the bases with only one out. But Lawley popped out to second and Centeno grounded out to first to send the game into extra innings.

    As Reading put the finishing touches on Portland, winning 5-2, the Mets entered extra innings.

    Adam Kolarek relived Satterwhite in the tenth and struck out the final two batters of the inning to get out of a jam with runners on first and second. In the bottom of the tenth, the B-

Mets once again tested fate as Tovar put himself in scoring position with a single and a stolen base, only to have Nimmo strike out and Herrera ground out to end the inning.

In the top of the 11th, the Rock Cats put pressure on the Mets, banging out four hits and stealing two bases. The Mets contributed an error, a failed fielder's choice, and a wild pitch to help the Rock Cats to a five-run 11th to seal a loss. As the Mets entered the clubhouse, they knew they had passed up a golden opportunity to apply pressure to Portland. It was the type of game they had won all season long, holding a four-run lead after five innings and a two-run advantage going into the ninth.

The deficit remained at two games, as Portland also lost. As the clock approached midnight, it was the type of a game where Burgamy and his teammates needed to think of an Etch-A-Sketch®. It was time to shake the game out of memory; tomorrow was another game.

Shockingly, the next night Satterwhite once again failed to protect a lead. This time he was handed a 3-2 lead going in to the ninth but when he was through with the inning the B-Mets were down, 5-3. Lynn Worthy summed up the strange events in his lead for the game story that night: "A cruel joke is being placed on the Binghamton Mets as the Eastern League's regular season nears its end. Two nights in a row they've lost games that were in their grasp in the ninth innings. Adding to the frustration, the B-Mets could have moved into a tie for first place had they won both games because the Eastern Division leader Portland lost on both nights."

No matter the failures of Satterwhite, Lopez was behind his closer. This was obvious in his comments the next day, before starting the four-game series on the road against Richmond. "The first game, Cody just made mistakes in the middle of the plate and got hurt against a good hitting ball club. Last night, the defense let him down," he said, referring to a two-base error by Taijeron that allowed a run to score and a grounder that Herrera bobbled, costing him a play at home. "I met with him and told him he will be the closer all the way through the championship. He's my guy," emphasized Pedro as he continued, "The team just needs a short-term memory. We've bounced back from really bad games and before you know it, we win six straight."

Satterwhite made no excuses for his back-to-back failures. "I've just got to make better pitches," he explained. "I've got to make better pitches when it matters. I haven't made those pitches and the other team has made me pay."

As the team got ready to head to Richmond, Greg Peavey, who earlier that evening was named the team's Pitcher of the Year, spoke for the team when he told the *Binghamton Press & Sun Bulletin*: "I think that we need to string together a couple wins in this next series just for confidence. These last two games have been unfortunate, but we're a great team. Hopefully, we'll go into Richmond and take care of business and get a full head of steam into the playoffs."

While Peavey was saying those words, however, shock was spreading through the clubhouse. Dilson Herrera was excitedly accepting handshakes from his teammates while front office personnel of the Binghamton Mets were looking at one another with quizzical visages.

Due to an injury to Daniel Murphy, Herrera was going to Flushing, Queens to play second base on a regular basis.

Lopez was sad and ecstatic at the same time.

The next day, Lopez elaborated. "Last night, hearing about Herrera, it was mixed feelings. When he and Nimmo and T.J. came up from St. Lucie, we were a different ball club, we took off as team. A lot of that goes to show what Dilson brought to the table, the leadership he brought to the team with all that energy." Lopez continued for another solid minute, sounding as if he needed to convince himself that all would be well.

"But at the same time I was so happy for him, and it was great seeing one of my kids go from AA to the big leagues. And as far as the team, it has worked so hard all season long, but there is no doubt in my mind that this team has the personnel to bring a championship home. Today, before I came to the park I jumped in the shower and asked the good Lord to give me the right words in my mouth and heart to say to this team. There is no doubt in my mind that when this thing is said and done, we will look back and be able to say we still made it."

While Herrera headed to Flushing, his ex-teammates headed to Richmond.

While the Mets were still chasing the Sea Dogs, the Flying Squirrels had a magic number of one to clinch first place in the Western Division. Richmond had also been hurt with the call-up bug, as earlier in August the team lost Matt Duffy to the Giants. Both teams wanted to finish the four-game series with momentum on their side and no more loss of players.

Little did the Mets know, however, that they'd be playing Etch-A-Sketch® every day on this final road trip.

The organizational innings limit on Matz prevented him from going more than five innings in the opener, and though he pitched well that Friday night, when he left the game he was on the short side of a 2-1 score. Richmond's starter, Adalberto Mejia held the B-Mets to one run in six innings and then turned the game over to the bullpen, which was superb. Edwin Quarite, Stephen Okert, and Hunter Strickland shut the Mets down, allowing only one hit over the final three innings. Strickland was especially impressive, striking out Tovar and Taijeron to end the game and in the process throwing only three pitches for balls in the entire inning. Strickland was closing out an outstanding minor league season, as he had 11 saves and a 2.02 E.R.A for the season. (He got called up to the San Francisco Giants for September, providing the bullpen with a lift as he went unscored upon in nine games.)

Portland won on this night, clinching first place. Even if the Mets swept Richmond and Portland lost the next three games, Portland would finish first with the tiebreaker (having a better record in head-to-head competition) going in its favor.

The next night, things got worse for the B-Mets. Leading 6-4 going into the bottom of the ninth, Lopez tuned the game over to Randy Fontanez to close it. Having used Satterwhite two out of the last three days, Lopez wanted to give Satterwhite some rest. But Fontanez had a nightmare in the bottom of the ninth. He walked the first batter, then gave up a single. Then on a comebacker to the mound, he threw the ball away, putting runners on second and third and allowing a run to score. Then Fontanez threw a wild pitch, allowing Richmond to tie the score.

Then second baseman and third place hitter Blake Miller raised his average to .318 by hitting a single to left on a 3-1 pitch from Fontanez. If anyone ever needed to "turn it over and shake it out," it was Fontanez, as there was no hiding his ugly line. Four batters faced, none retired, two hits, a walk, a throwing error and a wild pitch!

The last day of August saw the B-Mets losing streak reach five games, as the Richmond pitchers again held the Mets in check, winning 1-0. Starter Tyler Blach threw seven shutout innings and Quarite and Okert closed the door in the final two innings.

After the game Pedro Lope held a short team meeting, saying that as far as he was concerned, the season started on September 1st. He wanted to team to forget about the five losses, but prepare for the playoffs with a win.

Shortly after the team meeting, however, he and the team received a blow that was more difficult to accept than the previous three losses in Richmond.

Catcher Centeno and lefty reliever Dario Alvarez were no longer on the team.

They too had gotten the call to go to Flushing!

Though Lopez would not admit it, he was shocked. It was no surprise the N.Y. Mets wanted a third catcher to lengthen their bench in September, but most people thought Plawecki would get the call. What they had not factored in was the status of the Mets' 40-man roster. Because Plawecki only had two years in the minor leagues, the Mets did not have to add him to their 40-man roster in the offseason. So if they called him up in September, it would cost them a spot on the 40-man roster and they were already concerned that they did not have enough openings on their roster to protect all of their prospects. Centeno was already on the 40-man roster, so it made sense to call him up. This was similar to the earlier reasoning in calling up Herrera two days earlier. Herrera already had four years in the minors, so they were planning to protect him in the offseason, so his callup would not ultimately cost a spot on the 40-man roster.

The loss of Alvarez also stung Lopez. In the last few weeks Alvarez had become his number one lefty out of the pen.

As with Herrera, the Mets planned to put Alvarez on the 40-man roster in the offseason. Since they were planning to protect him, they were eager to take a look at him.

Before the final game of the season, Lopez admitted he was concerned. "The concern level is high, with the way things have gone down now the past five games, it's tough. You know after our meeting yesterday I got the call concerning Alvarez and Centeno after everyone left the clubhouse. I almost called another meeting at the hotel," Lopez admitted.

"But the main thing now is what are we going to do?" Lopez asked as he shifted his focus. "Are we going to shy away from the challenge? When all is said and done, I think we will be holding that championship trophy when everything is over… there's a good bunch of guys in that clubhouse. The team's been through a lot this year and this is just one more thing to overcome."

Lopez gave Tovar and Burgamy a day of rest. Newcomer Tim Peterson got the start on the mound, as Lopez wanted to give his staff a rest for the playoffs as well. 2012 first-round pick Gavin Cecchini got the start at short. Unfortunately, Lopez's strategy backfired, as Peterson lasted only one third of an inning, giving up five runs, so Lopez used six pitchers to finish the losing effort to Richmond, 12-4.

As the Mets rode the bus back to NYSEG Stadium during Labor Day's late afternoon, they were determined not to waste the labors of their season. They knew what they had to do.

Get out the Etch-A-Sketch®.

Chapter 11. A September to Remember

John Bernhardt, cohost of the one-hour *Tip Off* sports-talk radio show for WIOX FM 91.3 in Roxbury, N.Y., got to NYSEG Stadium in the early afternoon for the first playoff game against Portland. He settled into his seat in Section 1, seat B2, with an assortment of signs for later use in the night. As he watched Portland take batting practice, catcher Michael Brenly caught Bernhardt's eye in his batting practice routine.

"Brenly was a real character, he reminded me of Ceciliani. He was always goofing around with his teammates," explained Bernhardt. "At one point, he acted as if he were going to throw a ball at me into the stands, as he wound up in an exaggerated motion."

Later, as fans entered the stadium and filled the seats around him, Bernhardt handed out 50 or so signs that had "Six More Wins" written on them, in tribute to the season-long mantra. Bernhardt had sundry other signs with him this night too, so when the game started, he or one of his cohorts held up signs to entertain the crowd and, he hoped, spur the Mets to victory. If a Binghamton Mets player made a good play in the field, one of his cohorts stood with a sign that said "UN"-*picture of Buddy the Bee*-"LIEVABLE." And if things did not go as well as he had hoped, he or one of his recruits countered with a picture of Buddy the Bee with the letters "lieve" following it.

Bernhardt's actions were reminiscent of Karl Ehrhardt, who was unofficially known as the "Sign Man of Shea" at Shea Stadium from 1964 to 1981.

Bernhardt's face lights up as he recalls Ehrhardt. "He had some 1,200 cardboard signs with almost every saying imaginable. He would bring about 60 different signs to every game and would hold up a sign to accentuate the moment." Ehrhardt was a popular icon for the TV cameras to capture as he stood and held his signs for all to see. "Can You Believe It?" "Amazing!" and "Curses, Foiled Again!" were signatures of his signage wit. And when Tom Seaver dominated the mound in

1969, "Leave it to Seaver" was perhaps his most comforting sign. When the Mets recorded the final out of the 1969 World Series, Ehrhardt stood holding a sign that simply read "There Are No Words."

Ehrhardt even took on the front office when he thought it appropriate, once holding a sign that read "Grant's Tomb," reflecting his displeasure with then N.Y. Mets General Manager, M. Donald Grant.

Bernhardt's signs appeared to bring out the best in the B-Mets on this night.

In one of the greatest games ever played at NYSEG Stadium, in the first game of the Eastern Division Championship Series, the Binghamton Mets came back from a 5-1 deficit to defeat the Portland Sea Dogs, 8-5, on a three-run, walk-off home run by T.J. Rivera in the bottom of the ninth inning with two out.

For the first five innings of the game, Tyler Pill and Brian Johnson locked up in a classic pitcher's duel, with each pitcher allowing only one run. Second baseman Sean Coyle accounted for the Portland run with a solo homer in the fourth and T.J. Rivera knocked in the Mets' first run with a single in the third.

In the sixth inning, however, the game took a dramatic turn in favor of Portland. Rusney Castillo, the recently signed Cuban bonus baby, started the inning by sending a dribbler down the third base line that Dustin Lawley could not field cleanly; it was ruled a hit, as even if Lawley had come up with the grounder, Castillo may well have beaten the throw to first. Castillo stole second, but Pill bore down and got third baseman Mike Miller to ground back to the pitcher and then got Coyle to ground out to third. But Pill then yielded an RBI single to left fielder Keury De La Cruz, giving Portland a 2-1 lead.

From there things quickly worsened for the B-Mets. Catcher Blair Carson followed with another single. Pill fell behind first baseman David Chester, 2-1 when he decided to challenge him with a fastball. But Pill missed his mark and now was behind in the count, 3-1. Chester sat on another fastball and Pill challenged him again. This time Chester launched a huge home run over the left field fence, silencing the home crowd.

After Pill hit the next batter, Stefan Welch, Pedro Lopez came out to end Pill's evening.

Brian Johnson gave back one run in the sixth on an RBI double by Rivera. He finished the night strongly, though, retiring the Mets in order in the bottom of the seventh. Meanwhile Hansel Robles restored order to the night, throwing 2.1 innings of hitless and scoreless relief, striking out four hitters in the process.

In the bottom of the 8th inning, lefty setup man Robby Scott relieved Johnson and Tovar led off the inning with a double. One batter later, TJ Rivera singled, knocking in Tovar. After Burgamy walked, manager Billy McMillon brought in his closer, Noe Ramirez, to pitch to cleanup man and designated hitter Jayce Boyd. The B-Mets then received a huge break as Jayce Boyd hit what looked like a double play ball to second baseman Sean Coyle. But Coyle made a bad throw to shortstop Ryan Dent at the second base bag, and instead of the inning being over, the Mets had another run in and runners on first and third with one out.

Darrell Ceciliani then hit a sacrifice fly to center to tie the game, lifting the fans out of their seats with back slaps, hugs, and raucous clapping. The crowd was now frenetic, seemingly inhaling and exhaling with each pitch.

Ramirez got out of the inning without further damage, though, retiring Taijeron on a routine fly to left.

Lopez countered by bringing in Satterwhite, who rewards Lopez by throwing a scoreless ninth. Satterwhite did tease the crowd a bit, as he walked a batter and gave up a hit before getting the third out.

Ramirez started the bottom of the ninth by getting Dustin Lawley to flail at a 1-2 off speed pitch. Catcher Xorge Carrillo then hit a routine ground ball to third, but Mike Miller, moving a step to his left, let the ball go under his glove for an error. The Mets now had the winning run on first with one out. Double-A veteran Wilfredo Tovar then singled, putting runners on first and second, with one out.

Lefty hitting Brandon Nimmo now came to the plate and Kyle Johnson came into the game to run for Carrillo. The Henry

Street crowd made noise in anticipation, rhythmically clapping their hands—a single would win it. Nimmo was eager to atone for his night, as he was 0-4, with two strikeouts, a groundout and a fly out. He settled into the box as he always does, with his left foot at the back of the box and his right knee slightly bent.

Before getting into his hitting stance, he held his bat straight up, looking at the pitcher. Nimmo battled throughout the at bat, fouling off some outside pitches to stay alive. In the end, though, Ramirez prevailed, getting Nimmo to swing and miss at a low outside breaking pitch.

The night was getting long, the game just over three hours old when T.J. Rivera approached the plate. Rivera was the only thing separating Ramirez and the Sea Dogs from extra innings. Wilhelm Rathgeber fidgeted nervously in his seat as he called out support for Rivera.

With Brian Burgamy studying the action on the diamond from his spot on deck, Ramirez challenged Rivera with a first pitch fast ball and Rivera wasted no time, swinging at this first pitch. As soon as he heard the bat meet the ball, Burgamy looked out towards left and then started jogging toward the first base line, getting a better look at the action. Then, almost immediately, Burgamy turned to the B-Mets' dugout, raised his right fist in the air as he realized the ball was going to leave the park! As Rivera rounded first, Burgamy jogged behind him, almost going onto the field. Then Burgamy did an about face, jumping up and down on the first base line as he headed home to join the scrum that was gathering to greet Rivera.

As Rivera stepped on the plate, he was mobbed and mauled by his teammates, while the stadium denizens turned the corner of Henry and Fayette Streets into a block party.

"I was just looking to drive the ball somewhere," recalled Rivera after the game, noting he was anticipating a first-pitch fast ball, which is what Ramirez delivered.

That's Rivera on the far right, just escaping from his raucous teammates after his walk-off homer in Game 1.

As Rivera gave a post-game interview for being the player of the game after going four for five with five RBIs and a home run, he was doused with a bucket of ice water by his teammates.

Never before had ice felt so warm.

Portland Silences the Sign Man

In baseball, momentum is often measured by the day's starting pitcher and in the Binghamton Mets' case, that's exactly what happened in the second playoff game. Before the game, the Mets were riding high from Rivera's heroics. Greg Peavey was given the ball, but on this night he could not sustain the momentum. Though he was betrayed by sloppy infield and outfield play in the five-run second inning that Portland pasted on the Mets, Peavey was not sharp. His fastballs were thigh high and his breaking stuff was even higher. Portland greeted him with three homers in his two innings of work.

For Portland's catcher, Michael Brenly, it was payback time. Squatting behind the plate in Game One, he had only been a few feet in front of Bernhardt's placard-carry fans. Now, with a comfortable lead in the early innings, he caught Bernhardt's attention. "After the first three or four innings our signs were quiet," lamented Bernhardt. With Portland holding a 7-0 lead after five innings, smiles were scant in the stands. For Bernhardt, resignation set in.

"In the final two innings, when he warmed the Portland pitcher, Brenly would turn and stare at me motioning for the signs," explained Bernhardt. "At the start of each inning in his squat position he simply turned and stared for several seconds, then motioned his arms in a 'bring it' gesture that I took to mean, 'Where are your signs now?'"

Brenly succeeded in intimidating Bernhardt. "I just ignored him, but it was a tad uncomfortable. It let me know the signs had really touched a nerve with the Portland guys, which was not my intention at all. I was only trying to fire up the crowd and make it more exciting or the fans," explained Bernhardt months later.

Bernhardt's signs were not the only thing quieted this night.

The bats for the B-Mets were also silenced, garnering eight hits but no runs. Darrell Ceciliani symbolized the frustrating night for the Mets when he came up with runners on first and second and one out in the bottom of the sixth. Ceciliani, the life of the clubhouse and the unofficial sparkplug of the team, battled starting pitcher Justin Haley by fouling off a number of pitches down the left field line. Ceciliani just missed a run-scoring double as one of his line drives just fell outside the line.

Ceciliani refused to give in, though he was down in the count, one ball and two strikes.

When Haley finally gave him a pitch that he could pull, Ceciliani hit a hard grounder down the first base line; off the bat, it had "hit" written all over it. But Stefan Welch was guarding the line and with a lunge to the left he was able to snare the ball and start a 3-6-3 double play. As Ceciliani crossed the bag he grasped his helmet with both hands and threw it to the ground.

As Ceciliani's helmet bounced on the ground, the chances for a comeback had no bounce in them at all.

The Mets sent only nine hitters to the plate over the final three innings, netting only two hits, which were erased by double plays. Double plays were the subplot of the game's frustration for the Mets, as they hit into four of them; when it looked like they might get something started, the inevitable double play followed. The final score: Portland 7, Binghamton 0, and quite a few unused signs by Bernhardt.

Worse yet for the Mets, they now had to head to Portland, with the long bus ride giving them plenty of time to contemplate the daunting task of taking two out of three at Hadlock Field, where they had managed to only win two of nine during the regular season.

A Few Feet Short

Both teams line up for introductions in Portland before Game 3.

Trailing the Portland Sea Dogs, 6-3, going into the top of the ninth in the third game of the series, the B-Mets were determined not to surrender without a fight. Though Rivera started the inning harmlessly by grounding out to pitcher Aaron Kurtz, Burgamy came up with the type of professional at bat that you would expect from a veteran, as he worked out a walk. Boyd followed with a bloop single to right and suddenly, Ceciliani came up to hit, representing the tying run.

Darrell had struck out his first two at bats against starter Eduardo Rodriguez, succumbing to Rodriguez's 95 mph fastball and assortment of breaking pitches. He had worked out a walk against a tiring Rodriguez in the 7th and came around to score on the ensuing double by Taijeron to briefly tie the score, before Portland scored three times in the bottom of the seventh to take a commanding 6-3 lead. As Ceciliani strode to the plate in the ninth, he was three for nine in the series with an RBI.

Prankster Ceciliani was all business now. A base hit here and he could change the whole complexion of the game. Reliever Aaron Kurcz had been effective since taking over for Rodriguez, with Burgamy and Boyd being the first base runners he allowed.

Kurcz challenged Ceciliani on the first pitch with a fastball and Darrell got a piece of it, tipping it off the catcher's glove. Kurcz followed with nothing but fastballs and Ceciliani stayed alive by fouling the next three pitches off. Down in the count, 0-2, Ceciliani had to guard against a breaking pitch, but Kurcz was focused on simply challenging Ceciliani. When Ceciliani saw his fifth straight fastball, he was ready for it and hit it deep to center—but Shannon Wilkerson caught it easily, a few feet in front to the warning track. Ceciliani headed back to the dugout, wondering what might have happened if only his bat had been a bit quicker.

Two outs, two on, and Travis Taijeron now at the plate. Travis hails from California and in the beginning of the season, he had to adjust to the cold weather of Binghamton, even though he had spent half a season here last year. Taijeron loves to hit fastballs and is still adjusting to hitting off-speed deliveries.

Pitching coach Bob Kipper now visited the mound, no doubt with two thoughts on his mind. One was to remind Kurcz that Taijeron's strength was hitting the fastball and that he'd be sitting on this pitch. The other was to pump up Kurcz. "Be a pitcher out here. Set him up, then go for the kill with your best stuff."

Kurcz's command of his breaking pitches was not as crisp as Kipper had hoped with his first two deliveries. Within a minute, Taijeron was ahead in the count 2-0. Now he could sit on a fastball in a location that he liked. There was no question that Kurcz and finesse were not going to be partners at this point. Kurcz would go with his best against Taijeron's best—fastball against a "dead red" fastball hitter.

At 2-0, Taijeron did indeed get a fastball and when he first made contact, the 5,000 fans that filled Hadlock grew silent as their eyes looked high and deep into the night, studying the high fly that was headed to deep left center. Both center fielder Shannon Wilkerson and left fielder Keury De La Cruz headed to the left centerfield gap, with players from both teams looking out at the outfield from the top step of the dugout.

The B-Mets players were yelling "Stay Up, stay up, get outta here!"

And the Sea Dogs were thinking, "That's gotta be short, get down, baby, get down!"

Get down it did, as at approximately 9:05 PM, the ball nestled into De La Cruz's glove, on the warning track in left center. The B-Mets fell a few feet short of another dramatic home run in the series. As the fans cheered and the Sea Dogs quickly headed to the dugout, the B-Mets were left to think of what might have been.

For the first four innings, Stephen Matz and Eduardo Rodriguez had engaged in a classic pitcher's duel, with Rodríguez holding a 1-0 lead and holding the Mets hitless. Rodriguez was dominant, not allowing a hard hit ball and erasing his only base runner, Brandon Nimmo, on a fourth-inning walk, by getting Burgamy to ground into a double play.

Matz was almost as good, throwing four innings and giving up only one run on three hits before getting touched for two runs on three hits in the fifth inning.

The Mets finally broke through against Rodriguez in the sixth, as he started to tire and left some pitches up in the zone. With one out, Carrillo hit a hanging curveball off the wall in left center and after Tovar moved Carrillo over to third with a groundout, Nimmo, coming to the plate with a 1 for 10 albatross, brought Carrillo home with a double and went to third as Wilkerson had trouble picking up the ball. Nimmo scored shortly thereafter on a wild pitch as the Mets pulled within one.

In the top of the seventh, the Mets tied the game on a single by Ceciliani and a double inside the third base line by Taijeron, but the Sea Dogs strung together four hits in the bottom of the seventh to score three runs, giving them a 6-3 lead.

Ceciliani and Taijeron gave the Mets hope, but their drives fell a few feet short of giving them a win. Portland now held a 2-1 series advantage.

Grinding it Out

Saturday's game was moved up from 6 p.m. to a noon start due to a huge thunderstorm that was predicted for early evening. With teams as far apart as Akron, Richmond, Binghamton, and Portland participating in the Eastern League playoffs, the travel schedules were demanding enough, without throwing a rainout into the mix.

Early Saturday the sun shone brilliantly and, as fans trickled into the stadium at 10:30 that morning, the friendly ushers and staff had smiles waiting for all of them, even the dozen or so diehards who had made the trip from Binghamton to cheer on the boys in the orange and blue. The Binghamtonians were not hard to pick out, as they were adorned with their Binghamton shirts and caps. The ushers lamented that the change in starting time for the game would keep the crowd under 3000. "You won't see the stands packed like last night, but you should see a good game today," was a commonly-repeated sentence of the stadium staff.

The game started well for the Sea Dogs, as entering the fifth inning, they were leading, 2-1, and were only 15 outs from a victory celebration. Mike Aguilera, the Portland starter and Binghamton University draftee, had held the Mets to one run and four hits and at 1:15 p.m., as the fifth inning started, most Portland fans thought they would be celebrating by three o'clock. But Wilfredo Tovar and the Mets had other ideas. Tovar, the

September sparkplug, started the fifth by singling to right. Up strode Nimmo, carrying a .166 post-season average to the plate. In what was the turning point of the series for Nimmo and the Mets, Aguilera left a pitch up in the zone, and Nimmo drove it to deep center for a double. Burgamy followed with a hard single to left, scoring Tovar and sending Nimmo to third.

    Kipper visited the mound, forming an enclave with his battery and infielders. Aguilera listened and gave him reassuring words, letting Kipper know he could get back to hitting his spots. When Burgamy worked out a walk, however, manager McMillon had seen enough, and with the bases loaded, no one out and the game tied, 2-2, he wanted a fresh arm. He pulled Aguilera for righty Mike McCarthy. Aguilera is not one to light up the radar gun and when he starts to miss his spots, his runway is far shorter than that of a kid who hits 93 and higher on the radar gun.

    Center fielder Ceciliani now approached the plate. "With the bases loaded, I knew he had to come to me," explained Ceciliani. "I just reminded myself to let the game come to me, and not try to do too much."

    Patience proved to be the mantra of the day for the B-Mets for the next half hour. Ceciliani worked out the second of the six walks that would occur during the next thirty minutes. His walk gave the Mets their first lead of the series since the bottom of the third of Game 1, when they held a 1-0 lead until they relinquished it the next inning.

    McCarthy appeared to be settling in when he struck out Taijeron for the first out of the inning. But with Dustin Lawley at the plate, McCarthy threw a wild pitch, enabling Rivera to score the third run of the inning. After Lawley worked out another walk, Carrillo just missed icing the game with a long fly to right that was only a few feet short of the wall when Shannon Wilkerson gloved it for the final out. The B-Mets now led, 4-2.

    In the sixth inning, the wheels on the Sea Dogs' pennant-hoping bus came off. Tovar once again started it off with a single, this time to left. Nimmo then was hit by a pitch, and Rivera singled to left, with Lopez holding Tovar at third. Burgamy followed with another walk, scoring Tovar. Bases loaded, no one out, Portland now down by three runs. Manager

McMillon came out to the mound, taking the ball from McCarthy and handing it to righty Pete Ruiz.

Jayce Boyd worked out his first walk of the game, putting the Mets ahead 6-2. As Yogi Berra once said, it was "déjà vu all over again" as Ceciliani had the bases loaded as he approached the plate.

"Again, I knew they had to come to me, they had to throw me strikes," thought Ceciliani.

Both Rivera and Burgamy scored as Ceciliani stroked a hard ground-ball double down the right field line, breaking the game open and giving the Mets a six-run lead, at 8-2.

Ruiz, perhaps with the jitters now gone, then bore down and got both Taijeron and Lawley to pop out to first. Catcher Xorge Carrillo now approached the plate, with Boyd still at third and Ceciliani at second. Carrillo worked out the Mets' sixth walk of the game to again load the bases.

Portland's fans grow restless, moving their bottoms from cheek to cheek in their seats, with groans filling the summer air.

"C'mon, did you forget how to throw strikes?"

"Let's get this inning over with, stop the freebies already!"

Deflated faces fill the stands, with futility etched on practically every mien.

Wilfredo Tovar, who started the inning with a single, hits another one, a line drive to left, scoring Boyd and Ceciliani, making it a 10-2 game. More groans filter out to the field, the frowns get fuller, and Hadlock Field has become an asylum of frustration as its inhabitants wonder when this interminable half-inning will end.

Brandon Nimmo steps into the batter's box while the most exasperated fans leave their seats to pursue other items of attention on this Saturday afternoon. Before the frustrated fans are out of the concourse, Ruiz throws his second wild pitch of the inning, scoring Carrillo, moving Tovar to second, and giving the Mets an 11-2 lead.

Almost mercifully, Nimmo flies out to center.

Portland answered with a two-run home run by David Chester in the bottom of the eighth off of Jon Velasquez, but hit three routine grounders to short in the ninth inning. By the end of the game, half of the 3,077 fans remain in the park to see the bitter end of the 11-4 win for Binghamton. Tomorrow, it is a "winner takes all" day.

After the game, manager Pedro Lopez explained the hitting philosophy of the team. "I called a team meeting after last night's loss and told them that if we were going to lose, we were going to go down fighting. I told them to take each bat as if it were the last, to grind out everything." With the pressure on the Sea Dogs to produce a win to celebrate, the B-Mets focused on taking the game one at bat at a time.

The Winner Goes to Richmond…

Sunday, September 7th was a perfect day for a ball game in Portland, with temperatures in the 70's and the sun shining brightly. It also, however, was the first day of the NFL season, and many Portlanders preferred to watch their beloved New England Patriots play rather than see the Sea Dogs take on the B-Mets. But the 2,813 fans who came out to cheer on the Sea Dogs were focused on every pitch, showing that Hadlock Field had more than just its scoreboard reflecting Fenway's faithful.

Before the game Rusney Castillo signed autographs from the home plate side of the dugout for five to ten minutes, putting a smile on many faces. McMillon was giving the ball to Luis Diaz, the 22-year old Venezuelan, who had faced the B-Mets twice in July, striking out 16 in 12.2 innings of work, but going 0-1. Though his final stat line with Portland was impressive, with a 3.72 E.R.A. over 13 starts, he had to rely on two outstanding starts to finish the season to lower his E.R.A. from 4.21. Portland fans were squeamish over which Diaz would show up.

The Mets, meanwhile, were going with Gabriel Ynoa, a 21-year-old native of the Dominican Republic who was rated as the 15th best prospect in the Mets' organization at the beginning of the season. In 2013 Ynoa was voted the Mets' minor league pitcher of the year, as he posted a 15-4 record with a 2.72 E.R.A. for the Savannah Sand Gnats, the Sally League Champions. This year he split his time between St. Lucie and Binghamton with mixed results, as consistency was not his companion. With Binghamton, he pitched to a 3-2 record, with a 4.21 E.R.A. Ynoa's best pitch is his fastball, which he can dial up to 94 mph and the key to his success is how well he locates his changeup and curve.

At the start then, the teams looked evenly matched on the pitcher's mound: two South American pitchers not yet past their 23rd birthday whose work in AA was inconsistent but impressive.

Brandon Nimmo stepped into the batter's box at 1:05 and took Diaz's first pitch for a ball. Then, as Nimmo is known to do, he fouled off a bunch of pitches to the left side, four in a row to be exact. Nimmo's ability to work pitchers deep into counts and foul off those outside pitches are two traits that have endeared him to General Manager Sandy Alderson and Director of Minor League Operations Paul Depodtesta. They feel that as Nimmo matures he will learn to pull the inside pitches and increase his power while his ability to "stay behind the ball" will let him adjust to hitting breaking pitches from fellow lefthanders.

After fouling off his four pitches, Nimmo took two more balls, working the count to 3-2. On the eighth pitch in the at bat he doubled to right on a liner in the gap. There were a few youngsters in the stands who, though sporting Portland gear, were happy to see Nimmo lead off with a double. They had stayed alongside the dugout after yesterday's game and received not only Nimmo's autograph, but some baseballs as well, as Nimmo handed out baseballs and signed autographs for ten minutes until all the youngsters left with smiles.

With Nimmo taking a small lead off second, Rivera hit to the right side, but got it up in the air and not very deep, so Nimmo had to hold at second. But then Brian Burgamy hit a double to right center, giving the Mets the early 1-0 lead—it was only Burgamy's third hit of the entire series. Jayce Boyd then grounded out, third to first, getting in front of an outside curveball. But Ceciliani drew a five-pitch walk. That brought Taijeron to the plate and a visit to the mound from Kipper. This time Taijeron worked behind in the count, 1-2. When Diaz threw a low outside curve, Taijeron lunged and in an off-balance swing, he managed to drive a hard ground ball over third, scoring Burgamy, giving the Mets a 2-0 lead in the first 15 minutes of play.

Diaz escaped further damage by getting Lawley to end the inning with a fly to right.

The Sea Dogs got a run back off Ynoa as Castillo led off with a double and came around to score on a sacrifice fly to left by David Chester that was scalded.

The score remained 2-1 until the top of the fourth. Third baseman Lawley led off with a line drive to left on a 1-0 pitch that fell in front of Keury De La Cruz, who respected Lawley's power by playing a deep left field. Carrillo then put down a sacrifice bunt, forcing the first baseman, David Chester, to field it and throw to second baseman Mike Miller, who covered first. Wilfredo Tovar, the September base-hitting machine, now stepped to the plate and he worked the count to 3-2 before he hit a line drive single to center, knocking in Lawley. Nimmo followed with another single, and when right fielder Jonathan Roof threw past third, Tovar scored and Nimmo took second. The Mets now led 4-1.

Rivera attacked the first pitch, hitting a hard ground ball to the left of second. Shortstop Hector Meneses fielded the grounder and threw out Rivera, with Nimmo crossing to third.

If Hadlock were human, the slight breeze that filled the stands would have been a sigh of relief as there were now two outs with Burgamy coming to bat.

Burgamy worked out a six-pitch walk, however, passing the baton to Jayce Boyd. When Diaz hit Boyd with his next pitch, McMillon went to the mound and replaced one Diaz with another, this one named Dayan. The Hadlock habitants were squirming in their seats again, and they must have felt they went back in time about 24 hours. Just when they thought their hometown boys would get out of the inning, a walk and a hit batsmen had loaded the bases.

Amazingly, once again Ceciliani found himself hitting with the bases loaded. Dayan's first pitch to Ceciliani was low for a ball, which caused a continuum of fannies to move restlessly in their seats. Dayan's next pitch was also a ball.

"C'mon, throw strikes!"
"Make him a hitter!"
"Let's Go Dayan!"

Ceciliani knew Dayan had to come to him with a strike and when Dayan delivered a fastball thigh high, Ceciliani went with the outside pitch and lined a shot over De La Cruz's head for a bases-clearing double, giving Binghamton a 7-1 lead. As Ceciliani pulled into second, he looked into the Mets dugout and clapped his hands in a frenetic flurry.

His claps were death knells for Portland.

Dayan threw a wild pitch, sending Ceciliani to third and the groans in the stands grew louder. Taijeron prolonged Portland's agony with a line drive single to right to score Ceciliani before Lawley struck out.

Portland tried to get back into the game, scoring single runs in the fourth and fifth, and plating two runs in the sixth. But Hansel Robles settled things down by striking out four in 2.1 innings of relief.

Lopez then sent Satterwhite out to the mound in the bottom of the ninth to preserve the 8-5 lead. As Satterwhite prepared to make his first pitch of the inning to Hector Meneses, behind third base, about six rows up, a Portland middle-aged woman stood up and started to cheer for her team.

"C'mon, Hector, let's get this thing started right now," she called out as she loudly clapped her hands.

Meneses took the first pitch for a strike. The Portland fan was still on her feet as Meneses fouled off the next two pitches from Satterwhite. Coincidentally, or conveniently, she was blocking the view of a half dozen or so Binghamton fans who had made the trek together to take in the playoff game. After the third pitch of the inning, Binghamton Mets fan Kevin Healy spoke up, as he and his wife, Cyndy, could not see the field.

"Excuse me, down front, can you please sit down?"

Healy's request was ignored as Meneses took a pitch for ball one.

Politely, once again, Healy repeated his request.

"Excuse me, you are blocking our view. Can you please sit down in front?"

The Portland woman continued to clap as Meneses fouled off yet another pitch to stay alive.

Kevin was now growing frustrated, even more so than he was on the night from long ago when a fan behind him played the game's play-by-play on a transistor radio on the night Aaron broke Ruth's home run record. 'Excuse me, ma'am, can you please sit down in front?"

Suddenly, without provocation, the middle-aged lady turned and faced Healy, her jersey with "Portland Sea Dogs" on the front facing Healy and his travel mates from Binghamton. Her face twisted into a dare. "I'll sit down when you get that other group from your town to stop yelling," she demanded, before turning to watch the action on the field.

She was referring to a another small group of Binghamton fans, about five rows back and in the next section, who had been cheering loudly for Binghamton throughout the game. Healy looked at his wife and then at Denis Wickham, one of his traveling companions, with numbness filling his face.

Wickham now piped up. "C'mon, they've only been cheering for Binghamton, no one has been rude. At least not until now. Can't you please sit down?"

As if on cue, Meneses goes down swinging. One out.

The Portland fan now clapped louder as Rusney Castillo stepped into the batter's box.

Wickham continues pleading for Healy. "Can you please sit down in front?"

Satterwhite's first pitch to Castillo is a called strike. Wickham and Healy look at one another and shake their heads in disbelief. The Portland fan claps louder and yells, "C'mon Castillo, let's get this started!"

Satterwhite winds and delivers and Castillo fouls off a pitch to go 0-2. Healy tries one more time, "Ma'am, why are you being so rude? Can't you please sit down?"

Now her husband stands alongside her. Healy and Wickham look at each other in frustration and get up from their seats so they do not miss any more action. Castillo goes down swinging on Satterwhite's third pitch to him. Two out.

Mike Miller now steps to the plate. He turns on Satterwhite's first pitch and hits a double over the head of Nimmo in left. Applause fills Hadlock and the woman in front of Healy and Wickham barks, "C'mon, it's never too late. Let's keep this thing going!" She is loud, animated, and agitated, feeling that if she claps and yells long enough, the season will not die. Left field Keury De La Cruz now steps to the plate.

The row of Binghamton fans has given up on getting the Portland fan to sit down. They too are standing in order to see the action.

La Cruz works the count to three and two. Then, at approximately 4:18, De La Cruz hits a grounder to short. Tovar gobbles it up and easily throws him out.

Carrillo is now picking up Satterwhite, as the Portland woman who would not sit down quickly leaves with her husband, without even a glance at the Binghamton fans.

The Mets now are turning the mound into a mountain of celebration. In the middle of what is now a stunned and silent Hadlock Field, save for a dozen or so Binghamton fans, the B-Mets celebrate, jumping on top of one another and pounding each other in relief and jubilation.

As the Mets head to the clubhouse, they do so with a hurried gait, as a bus ride through the night to Richmond awaits them. After a half hour or so in the clubhouse, Lopez comes out to thank the Binghamton fans who made the trip and waited outside to glimpse their hometown heroes boarding the team bus.

On to Richmond!

If it's Monday, We Must be in Richmond?

As the sun rose on Monday, September 8th, the Binghamton Mets, bleary-eyed and weary from an emotional win and celebration the day before in Portland, were opening their eyes and turning restlessly in their seats as the team bus entered the city limits of Richmond. There was no sense in battling the day for a few more moments of alleged sleep. Ask any of the players how long it takes to get to Richmond from Portland and they'd give you a rough estimate that sounded like a question. The Eastern League would never schedule a road trip from Portland to Richmond during the regular season. The trip is approximately 650 miles and if all goes well, with only one stop for food on the way, the trip can be made in 11 hours. In the bushes, first-class travel is an oxymoron.

    The Mets used the off day to get some much needed rest and for Tim Heiman, part of the day was spent doing laundry. Heiman had been told that if the Mets won in Portland, the bus would stop in Binghamton on its way to Richmond, allowing Heiman to get a change of clothes. A change in plans, however, called for the B-Mets to drive straight through to Richmond, so Heiman was short some clean threads.

    2,839 fans showed up on Tuesday night at Richmond's ballpark, The Diamond, to watch their Flying Squirrels take on the Mets. The Mets put Tyler Pill on the mound and the Squirrels countered with Clayton Blackburn, a hard-throwing southpaw who was rated as the 10th best prospect in the Giants' organization entering the season. Blackburn turned 21 in January and was signed out of high school in the 2011 draft in the 16th round, as the Giants convinced him to sign for $150,000 and reject his scholarship to the University of Oklahoma.

    Without a designated hitter in this series, Lopez started Boyd at first and put Burgamy at third, leaving Lawley on the bench. Lopez was just waiting for one of the trio to shake the post-season doldrums, as entering the game Boyd was hitting .158, Burgamy was sitting at .176, and Lawley was rock bottom at .105.

    The Mets jumped out to a 1-0 lead in the second inning, after leaving the bases loaded in the first without scoring, as Taijeron was caught looking at a pitch on the outside corner. Brandon Nimmo knocked in the second-inning run with a single to right on the first delivery from Blackburn, knocking in Tovar, who had reached on a force out. Richmond tied the game in the bottom of the third on a single by center fielder Daniel Carbonell.

    The Mets broke the tie in the top of the fifth, scoring two runs to take a 3-1 lead. Ceciliani knocked in a run with a single and Carrillo hit a sacrifice fly to score the other run. In the bottom of the fifth, right fielder Tyler Horan hit a one-out double to right and then manager Russ Morman sent up Myles Schroder to pinch hit for Blackburn, whose pitch count was at 92 after giving up three runs on eight hits in five innings of work. Schroder delivered a run-scoring single to right, but was thrown out at second as Carrillo was able to gun him down after receiving Taijeron's late throw from right field.

The Biggest Double Play of the Year

The defining moment of the game came in the top of the seventh. Righty reliever Paul Sewald started the inning, relieving Pill, who handed him a 3-2 lead. Along with replacing Pill, Lopez tightened up his infield defense by moving Burgamy to first, sending Boyd to the bench, and inserting Lawley at third.

Sewald, who was a 10th-round pick in the 2012 draft and was appearing in only his third game for Binghamton, walked left fielder Devin Harris on five pitches to start the inning. Abbot and Lopez exchanged knowing glances, thinking this is not the way to preserve a one-run lead. Sewald's first pitch to power hitting first baseman Angel Villalona is a ball, eye-high in the center of the plate. Six pitches thrown by Sewald and five of them are balls. Villalona was now in the driver's seat, looking for a fastball, knowing Sewald had to find the plate.

Villalona gets his heater, but disappoints the Richmond rooters by popping up to Tovar. One out now with a runner at first. Lopez and Abbot are thinking, "OK, we got an out, now just throw strikes, Paul. That first out is the toughest to get."

Catcher Tyler LaTorre now finds his way to the plate, but Sewald's next three pitches do not. If this inning were a movie, it could be titled "The inning of living dangerously," as LaTorre draws the second walk of the inning.

Lopez has seen enough. He removes Sewald and brings in tall lefty reliever Chase Huchingson. Morman counters by sending righty hitter Elliott Blair to pinch hit for lefty Tyler Horan. Huchingson just misses with an outside fastball on the first pitch. But then each pitch he throws is higher and more outside than the last one. Blair works out a four-pitch walk.

The bases are loaded with only one out.

Righty batter Mitch Delfino now approaches the plate as a pinch hitter for pitcher Tyler Rogers. Huchingson takes a deep breath to help him regain focus, the fans all the while sensing a lead change. Delfino tells himself, "Make him come to you, make him throw a strike."

"The first hitter I walked, but I had a lot of movement on the ball, so I told myself just to move the ball to the middle a little more. When Delfino came to the plate, I stepped off and told myself just to throw strikes," explained Huchingson. In take mode all the way, Delfino watches the first pitch go down the middle for a strike. Lopez and Abbot, and the entire Mets bench breathe a sigh of relief. But Huchingson's next two deliveries are outside.

With the count 2 and 1, Delfino is looking for a fastball, for a pitch he can drive. Huchingson is able to throw a pitch on the inside corner and Delfino hits a grounder to second baseman T.J. Rivera, who is able to start a 4-6-3 double play.

Huchingson does a fist pump as he exits the mound, knowing he has made his best pitch of the season. The Mets go on to score two runs off of Kyle Crick in the eighth and cruise to a 5-1 win.

"We have a little bit of magic about us," stated Huchingson after the game. "I am cherishing every moment along the way, seizing the moment. It's great to be here and we have a lot of comradery going on both on and off the field, everyone is feeding off the energy."

Peavey and Carrillo Step Up

Things do not get any easier for the Mets the next day, as they face Adalberto Mejia, who is the fourth-rated prospect in the Giants' system. Mejia just turned 21 in June and though he had the highest E.R.A of all the Squirrels' starters during the season, Mejia is highly regarded, as he consistently throws in the low nineties and throws an effective changeup and breaking pitch. He had an outstanding season for San Jose in 2013, where his strikeout-to-walk ratio was four to one. The Mets counter with Peavey, who has dominated AA batters, but in his cups of coffee at AAA, the hitters have dominated him. Peavey is buried in the depth charts of the pitching-rich Mets' organization, but with a good post season, he can make front office executives think twice about his prospects for cracking the AAA rotation next year.

    Generally, Peavey is one of those pitchers who needs an inning or two to get settled and have his pitches hit his spots. When he takes the mound, B-Mets fans say to themselves, "If we can get out of the first couple of innings with only a run or two, we'll be in good shape!"

    4, 269 fans are at the game this night, knowing it is the final time they will get to see the Squirrels in action, win or lose. It's 81 degrees, with a slight breeze blowing from right to left, an ideal night for a game. For the second game of the series, Lopez sends Boyd to the bench and gives Lawley the start at third, with Burgamy moving to first. He also tinkers with the order a bit, moving Taijeron to cleanup and putting Lawley sixth in the order. As usual, Carrillo and Tovar hold down the seventh and eighth spots in the order. Putting Tovar eighth in the order has been a luxury for Lopez.

    In the second inning, Xorge Carrillo, coming off a quietly excellent game the night before, where he went 1 for 3 with an RBI, gets the Mets on the board with a home run following a Lawley walk. It is his first home run since June 30th and only his third for the season. Peavey is excellent this night, as he throws seven innings, without issuing a walk and striking out nine, giving up only one run on five hits. The Mets break the game open with three runs in the top of the eighth on a three-run homer by Taijeron.

    Randy Fontanez and Cody Satterwhite throw two scoreless innings to seal the 5-1 win. The game is over in under three hours and by 11 PM the Mets are on their way back to Binghamton where they are expected to arrive at around 6 a.m.

A contingent of fans is planning to meet the team bus, but their plans go awry when the bus breaks down outside Harrisburg at around 3 a.m. The bus finally pulls in to Binghamton at around 8:30 a.m., but with an off day on Thursday, the Mets can rest up before taking the field on Friday, September 12th.

Matz Breaks the Rules, then the Bats of the Squirrels

It's 35 minutes before game time when Steven Matz, 22-years-old and the 2014 N.Y. Mets' minor league pitcher of the year, steps out of the Binghamton dugout and makes a quick right to head to the bullpen to warm up for a potential championship-clinching start. The stands are one-third full and the walk-up crowd outside the stadium curves along Lewis Street, signaling spectators will be standing in the stadium tonight. As Matz takes a few steps down the right-field line, fans, three generations of them, call out his name for an autograph. Matz glances over and signs his name on what is thrust in front of him, breaking an unwritten, but strict rule for the starting pitcher of the day—*No autograph signing if you're starting, no distractions! It's only a half-hour before game time when you start to warm up. Get your game face on and focus on what you are about to do.*

Matz nods in acknowledgement of the good wishes and the mewling from the fans. He looks as if he is about to walk out of his home to retrieve the mail. Matz is the polar opposite of teammate Darrell Ceciliani, who is perpetually breaking out in a smile and clapping his hands. For Ceciliani, adrenaline pours from all his pores; for Matz, adrenaline needs no apparent outlet. If Matz were a movie star, he'd be Gary Cooper in *High Noon*—no, check that, he has the quiet grace of Cooper, but lacks the gravitas; he's more like Jimmy Steward in *Destry Rides Again*—reserved, calm, outwardly nonchalant, with a fire burning inside.

Abbott is waiting for him in the right-field corner, outside the bullpen. Xorge Carrillo is practicing blocking phantom pitches in the dirt, as he crouches and scrambles, crouches and goes to his knees down the right-field line. Abbot looks as if he hasn't a care in the world and Carrillo, when he is done with his gymnastics routine, ambles over to the fence to sign a few autographs.

"You won't have to worry about blocking Matz's pitches tonight," calls out an observant fan.

Carrillo glances at him and says, "Oh no, I gotta be ready, that's part of the plan, they'll be some bouncing tonight."

Scouts watching Matz this year have been impressed with the development of his curveball, he is throwing it more often, showing outstanding command. Largely because of this he will be moving up the prospect ladder from the # 11 position he had at the beginning of the season. His curveball has made his fastball and changeup more effective and the changeup has made marked improvement this year as well. At times this year Matz has abandoned his 93-95 mph fastball to get batters flailing at his breaking stuff. And part of his command of his breaking pitch is to put it in the dirt, to get batters flailing at impossible pitches to square up. Carrillo knows this; hence the gymnastics routine before Matz throws his first warmup pitch.

After Matz grants all the autograph requests, he starts his stretching under the focused eyes of Abbot. As the stands fill, the Mets players come out, with virtually everyone stopping to interact with the fans a bit. Tonight's routine is just like any other night for them. For the Greater Binghamton Area, however, the routine is anything but *routine*; it's been 20 years since Chris Roberts, a crafty lefty from long ago, clinched an Eastern League Championship with a 7-2 win over Harrisburg.

On the mound opposite Matz tonight is Ty Blach, another highly-regarded southpaw for the Giants. He is more the crafty lefty type, relying on great command and a fastball that sits in the 89-91 range. He's been an ace wherever he's pitched and he is stingy with his walks, but free with his scripture. (He follows his autograph with *Matt: 6:33 --But seek ye first the kingdom of God, and his righteousness; and all these things shall be added unto you.*)

It's 7:05 when Matz throws his first pitch to Daniel Carbonell, a top rated prospect and Cuban refugee who signed with the Giants earlier this year—it's 95-mph, a strike, and a harbinger of the hits that will not fall for the Squirrels this night. Matz throws nothing but fastballs to Carbonell—95, 95 96, 94, 94, 94, and the last one Carbonell grounds back to Matz for a *1-3* notation in a scorecard.

    Shortstop Kelby Tomlinson grounds out, second-to-first before Blake Miller works out a walk from Matz, as the lefty misses with a 3-1 fastball. Third baseman and cleanup hitter Mario Lisson, who had 18 homers and 76 RBIs in only 376 at bats during the regular season, now steps to the plate. Looking for fastballs from Matz, Lisson takes two curves at 74 and 76 mph, and is behind, 0-2.

    Sandy Alderson, the N.Y. Mets General Manager, is watching the game from the stands tonight and he notices the curveballs thrown in typical fastball counts. The ability to get ahead with the curveball is something some major league pitchers have yet to master. Just mention the name of lefty Oliver Perez to any New York Mets fans in the stands and their faces will contort in misery as they conjure up images of Perez throwing ball after ball during his last two years with the parent club.

    The curveballs enable Matz to strike out Lisson with a 93 mph fastball. Matz walks off the mound to cheers while the crowd buzzes with excitement, needing no assistance from "Buddy the Bee," one of the team's mascots. Over 5900 fans have packed the stands and they are hungry for more than hamburgers and spiedies on this cold September evening. Many are dressed for football, complete with sweatshirts, knit caps, and gloves, as the temperature is 53 degrees at the game's first pitch.

    In the bottom of the first, Johnson and Burgamy sandwich an out by Rivera with singles, bringing up cleanup hitter and right fielder Travis Taijeron. Blach is fully aware of the scouting report on Taijeron—like most young power hitters, he can turn around a fastball, but is prone to chasing breaking pitches out of the strike zone. But Blach's command is a bit off and Travis is not fishing this early in the game. Two curveballs later Travis is ahead in the count 2-0. Now Travis can sit on the fastball—he gets one and he turns on it, sends it deep to left, down the line, and over ten thousand eyes follow the orb against the darkness of the night.

Many in the crowd rise to their feet and shout, "Get out, get out!"

Shouts from the Richmond bench plead "Get down! Get down!"

The ball follows the commands of the Richmond bench, settling in the glove of left fielder Devon Harris, two-feet shy of the wall and, as it does so, the stadium fills with groans.

Matz squishes the Squirrels in the second, with two strikeouts and a groundout. Blach returns the 1-2-3 favor by getting Nimmo, Carrillo, and Tovar with a strikeout, fly out, and groundout. In the third, catcher Tyler LaTorre, a 31-year-old veteran who has had three stints in AAA, looks foolish swinging on a 94-mph fastball, as Matz shows no mercy, setting up his strikeout pitch with a 74-mph curve. Pitcher Blach then feebly grounds out to first. As Carbonell quickly enters the batter's box, Morman grimaces. After the first pitch to Carbonell, manager Russ Morman, standing in the third-base coaches' box, calls over one of his players to the edge of the dugout.

"After this at bat, be sure to tell Carbonell when the pitcher makes an out and runs, he has to take some time getting into the box. This is the first time he has ever batted in a NL game where the pitcher is hitting." Morman's worst fears play out when Carbonell strikes out quickly and Blach has to get back to the mound in a hurry.

Matz is the first batter in the bottom of the third and he shows he is an all-around athlete when he puts a good swing on a pitch and lines out to center. Kyle Johnson flies out to right, but Rivera gets a single and Burgamy steps to the plate. Burgamy just gets under a fastball, sending it high and deep to center, but Carbonell catches the ball without any trouble.

The first three innings take 44 minutes to complete; both pitchers get the ball, toe the rubber and waste little time in delivering their pitches.

Matz continues to dominate the middle three innings, his only blemish being another walk to Miller in the fourth. The Mets, meanwhile, nurse out a run in the bottom of the fourth when Taijeron leads off with a single and, after Lawley strikes out swinging, Nimmo hits a ground ball up the middle that looks like it will be a double play, as Tomlinson, the shortstop, is shaded toward second. But the baseball gods of Binghamton are smiling, with a grin almost as wide as a Ceciliani smile—the ball hits the second base bag, and takes a high bounce into center field, allowing Taijeron to race to third, putting Nimmo on first. Xorge Carrillo then takes a fastball to center field, deep enough for Taijeron to cross the plate with the game's first run. The fans are cheering now, patting one another on the back, supporting each other with hugs. Some bold fans dare to state, "With the way Matz is pitching, one run might be enough!"

    The Mets go down in order in the fifth and sixth. Rhythmic chants of "Let's Go Mets" fill the stadium as Matz takes the mound for the seventh. He still hasn't given up a hit and the stadium knows it, as it claps, stomps, and shouts with Matz's every pitch. The game is not even 90 minutes old!

    Miller leads off for the Squirrels in the seventh, determined to put some vibrancy into the playoff picture for the Squirrels. Through 24 innings of the series, the Squirrels have been held to three runs. Miller, a .304 hitter during the season, has drawn two walks so far, which is the closest Richmond has come to staging a rally. But Matz is determined not to walk him again. He starts Miller with a curve, then follows with a few fastballs. Matz leaves one belt high and Miller squares it up. "Get out!" yells a player from the Richmond dugout. But the hardest hit ball of the night falls harmlessly into left fielder Kyle Johnson's glove. Eight outs away.

    Matz, after getting ahead 0-1, to Lisson, leaves a fastball up in the zone to Lisson, who fouls it off. Then, perhaps showing signs of fatigue, Matz hangs a curveball to Lisson, but Lisson gets under it and flies to center. Lopez and Abbot glance at one another for the thousandth time during the season. While the crowd sees two batters, two outs, and seven outs to get, the coach's eyes are trained to spot any sign of fatigue. One of the things they look for is not so much a drop in velocity, but signs of pitchers losing control, leaving their pitches up in the strike zone. Fatigue causes a pitcher's mechanics to break down and any breakdown in mechanics, no matter how small, often leads to pitches out of the strike zone. Until now, Matz has been low in the strike zone, so now Matz's every move is scrutinized and there is even activity in the Mets' bullpen, with Robles starting to stretch.

Up steps Devon Harris, a strikeout victim his previous two trips to the plate. Matz starts him with heat and gets ahead in the count, 0-2. The crowd rises with two strikes and starts another rhythmic clap. But when Matz misses with a close pitch, he grimaces quickly and looks off to third. He thought he had Harris, but the umpire differed in opinion. Matz and the crowd are pumped for every pitch. The crowd starts another rhythmic clap. Harris flails at a breaking ball and Matz gleefully hops off the mound.

Matz grimaces as he thinks he has Devon Harris struck out in the eighth.

Eric Bloom, an eighth grader and big fan of the B-Mets from Chenango Valley, holds up a Bernhardt sign that says "One More Win!" As fans on the right-field side get up for the seventh inning stretch, some point to a banner that was just put up before the game:

Welcome Back, B-Mets. Our Team. Our Town. Our Pride.

Right now Steven Matz is the pride of all of New York State, having grown up on Long Island, and now pitching in the Southern Tier of New York.

The Mets go meekly against Blach in the 7th, as Nimmo strikes out and Tovar grounds into a shortstop-to-second-to-first double play, after Carrillo had drawn a walk. Matz comes out to start the eighth. Hansel Robles is warming in the bullpen.

Meanwhile, Ron Matz, 51, and the proud father of Steven, is thinking only of outs. He cheers as if he were 12 again. Steven has his father clapping, cheering, and yelling as he strikes out Angel Villalona for his 11th strikeout with a 93-mph fastball. Steven now officially has his longest stint in AA ball; up until tonight, the deepest he had gone into a Double-A game was seven innings.

Right fielder Elliott Blair now steps to the plate. Blair has struggled since he was called up from San Jose, hitting only .240 in 96 at bats. The playoffs have not been any kinder, as he carries a .200 average in only five at bats. But Blair is able to turn a high fastball from Matz into a solid hit to right center and, as soon as Matz sees it headed for the outfield grass, he jumps up and down on the mound, in a moment of angst. As soon as the ball hits the ground, however, he is composed again, and most of the stadium does not even know he jumped in disappointment, as they were too busy following the ball. As the ball is thrown into the infield, the crowd stands in unison, applauding the no-hit bid.

Matz soaks it in only for a few seconds. No need to slow things down now. Pedro Lopez and Glen Abbott make no move in the dugout. The kid is staying in.

Only after catcher Tyler LaTorre hits a slow grounder that manages to make it to right field does Lopez stir.

With Robles ready in the pen, and righty pinch hitter Mitch Delfino announced to bat for Ty Blach, Lopez comes out to get the ball from Matz.

As Matz walks off the mound, the stadium breaks out in a perfectly timed cheer "STE-VEN…MATZ! STE-VEN…MATZ! STE-VEN…MATZ."

Bernhardt, sitting behind home, does a great imitation of Karl Ehrhardt from long ago and proudly displays a sign that reads "The Left Hand from God."

Binghamton Mayor Richard David stands and blends in with the crowd, as he applauds Matz, even though if elections were held right now, Matz would be mayor of the city in a landslide. Matz is Jimmy Stewart again as he walks off the mound, stoic and unassuming as he walks into the dugout, not even hesitating to acknowledge the filled stadium that is now on its feet. "I'm just doing my job out there," he'll say later.

Lopez gives the ball to Robles, who has been tremendous in the bullpen since being removed from the starting rotation in the middle of the season. Not worried about pacing himself, he has added a mile or two to his fastball, though he still battles inconsistent command of his breaking stuff. Lefty hitting Tyler Horan is now sent to pinch hit for Delfino. Robles gets the crowd cheering again by striking out Horan. Some fans exchange high fives and yell out, "Four more outs!"

Don Carbonell, 0-3 on the night, now steps to the plate. Robles goes right after him, throwing nothing but fastballs between 93-95 mph. On the fifth fastball, Carbonell singles hard to right field to bring home Blair with the tying run.

When Burgamy cuts off the throw home, he fires to Lawley, who tags La Torre, caught between second and third. Richmond does not seem to mind however, breathing a sigh of relief not only in getting the game tied, but in getting Matz off the mound as well. The Richmond players are patting each other on the back and yelling encouragement to one another as they take the field for the bottom of the eighth.

Ceciliani leads off the bottom of the eighth by working out a 3-2 walk off of righty reliever Tyler Rogers. Kyle Johnson, after showing he was going to sacrifice bunt a few times, also works out a walk. A large factor for the B-Mets' four-game winning streak in the playoffs has been their ability to draw walks and grind out the at-bats, forcing the pitchers to come to them. Lopez is content in the dugout, thinking "If we continue with this approach, we are going to be OK." Morman is not content with the two walks issued by Rogers, however, and he brings in right hander Cody Hall.

Rivera now steps to the plate and does the right thing by taking a strike. Shortly thereafter, he lays down a successful sacrifice bunt, pitcher to first. Burgamy, the team MVP of the season, now slowly approaches the plate. Morman signals four pitches from the dugout and Burgamy jogs to first, loading the bases.

Now it's up to Taijeron, newly anointed cleanup hitter. Though less than two hours ago, his long fly to left in the first inning seems an eternity ago. What he wouldn't give for a similar result now, though. Binghamton's fans do their best imitation of fans at Citi Field, focused on each pitch, electricity filling the stadium.

Taijeron's bat has no thunder in it, however, as he flies out to shallow right field, with all runners holding. When Hall strikes out Lawley, catcher Tyler La Torre pumps his first in pleasure and the entire Richmond bench erupts with shouts of relief and desire.

Lopez plays by the book in the top of the ninth, bringing his closer, Satterwhite, into the game with hopes of holding the Squirrels at bay so the Mets can win it in the bottom of the ninth. Kelby Tomlinson leads off as Satterwhite looks in for the sign. Satterwhite hangs a curve but Tomlinson only musters a routine fly to center. Carrillo looks out to Satterwhite, his glance telling Satterwhite, "Keep it down! Finish off those pitches."

Satterwhite has the perfect closer's mentality. As he cradles the ball in his hand, he has already forgotten about the hanging curve. Satterwhite knows success is all about the next pitch you throw, not the one you just threw.

Next, pesky Blake Miller gets a single off a 95-mph fastball and the Richmond bench becomes animated as Lisson steps to the plate. Satterwhite starts Lisson off with a breaking ball, as the scouting report says Lisson prefers to sit on the fastball. Cody, having trouble with commanding his curve, hangs this pitch as well, but Lisson only fouls it off. Satterwhite is living dangerously, but his body language does not let anyone know it. Unruffled, he gets Lisson to fly to right. Next up is

Devon Harris, who has not hit the ball all night, striking out three times. When he hits a routine grounder to first, the stadium again erupts in cheers.

Lopez calls out to his team before he heads for the third base coaching box. "We're going to finish it the way we started it!" Strength and conditioning Coach Jason Griffin knits his brows and compresses his face, as he mutters "Huh?"

"Walk-off" proclaims Lopez, recalling Rivera's walk-off hit in the first playoff game against Portland. "It's going to happen," are his last words as he pops out of the dugout.

Lefty reliever Steven Okert is now on the mound for the Squirrels. Nimmo leads off, and for the fourth time tonight he has to face a lefty. There are no spark plugs in his engine tonight, as he strikes out for the third time. Carrillo energizes the stadium with a single and when Tovar follows with a single of his own, the stadium erupts.

Jayce Boyd now emerges from the dugout to pinch hit for Satterwhite and Gavin Cecchini pinch runs for Carrillo at second. Boyd has been one of the leading hitters for the Mets all season, but a cool bat during the playoff run relegated him to the bench even though the Squirrels started a lefty.

At 9:34 PM Boyd works the count to 2-2 and then strokes a line drive into the gap in right center, scoring Cecchini!

By 9:35 the on field celebration is in full swing, with the players jumping on one another and pounding each other's backs. Five minutes later the champagne is spraying, with everyone bathing in its bubbles.

As the champagne's spray spreads over the infield and the fans stand and applaud in the stands, no one cares that the Friday night fireworks show is being delayed. The crowd has had a full share of fireworks for one night.

In a post-game interview with the *Press & Sun-Bulletin*, Lopez expounds on his prediction to Lynn Worthy:

"I wish I could do that with the lotto numbers. I could probably be a millionaire right now, but you know what, I'll take it. I feel like a millionaire. I'm so happy for these guys because they have worked so hard for months. It's been a great ride, I won't ever forget it!"

Jayce Boyd is in the middle of the pile as the scoreboard has yet to catch up to the events of the night.

As the celebration moves to the clubhouse, reporter Lynn Worthy is happy he has come down to the clubhouse to hear from hitting coach Luis Rivera, as the coach gives him a perfect close to his "Big Effort, Big Result" story that will run in the morning's paper. Rivera captures the joy of winning a championship and the transient and challenging fate of being a minor leaguer:

"It's outstanding. The guys worked hard. It feels good to see them win the championship and move on. Some of them are going to go to Triple-A. Some of them are going to go on to the big leagues. Some will go back. Some maybe will get released. I don't know. That's not in my hands. It just feels good to see them be successful and improve."

Epilogue

The inhabitants of the 2014 roster for Binghamton no doubt will continue the pipeline to New York. In September 2014, before the Binghamton Mets played their first playoff game, three players had already been called up to the New York Mets: second baseman Dilson Herrera, lefty pitcher Dario Alvarez, and catcher Juan Centeno.

Only administrative details prevented catcher Kevin Plawecki and shortstop Matt Reynolds from getting a call to Flushing as well. Because both Reynolds and Plawecki were drafted as recently as 2012, neither needed to be placed on the 40-man roster to be protected from December's Rule 5 minor league draft. By not calling up either one, the NY Mets were able to protect two other prospects from November's Rule 5 draft.

As it was, the Mets wound up losing 5 players in the November draft: Juan Centeno was drafted by the Brewers in the major league portion of the draft and pitchers Randy Fontanez, Greg Peavey, and Logan Verret, and catcher Cam Maron were lost to other teams in the minor league portion of the draft.

Second baseman Wilfredo Tovar also got a call to New York in 2014 (he also got 12 at bats with the big league team in September of 2013 as well). Tovar hit over .300 while playing outstanding middle infield defense for Binghamton. Though not regarded as a star, Tovar is seen as having a bright major league career ahead of him as an excellent fielding utility infielder. If he can learn to draw more walks and not get "homer happy," he has supporters who think he can carve out a career as a starting shortstop with a team that does not need too much offense at the position.

Top prospects Dilson Herrera, Steven Matz, and Brandon Nimmo helped the B-Mets earn its 2014 championship through their call-ups from the Florida State League in the middle of June. Many see them playing key roles in the future success of the New York Mets. The presence of Matz already has the New York City media discussing the potential trade value of Jon

Niese, the Mets' lone left starter. If Niese is traded, the media has speculated that Matz could step right into his role. 2014 was seen as a sort of "breakout" year for Nimmo, as he made the Florida State All-Star team and displayed periods of excellence at Binghamton, especially during the playoffs, where he raised his level of play.

    2014 was not the first time that farmhands from Binghamton are being asked to revitalize the parent franchise. In the offseason of 1994, the front office pundits in New York City were pointing to the 1994 Eastern League Champion Binghamton Mets and the wealth of talent on that team as a path for prosperity. Future general manager of the N.Y. Mets, Steve Phillips, then the Mets director of minor league development, was on hand to see lefty Chris Roberts clinch that 1994 Eastern League Championship and in a victory celebration that took place on the field, he exhorted: "You fans all year have had the privilege of seeing this team at work and quite frankly, it is a team with as much talent as you may ever see on a minor league field."

    That 1994 team was laden with talent. Of the 34 players who wore Binghamton's uniform, incredibly, 18 of them wound up in the big leagues at some point. The players ranged from the obscure to the well-known. Utility infielder Pablo Martinez symbolized the obscure, reaching the big leagues in 1996 with the Atlanta Braves, getting into four games and going hitless in his two at bats in the "Show." Representing the well-known big leaguers were the trifecta of Edgardo Alfonzo, Jay Payton, and Jason Isringhausen. Payton, the first round draft pick of the Mets in 1994, played in the majors for twelve years, hitting .279 with 119 HRs and 522 runs batted in. Shortstop-second baseman Edgardo Alfonzo also played a dozen years in the majors, putting up even better numbers than Payton, hitting .284, with 146 homers and 744 runs batted in. Isringhausen, who teamed with Bill Pulsipher to lead the B-Mets pitching staff in '94, went on to a 16-year big league career, accumulating 300 saves along the way.

Passing through Binghamton. Jay Payton sits, while from left to right, Bill Pulsipher, Paul Wilson, and Jason Isringhausen pose for the press. (Photograph courtesy of Binghamton Mets.)

That '94 team included bona-fide prospects at every other position: Alberto Castillo at catcher, Edgardo Alfonzo at second; Rey Ordonez at shortstop, Ricky Otero and Jay Payton in the outfield. Joe Roa, who pitched in 120 big league games was an afterthought on that team; only arm woes prevented lefty Chris Roberts from reaching the big leagues.

Dwight Gooden even started one game on a rehabilitation assignment, throwing five shutout innings. (Ironically, a few days later Gooden tested positive for drugs and was suspended for the rest of the 1994 season.)

That 1994 team sent seven pitchers to Flushing alone (Juan Castillo, Joe Crawford, Jason Isringhausen, Robert Person, Bill Pulsipher, Joe Tam, and Joe Vitko), along with nine position players (Edgardo Alfonzo, Jeff Barry, Alberto Castillo, Charlie Greene, Pat Howell, Rey Ordonez, Ricky Otero, Jay Payton, and Doug Saunders).

But in terms of leading the Mets out of the wilderness, that '94 team did not live up to expectations. Tommy John surgery and arm trouble derailed Pulsipher's promising career, limiting him to 327 innings pitched and only 13 wins. Phillips got desperate in pursuing the 2000 National League pennant and traded the still unproven Isringhausen for the forgettable Billy Taylor, precluding the Mets from seeing the benefits of Izzy's 300 major league saves. Jay Payton became a solid major league player, but he never quite roamed center field as well as his predecessors of Tommie Agee, Mookie Wilson, or Lenny Dykstra.

When the N.Y. Mets got to the World Series in 2000, Payton and Alfonzo were the only members of the '94 team that played a prominent role.

The ensuing years will let us know the final success of the 2014 Binghamton Mets team. For no matter the excitement that the team generated on the warm summer nights in Binghamton, ultimately the minor leagues exist to develop big leaguers.

For the city of Binghamton, though, the team has left a legacy of fulfillment, hope, and revitalization. The town is on a rebound, and its denizens feel so too are the Binghamton Mets and its parent, the New York Mets. Binghamtonians are looking for the farm system to continue to flourish, with the likes of high draftees Gavin Cecchini, Michael Conforto, and Dominic Smith playing their way to Binghamton. For Binghamton public officials, business leaders, and everyday citizens, the 2014 Eastern League Championship from the Binghamton Mets is just another example of a town on the rebound and a symbol of determination.

In one of his final articles on the season, Lynn Worthy explained how the team in a sense was one of destiny and how it captured the hearts and minds of Binghamton's faithful. "It's easy now to say the season was meant to end the way it did. Predictions after the season are always brilliant, but it is funny that not only did the championship come 20 years after the previous title, but it also came in the 100th season of baseball in the Southern Tier. The clinching game also came in Binghamton, where the Eastern League formed in March 1923."

In the middle of September Worthy was a guest speaker for a monthly meeting of the Binghamton Mets Booster Club, where the meeting started with plastic cups handed out and champagne bottles opened to fill each cup with some bubbly in toast to the 2014 Eastern League Champions. Noted Worthy, "As the invited guest speaker for the night at the meeting, I could only describe it as a special thing to see a group of roughly 22 people raising a glass to a championship that arguably meant just as much to them as it did to the players." In the article, Worthy wrote his final words of the year documenting the 2014 magical season:

"What made this celebration special is these folks operated almost entirely behind the scenes with no applause or accolades. While many of the players and staff were headed out of town by the next morning after the championship-clinching game, these folks are here all year round....The bottom line of a banner the Boosters bought and hung up outside the clubhouse before the final game at NYSEG Stadium captures the sentiment perfectly. It reads, "Our TEAM. Our TOWN. Our PRIDE."

At the December 2014 winter meetings, N.Y. Mets General Manager Sandy Alderson recognized the B-Mets as the organization's Minor League affiliate of the Year. Alderson praised the entire B-Mets staff for doing an outstanding job taking care of the players, coaching staff, and visiting members of the front office throughout the season.

"They treat us like family when we come to visit Binghamton," said Alderson, as he not only noted how much pleasure he got in watching the Mets win the championship on September 12, but with his final four words he also came up with the potential mantra for the upcoming season.

"The 2014 season was an incredible one for the Binghamton Mets," noted Alderson. "I was fortunate enough to attend the championship game in Binghamton, and it was magical. The game was tight throughout and the capacity crowd showed its enthusiastic appreciation for the exciting play. It was a great night for the Mets and, more importantly, for the city of Binghamton. Congratulations to the entire B-Mets organization. *Let's repeat in 2015!*"

Appendix A. Player Profiles

This appendix contains brief profiles on all players who saw game action for Binghamton in 2014, with the exception of the major leaguers who had rehabilitation stints in Binghamton: Travis d'Arnaud, Juan Lagares, Daisuke Matsuzaka, and Eric Young.

Alvarez, Dario. Lefty reliever. 2014 B-Mets Record: 1-0, 0.00 E.R.A. Born: 1/17/1989. Late-season addition to B-Mets went unscored on in five appearances. Established himself as the # 1 lefty out of the pen for Lopez in his small sample of work before the N.Y. Mets called him up in September. Started the season in Savannah and finished it by making four appearances for New York in September!

Bennett, Hamilton. Right handed reliever. 2014 B-Mets Record: 0-0, 3.38 E.R.A. Born: 6/26/1988. Pitched in ten games for Binghamton before his early season release. Drafted in the 29th round in the 2010 amateur draft, one round ahead of Josh Edgin. Despite having a lifetime E.R.A of 3.01 in five minor league seasons, Bennett was not able to hook on with a minor league team after being released by Binghamton.

Bowman, Matthew. Right-handed starting pitcher. 2014 B-Mets Record: 7-6, 3.11 E.R.A. Born: 5/31/1991. Drafted in the 13th round of the 2012 amateur draft. Results improved dramatically once he began trusting his fastball. Likes to pitch to contact, is at his best when he stays low in the zone, and gets a large number of ground balls. His 2014 success will move him up the prospect charts; has a Tim Lincecum-type delivery. Slated to be in the Las Vegas rotation in 2015.

Boyd, Jayce. Right handed hitting 1B, DH. 2014 B-Mets Record: .293, 8 HR, 59 R.B.I. Born: 12/30/1990. Drafted in the sixth round out of Florida State University in 2012. Has established reputation as high average and contact hitter.

Provided walk-off double to win the Eastern League Championship against Richmond in Game 3. Started slowly in 2014, but came on strong to be a key contributor. Popular with the fans, signs his autographs with a smiley face and has been described as having matinee-idol looks.

Bradford, Chase. Right-handed reliever. 2014 B-Mets Record: 1-2, 2.02 E.R.A. Born: 8/5/1989. Served as Binghamton's closer until his call-up to Las Vegas. Excellent strikeout-to-walk ratio throughout his minor league career, a real "strike thrower." In 2013 he pitched to a 0.71 E.R.A in 25 innings for Binghamton and he followed that up with an 11-save season and 2.02 E.R.A. in 26 innings in 2014 for the B-Mets. He finished 2014 for Vegas, going 3-2 with 5 saves and a 3.52 E.R.A in 46 innings, striking out 41 and walking four.

Burgamy, Brian. Switch-hitting infielder/outfielder: 2014 B-Mets Record: .276, 23 HR, 76 R.B.I. Born: 6/27/1981. In 2014 Burgamy returned to organized ball for the first time since 2008. Mainstay in the lineup throughout the year, played LF, 3B, 2B, and 1B, and DH. Quiet leader on the team, veteran presence a great asset throughout the season. A student of the game.

Carrillo, Xorge. Right-handed hitting catcher. 2014 B-Mets Record: .283, 2 HR, 19 R.B.I. Born: 4/12/1989. Carrillo opened eyes with his 2014 season, as he supplied excellent defense and was voted the MVP of the championship series against Richmond. He backed up Plawecki in the first half, and became the first-string catcher when Plawecki was promoted to Vegas. Drafted by the Mets in the 14th round of the 2011 draft out of Arizona State University.

Cecchini, Gavin. Right-handed hitting shortstop. 2014 B-Mets Record: .250, 0 HR, 0 R.B.I. Born: 12/22/1993. Called up at the end of the season, he went one for four for B-Mets. Scored the winning run on Boyd's championship-clinching hit as he came into the game as pinch runner. Will be Binghamton's starting shortstop in 2015.

Ceciliani, Darrell. Left-handed hitting outfielder. 2014 B-Mets Record: .289, 7 HR, 54 R.B.I. Born: 6/22/1990. 2014 saw Ceciliani return to the B-Mets for his second tour of duty, where he improved on his 2013 line of .268-6-44, though his 16 steals in '14 were a drop of 17 from 2013. Brandon Nimmo's presence cut into Ceciliani's playing time and also increased his exposure to LF. Ceciliani is a grinder between the lines and a maestro in the clubhouse, where he keeps everyone lose with his energy and "puckish" nature. His value to the B-Mets went well beyond his contribution on the field. He was a fourth-round pick in the 2009 draft.

Centeno, Juan. Right handed hitting catcher: 2014 B-Mets Record: .286, 0 HR, 8 R.B.I. Born: 11/16/2989. Split 2014 between Binghamton and Las Vegas, with most of his time spent in Vegas. He gave the B-Mets team a lift with his play when he joined the team in August. Appeared in 21 games for the Binghamton Mets. Drafted in the 32nd round of the 2007 draft out of Antonio Luchetti High School in Puerto Rico. Claimed by Milwaukee Brewers off of waivers from NY Mets on 10/31/2014.

Chism, TJ. Lefty reliever. 2014 B-Mets Record: 1-0, 7.65 E.R.A. Born: 8/9/1988. Suffered through disappointing stint with Mets in '14, after serving as the closer for St Lucie in 2013, garnering 13 saves. His father, Tom, was a minor leaguer for over seven years for the Baltimore Orioles and was a teammate of Cal Ripken in the minors. T.J. split the year between St. Lucie and Binghamton in '14.

Clark, Matt. Left-handed hitting 1B/OF. 2014 B-Mets Record: .297, 10 HR, 47 R.B.I. Born: 12/10/1986. Veteran performer was outstanding for Binghamton before he asked to be released so he could sign with Milwaukee to play for Nashville (AAA). Finished the year with the Brewers, where he made his major league debut on September 2, 2014.

Cuan, Angel. Lefty-handed starting pitcher. 2014 B-Mets Record: 3-5, 6.23 E.R.A. Born: 5/29/2989. Saw limited action for the B-Mets in '14 as a spot starter. Voted the most inspirational pitcher on the team. The diminutive lefty has been in the organization since 2008, viewed as an organizational player.

Fontanez, Randy. Right-handed reliever. 2014 B-Mets Record: 0-1, 4.86 E.R.A. Born: 5/18/1989. Drafted by the N.Y. Mets in the 27th round of the 2011 draft out of the University of South Florida. He joined the B-Mets on June 19th, after registering 10 saves for St. Lucie and registering a 2.56 E.R.A, in 31 innings. Selected by the Los Angeles in the minor league portion of the Rule 5 draft from the Mets on December 11, 2014.

Forsythe, Blake. Right-handed hitting catcher. On opening day roster, but released before playing a game for Binghamton. Finished 2014 playing for the Midland RockHounds in the Texas League for the Oakland Athletics organization.

Fraser, Ryan. Right-handed reliever. 2014 B-Mets Record: 3-2, 6.39 E.R.A. Born: 8/27/1988. The 6' 3" blonde-haired long reliever returned for his third year in Binghamton in 2014, splitting his time between St, Lucie and Binghamton. Fraser has struggled the past two seasons, seeing his E.R.A climb each year in AA (3.48 in '12, 5.63 in '13, and 6.39 in '14). Drafted by the Mets in the 16th round of the 2010 draft, out of the University of Memphis.

Fulmer, Michael. Right-handed starter. 2014 B-Mets Record: 0-1, 16.20 E.R.A. Born: 3/15/1993. Drafted by the N.Y. Mets in 2011 with the 44th overall pick. Was not effective in his one start for the B-Mets. Should be part of the B-Mets rotation in 2015.

Gorski, Darin. Lefty starting pitcher. 2014 B-Mets Record: 4-2, 2.22 E.R.A. Born: 10/6/1987. Crafty 6' 4" pitcher whose progress has been adversely affected with shoulder issues. Has consistently excelled at AA and lower, but still adjusting to AAA, where hitters have proven to be more patient, resulting in higher W.H.I.P (Walk and hits per innings pitched), and consequently a higher E.R.A. Gorski's age, along with pitching-rich Mets organization means Gorski will probably need to convert to a reliever to make the New York big league roster. Went 2-3 with a 4.56 E.R.A. in nine starts for Vegas in 2014.

Gronauer, Kai. Right-handed hitting catcher. 2014 B-Mets Record: .176, 1 HR, 4 R.B.I. Born: 11/28/1986. Returned to Binghamton for third tour of duty in 2014. He split the season between Las Vegas and Binghamton. Quintessential organizational player.

Herrera, Dilson. Right-handed hitting infielder. 2014 B-Mets Record: .340, 10 HR, 48 R.B.I. Born: 3/3/ 1994. The 5' 10" second baseman immediately went on a hitting tear upon his arrival on 6/19. He joined the big league club in September, and showed flashes of brilliance in Flushing, though only hitting .220. When he was called up, the B-Mets immediate reaction was one of "Oh NO!" as Herrera was their unparalleled spark plug. But T.J. Rivera manned 2B in expert fashion, and Lawley and Taijeron picked up at bats in the post season and performed well.

Huchingson, Chase. Lefty middle reliever. 2014 B-Mets Record: 4-1, 3.10 E.R.A. Born: 4/14/1989. Though 6' 5," the lefty specialist is a soft tosser, relying on command for success. He delivered a key double-play ball in the first game of the Eastern League Championship Series. Though he was drafted in the 23rd round of the 2008 draft by the Astros, he did not sign until July 2010 as a non-drafted free agent with the New York Mets.

Johnson, Kyle. Right-handed hitting outfielder. 2014 B-Mets Record: .269, 4 HR, 39 R.B.I. Born: 11/9/1989. The 6'0" Johnson was a mid-season selection to the Eastern League AA All-Star team, but saw his playing time diminished with the arrival of Nimmo and the hot hitting of Ceciliani in the second half of the season. A true student of the game, he learned from the professional approach Burgamy brought to each at bat. A player whose value goes beyond his statistics, as evidenced by his history of high on base percentages. Drafted by the Angels in the 25th round of the 2012 draft, he was traded to the Mets for Collin Cowgill on June 25th, 2013.

Kolarek, Adam. Lefty reliever 2014 B-Mets Record: 1-2, 6.07 E.R.A. Born: 1/14/1989. The 6' 3" lefthander had a disappointing season for Binghamton in 2014 after he pitched to a 3-3 record and 1.71 in 44 innings in 2013 at Binghamton. Shared lefty specialist duties with Chase Huchingson, but by end of season, Huchingson (and Alvarez) supplanted him as the first long lefty out of the pen.

Lara, Rainy. Right handed starting pitcher. 2014 B-Mets Record: 6-4, 4.31 E.R.A. Born: 3/14/1991. The 6' 4" right hander was signed out of the Dominican Republic in 2010 at 19 and has made steady progress in the minors. Prior to 2014, he was outstanding in Brooklyn and Savannah, and performed steadily in St. Lucie. In 2014 he showed flashes of excellence at Binghamton.

Lawley, Dustin. Right-handed 3B, LF: 2014 B-Mets Record: .239, 20 HR, 69 R.B.I. Born: 4/11/1989. Mainstay in the Binghamton lineup, he backed up his 25-homer 2013 St. Lucie season with 20 homers for Binghamton, but struck out 28% of the time, with an OBP of .292. Drafted in the 19th round of 2011 draft out of University of West Florida. Started 2014 season as the 26th ranked prospect in the organization, but was not protected on the 40-man roster in November of 2014.

Leathersich, Jack. Lefty reliever. 2014 B-Mets Record: 3-3, 2.93 E.R.A. Born: 7/14/1990. The 5' 11" lefty has established a reputation as a strikeout artist, striking out 334 batters in 197 innings during a 4-year minor league career. In 2013 and '14 he dominated at Binghamton, but struggled in AAA Vegas, though he kept his strikeouts at a high level. Due to his uncanny strikeout ability, Leathersich was added to the 40-man roster in November 2014.

Maron, Cam. Right handed hitting catcher. 2014 B-Mets Record: .000, 0 HR, 0 R.B.I. Born: 1/20/1991. Joined B-Mets after Juan Centeno was called up to the major league club in September so he could back up Xorge Carrillo. Only saw action in one game, getting two at bats. Drafted out of Hicksville High School (Billy Joel's alma mater) in the 34th round of the 2009 amateur draft. Selected by the Cincinnati Reds in the minor league portion of the Rule 5 draft on December 11, 2014.

Matz, Steven. Lefty starter. 2014 B-Mets Record: 6-5, 2.27 E.R.A. Born: 5/29/1991. The 6' 2" lefty quickly established himself as the ace of the staff after joining Binghamton on 6/19. Drafted by the Mets in the second round of the 2009 draft, his career has been slowed by injury, including Tommy John surgery. His outstanding season in 2014 firmly established him as the top lefty pitching prospect in the Mets' system, as he showed increased command of his secondary pitchers. He sports a 93-95 mph fastball, along with a curve, slider, and change.

Mazzoni, Cory. Righty starter. 2014 B-Mets Record: 2-0, 4.50 E.R.A. Born: 10/19/1989. Started two games for Binghamton on a rehabilitation assignment, before joining Las Vegas where he went 5-1. Hard thrower who eventually might be moved to the bullpen due to logjam of pitching talent in the organization. Should start 2015 in Las Vegas rotation.

Nimmo, Brandon. Left-handed hitting outfielder. 2014 B-Mets Record: .238, 6 HR, 26 R.B.I. Born: 3/27/ 1993. Called up by the B-Mets on June 19th, Nimmo immediately became a fan favorite, flashing an engaging smile and always having time for the fans. Nimmo showed a good eye at the plate, posting an on-base percentage of .339, as well as the ability to go to left field. He hit 12 doubles in 240 at bats, showing power potential. One of the biggest things in his favor is his age, as entering 2015 he will only be 22.

Panteliodis, Alex. Lefty starter. 2014 B-Mets Record: 0-1, 12.27 E.R.A. Born: 7/74/1990. Made one spot start for Binghamton. Drafted in the 9th round of the 2011 draft. Pitched for Savannah, St. Lucie and Binghamton in 2014. Candidate for Binghamton rotation in 2015.

Peavey, Greg. Right handed starter. 2014 B-Mets Record: 11-3, 2.90 E.R.A. Born: 7/11/1988. The 6' 2" right hander was a fan favorite in Binghamton, sporting boyish looks and a perpetual smile. Until the arrival of Steven Matz, Peavey played the role of the ace of the staff. He has struggled in his AAA stints, diminishing his prospect status. He was selected by the Minnesota Twins in the minor league version of the Rule 5 draft on December 10th, 2014.

Peterson, Tim. Right handed reliever. 2014 B-Mets Record: 0-1, 108.00 E.R.A. Born: 2/22/1991. Gave up four earned runs in one-third of an inning in his only appearance for Binghamton. Started the season in excellent fashion in Savannah, also pitched in St. Lucie. Candidate for Binghamton bullpen in 2015.

Pill, Tyler. Right handed starter. 2014 B-Mets Record: 9-5, 3.83 E.R.A. Born: 5/29/1990. Mainstay of Binghamton's starting staff all season, overcame a 0-5 start to finish second on the team in wins. Has an excellent command of the strike zone, walking only 29 batters in 124 innings in 2014. Drafted by the Mets in the 4th round of the 2011 draft out of California State University in Fullerton, he merits a promotion to AAA in 2015.

Plawecki, Kevin. Right-handed hitting catcher. 2014 B-Mets Record: .326, 6 HR, 43 RBI. Born: 2/26/1991. Drafted out of Purdue University with the 35th overall pick in the 2012 draft, which was part of the compensation for losing Jose Reyes to free agency. Started 2014 as the fifth-best prospect in the organization and was the opening day catcher for Binghamton. Started slowly in April, but bat came alive in May and June, as he was a key contributor in the heart of the order. Promoted to

Vegas in mid-June, where he also finished strong, putting him in line for a major league roster spot in 2015.

Reynolds, Matt. Right-handed hitting middle infielder. 2014 B-Mets Record: .355, 1 HR, 21 R.B.I. Born: 12/3/1990. Drafted in the second round in the 2012 draft with one of the compensatory picks for the Mets losing Jose Reyes to free agency. He earned a mid-season promotion to Las Vegas, where he continued to hit for a high average. He is a line-drive, contact hitter who goes to right field well and has good plate discipline. Can play 2B, SS, or 3B, with 2B perhaps being his best defensive position.

Rivera, T.J. Right-handed hitting middle infielder. 2014 B-Mets Record: .358, 1 HR, 28 R.B.I. Born: 10/27/1988. Native of the Bronx, his father is a diehard Mets fan. Has consistently hit in the minors, known as a "grinder." His play was instrumental in B-Mets becoming champions. Hit walk-off, three-run homer in Game 1 of the Eastern Division Championship Series. His ability to hit for average and infield versatility should get him to the big leagues as a utility infielder.

Robles, Hansel. Right-handed starter/reliever. 2014 B-Mets Record: 7-6, 4.31. E.R.A. Born: 8/13/1990. The 5' 11" inch Robles was inconsistent as a starter for the B-Mets in 2014, alternating between brilliant and bewildering. But once he became a reliever on July 19th, he excelled. By the end of the season he was entrenched as the setup man for closer Cody Satterwhite. Finished the season throwing 26 innings in relief, with 34 strikeouts and only 7 walks, pitching to a 1.38 E.R.A! He and Satterwhite were instrumental in the B-Mets' 5-game winning streak in the post season. Added to the 40-man roster in November 2014, look for Robles to remain in the bullpen due to his dominance as a reliever in 2014.

Sandoval, Ryan. Right-handed utility infielder. 2014 B-Mets Record: .262, 1 HR, 12 R.B.I. Born: 8/10/1987. The 5' 10" organizational infielder appeared in 38 games in '14 but is best remembered for teaming with Ceciliani for changing Plawecki's walk-up song in June of 2014. Sandoval has never been able to match his 2010 season with Brooklyn, when he hit .330. Drafted in the 30th round of the 2007 draft out of Chabot College, Sandoval was released in the middle of the 2014 season.

Satterwhite, Cody. Right-handed closer. 2014 B-Mets Record: 3-2, 15 saves, 2.33 E.R.A. Born: 1/27/1987. The 6' 4" power right hander took over the closer's role after Bradford's promotion to Vegas. Unscored upon in first 6 weeks of the season, as well as in the Mets' playoff run. He was the 2008 second-round pick of the Tigers, but has battled injuries throughout his career, missing all of 2010 and 2012 due to injury. Despite his success in 2014, he was left off the Mets' 40-man roster, as being 28-years-old with a history of arm problems were factors working against him.

Sewald, Paul. Righty reliever. 2014 B-Mets Record: 1-0, 4.50 E.R.A. Born: 5/26/1990. The 6' 2" pitcher was drafted in the 10th round of the 2012 draft and pitched in three games for the B-Mets. Had an outstanding season for St. Lucie, where he went 4-1, with a 1.73 E.R.A. and accumulated 11 saves. His Class A season earned him a late season ticket to Binghamton. He should start the 2015 season in the Binghamton pen.

Taijeron, Travis. Right-handed hitting outfielder. 2014 B-Mets Record: .248, 15 HR, 64 R.B.I. Born: 1/20/1989. The 6' 2" outfielder held down right field for most of the year for the B-Mets, placing 6th on the team in games played and third in HRs and RBIs. He teamed with Ceciliani and Nimmo to form a formidable outfield in the post season. Drafted in the 18th round of the 2011 draft by the Mets, Taijeron has shown big-league power but will need to cut down on his strikeouts to get a serious look with the big club.

Tovar, Wilfredo. Right handed hitting shortstop. 2014 B-Mets Record: .282, 2 HR, 29 R.B.I. Born: 8/11/1991. Generously listed at 5' 10," Wilfredo returned for his third stint with Binghamton in 2014. Regarded as the finest fielding infielder in the organization, Tovar primarily played second until he was sidelined with a broken finger. Upon his return, with Matt Reynolds having moved up to Vegas, Tovar anchored the shortstop position. A member of the 40-man NY Mets' roster, he has hit .167 in 18 at bats during his brief cups of coffee with the NY Mets in '13 and '14.

Vaughn, Cory. Right-handed hitting outfielder. 2014 B-Mets Record: .190, 3 HR, 10 R.B.I. Born: 5/1/1989. Though he had a disappointing first half, he got the call to Las Vegas in June. At Vegas, he improved to .228, with 7 homers and 30 RBIs. Outstanding personality, he was a teammate of Stephen Strasburg at San Diego State, where their manager was the late Hall of Famer, Tony Gwynn.

Velasquez, Jon: Right-handed reliever. 2014 B-Mets Record: 4-4, 4 saves, 3.44 E.R.A. Born: 10/15/1985. In 2014 Velasquez returned to organized ball for the first time since 2011. Relying on a fastball, changeup, and cutter, Velasquez, a Bronx native, spent the entire season in the B-Mets bullpen, falling in behind fellow right handers Cody Satterwhite and Hansel Robles.

Ynoa, Gabriel. Right handed starter. 2014 B-Mets Record: 3-2, 4.23 E.R.A. Born: 5/26/1993. Mid-season addition to Binghamton, performed well in 11 starts. Slated to return to the B-Mets rotation in 2015.

Zapata, Neil. Right handed hitting catcher. 2014 B-Mets Record: .185, 0 HR, 1 R.B.I. Born: 12/13/1990. Zapata was briefly called up from Savannah to help out with an injury crunch. He appeared in 4 games for the B-Mets, playing 3B for the first time in his career. An organizational player, he has been in the Mets' system since 2009.

Appendix B. Game-by-Game Log

Author's Note: *Reprinted from the Binghamton Mets web site (bmets.com)*

April

3 vs. Akron, L 1-7 (WP: C. Anderson; LP: D. Gorski)

4 vs. Akron, Postponed: Inclement Weather

5 vs. Akron, W 6-3 (WP: R. Lara; LP: J. Colon; SV: C. Bradford)

5 vs. Akron, L 0-3 (WP: T. Murata; LP: T. Pill; SV: E. Tejeda)

6 vs. Akron, W 5-4 (WP: J. Leathersich; LP: W. Roberts; SV: C. Bradford)

7 vs. Erie, Postponed: Inclement Weather

8 vs. Erie, W 7-2 (WP: C. Satterwhite; LP: N. Avila)

9 vs. Erie, W 7-2 (WP: M. Bowman; LP: J. Ferrell)

10 @ New Hampshire, W 9-1 (WP: D. Gorski; LP: A. Bibens-Dirkx)

11 @ New Hampshire, W 7-0 (WP: R. Lara; LP: S. Copeland)

12 @ New Hampshire, L 4-9 (WP: C. Lawrence; LP: T. Pill)

13 @ New Hampshire, W 6-0 (WP: H. Robles; LP: A. Sanchez)

14 @ Portland, L 4-9 (WP: R. Scott; LP: G. Peavey)

15 @ Portland, Postponed: Rain

16 @ Portland, Postponed: Wet Grounds

17 vs. New Hampshire, W 4-1 (WP: M. Bowman; LP: S. Copeland)

18 vs. New Hampshire, L 3-6 (WP: T. Davis; LP: J. Velasquez; SV: G. Infante)

19 vs. New Hampshire, W 3-2 (WP: J. Church; LP: R. Bleier; SV: C. Bradford)

21 vs. Portland, L 4-7 (WP: H. Owens; LP: T. Pill; SV: M. Celestino)

22 vs. Portland, L 3-5 (WP: R. Scott; LP: J. Velasquez)

23 vs. Portland, Postponed: Inclement Weather

24 vs. Portland, W 5-4 (WP: C. Bradford; LP: M. Celestino)

25 @ Erie, Postponed: Rain

26 @ Erie, W 8-1 (WP: M. Bowman; LP: J. Ferrell; SV: A. Kolarek)

26 @ Erie, L 5-6 (WP: C. Knebel; LP: C. Bradford)

27 @ Erie, W 9-6 (WP: J. Velasquez; LP: T. Collier; SV: C. Bradford)

28 @ Akron, L 0-4 (WP: W. Roberts; LP: T. Pill)

29 @ Akron, L 3-4 (WP: J. Cooper; LP: J. Leathersich; SV: T. Sturdevant)

30 @ Akron, Postponed: Rain

May

2 vs. Portland, W 5-1 (WP: G. Peavey; LP: M. Augliera)

3 vs. Portland, W 3-2 (WP: D. Gorski; LP: H. Owens; SV: C. Bradford)

3 vs. Portland, L 3-9 (WP: B. Johnson; LP: M. Bowman)

4 vs. Portland, L 1-4 (WP: M. McCarthy; LP: R. Lara; SV: M. Celestino)

5 @ New Hampshire, L 0-5 (WP: S. Copeland; LP: T. Pill)

6 @ New Hampshire, L 4-6 (WP: R. Bleier; LP: H. Robles; SV: S. Gracey)

7 @ New Hampshire, W 6-0 (WP: G. Peavey; LP: C. Lawrence)

8 vs. Harrisburg, W 12-6 (WP: D. Gorski; LP: B. Schwartz)

9 vs. Harrisburg, L 3-4 (WP: N. Holland; LP: C. Bradford; SV: W. Madrigal)

10 vs. Harrisburg, W 5-2 (WP: R. Lara; LP: P. Espino; SV: J. Leathersich)

11 vs. Harrisburg, W 2-1 (WP: T. Pill; LP: A. Cole; SV: C. Bradford)

13 vs. Altoona, L 3-10 (WP: T. Sample; LP: H. Robles)

14 vs. Altoona, W 5-3 (WP: G. Peavey; LP: J. Rodriguez; SV: C. Bradford)

15 vs. Altoona, W 3-2 (WP: C. Satterwhite; LP: Q. Miller)

16 @ New Hampshire, W 8-6 (WP: J. Velasquez; LP: D. Antolin; SV: C. Bradford)

17 @ New Hampshire, W 6-5 (WP: R. Lara; LP: M. Boyd; SV: C. Satterwhite)

18 @ New Hampshire, W 9-8 (WP: A. Kolarek; LP: T. Davis; SV: J. Church)

19 @ Portland, W 5-0 (WP: H. Robles; LP: H. Owens)

19 @ Portland, L 2-8 (WP: M. McCarthy; LP: A. Cuan)

20 @ Portland, L 1-2 (WP: B. Johnson; LP: D. Gorski; SV: N. Ramirez)

21 @ Portland, L 1-5 (WP: K. Couch; LP: L. Cessa)

21 @ Portland, L 5-6 (WP: R. Scott; LP: M. Bowman; SV: J. Valdez)

22 @ Portland, L 5-6 (WP: A. Kurcz; LP: C. Satterwhite)

23 vs. New Britain, W 3-2 (WP: J. Velasquez; LP: C. Johnson; SV: C. Bradford)

24 vs. New Britain, W 8-6 (WP: J. Church; LP: A. Salcedo; SV: C. Bradford)

25 vs. New Britain, W 3-1 (WP: A. Cuan; LP: S. Gilmartin; SV: C. Satterwhite)

26 vs. New Britain, W 5-0 (WP: D. Gorski; LP: V. Vasquez)

27 vs. New Hampshire, W 7-5 (WP: T. Pill; LP: M. Boyd; SV: C. Bradford) (Completion on 5/28/14 at 5:30 PM)

28 vs. New Hampshire, W 7-5 (WP: T. Pill; LP: M. Boyd; SV: C. Bradford) (Completion of game suspended on 5/27/14)

28 vs. New Hampshire, L 2-5 (WP: C. Lawrence; LP: R. Lara; SV: R. Boone)

29 vs. New Hampshire, W 7-2 (WP: H. Robles; LP: A. Sanchez)

30 @ New Britain, L 0-4 (WP: S. Gilmartin; LP: A. Cuan)

31 @ New Britain, L 2-3 (WP: V. Vasquez; LP: M. Bowman; SV: L. Oliveros)

June

1 @ New Britain, L 1-6 (WP: P. Dean; LP: A. Panteliodis)

3 @ Altoona, W 15-6 (WP: T. Pill; LP: Z. Dodson)

4 @ Altoona, L 5-6 (WP: J. Rodriguez; LP: H. Robles; SV: Q. Miller)

5 @ Altoona, L 5-8 (WP: A. Sampson; LP: A. Cuan; SV: R. Beckman)

6 vs. New Britain, L 3-6 (WP: V. Vasquez; LP: M. Bowman; SV: L. Oliveros)

7 vs. New Britain, L 4-6 (WP: A. Salcedo; LP: J. Leathersich; SV: M. Hamburger)

8 vs. New Britain, W 7-3 (WP: C. Satterwhite; LP: C. Johnson)

9 @ Akron, L 2-10 (WP: D. von Schamann; LP: H. Robles; SV: B. Price)

10 @ Akron, W 8-1 (WP: A. Cuan; LP: C. Anderson)

10 @ Akron, W 10-5 (WP: T. Chism; LP: M. Packer)

11 @ Akron, W 12-6 (WP: M. Bowman; LP: T. Murata)

12 @ Akron, W 11-3 (WP: G. Peavey; LP: J. Colon)

13 vs. Erie, Postponed: Rain

14 vs. Erie, W 4-2 (WP: T. Pill; LP: K. Ryan; SV: A. Kolarek)

14 vs. Erie, W 6-0 (WP: H. Robles; LP: N. Avila)

15 vs. Erie, L 3-5 (WP: W. Palacios; LP: A. Cuan; SV: J. Valdez)

17 vs. Richmond, W 5-1 (WP: M. Bowman; LP: T. Blach)

18 vs. Richmond, W 6-1 (WP: G. Peavey; LP: J. Snodgrass)

19 vs. Richmond, W 6-0 (WP: T. Pill; LP: K. Crick)

20 @ Bowie, W 12-4 (WP: H. Robles; LP: J. Pettit)

21 @ Bowie, W 7-6 (WP: R. Fraser; LP: A. Vasquez; SV: C. Satterwhite)

22 @ Bowie, L 0-2 (WP: Z. Davies; LP: M. Bowman; SV: O. Drake)

23 vs. Reading, W 12-8 (WP: J. Velasquez; LP: J. Biddle)

24 vs. Reading, W 2-0 (WP: G. Peavey; LP: S. Gonzalez; SV: C. Satterwhite)

25 vs. Reading, Postponed: Rain

26 @ Altoona, L 1-3 (WP: J. Rodriguez; LP: H. Robles; SV: K. Kasparek)

27 @ Altoona, W 8-2 (WP: T. Pill; LP: A. Sampson)

28 @ Altoona, W 8-7 (WP: S. Matz; LP: Z. Dodson; SV: C. Satterwhite)

29 @ Altoona, W 7-4 (WP: M. Bowman; LP: P. Ludwig)

30 @ New Britain, W 8-3 (WP: R. Lara; LP: T. Rogers)

July

1 @ New Britain, L 6-9 (WP: J. Wheeler; LP: H. Robles)
2 @ New Britain, Postponed: Rain
3 @ New Britain, W 6-4 (WP: C. Huchingson; LP: C. Johnson; SV: C. Satterwhite)
3 @ New Britain, Postponed: Rain
4 vs. Erie, L 6-9 (WP: R. Robowski; LP: R. Fraser; SV: J. Valdez)
5 vs. Erie, L 0-2 (WP: T. Collier; LP: S. Matz)
5 vs. Erie, W 4-0 (WP: H. Robles; LP: G. Knudson)
6 vs. Erie, L 9-10 (WP: W. Startup; LP: C. Huchingson; SV: K. Faulk)
7 vs. Portland, W 11-4 (WP: C. Mazzoni; LP: B. Johnson)
8 vs. Portland, Postponed: Rain
9 vs. Portland, W 6-1 (WP: A. Cuan; LP: M. Augliera)
9 vs. Portland, W 1-0 (WP: G. Ynoa; LP: M. McCarthy)
10 vs. Portland, W 13-3 (WP: S. Matz; LP: L. Diaz)
11 @ Erie, L 3-7 (WP: K. Ryan; LP: R. Lara; SV: A. Nesbitt)
12 @ Erie, W 9-3 (WP: C. Mazzoni; LP: S. Smith)
13 @ Erie, W 5-4 (WP: R. Fraser; LP: G. Knudson; SV: C. Satterwhite)
14 @ Erie, W 11-4 (WP: G. Ynoa; LP: J. Ferrell)
17 vs. Trenton, W 8-4 (WP: S. Matz; LP: M. Banuelos)
18 vs. Trenton, L 5-6 (WP: Z. Nuding; LP: A. Kolarek; SV: D. Moreno)
19 vs. Trenton, L 1-6 (WP: L. Severino; LP: M. Bowman)
20 vs. Trenton, W 5-2 (WP: G. Peavey; LP: D. Camarena; SV: C. Satterwhite)
21 @ Portland, L 4-6 (WP: M. McCarthy; LP: R. Fraser; SV: R. Scott)
22 @ Portland, L 3-4 (WP: P. Ruiz; LP: J. Velasquez)
23 @ Portland, W 4-2 (WP: S. Matz; LP: M. Augliera; SV: C. Satterwhite)
24 @ Trenton, L 5-6 (WP: F. Rondon; LP: J. Leathersich)
25 @ Trenton, W 6-1 (WP: G. Peavey; LP: D. Camarena)
26 @ Trenton, W 10-7 (WP: R. Fraser; LP: P. Wetherell; SV: C. Satterwhite)
27 @ Trenton, L 3-7 (WP: J. Heredia; LP: R. Lara)
28 vs. New Hampshire, L 1-5 (WP: K. Graveman; LP: S. Matz; SV: B. McFarland)
29 vs. New Hampshire, W 4-3 (WP: C. Huchingson; LP: G. Infante)
30 vs. New Hampshire, L 2-7 (WP: C. Lawrence; LP: G. Peavey; SV: M. Storey)
31 vs. Bowie, W 9-4 (WP: M. Bowman; LP: M. Bischoff)

August

1 vs. Bowie, W 9-8 (WP: J. Leathersich; LP: O. Drake)
2 vs. Bowie, W 2-1 (WP: J. Leathersich; LP: S. Hensley; SV: C. Satterwhite)
3 vs. Bowie, L 2-8 (WP: Z. Davies; LP: S. Matz)
5 @ Richmond, W 9-6 (WP: T. Pill; LP: A. Mejia)
6 @ Richmond, W 5-1 (WP: G. Peavey; LP: C. Stratton)
7 @ Richmond, W 3-0 (WP: H. Robles; LP: J. Casilla; SV: C. Satterwhite)
8 @ Harrisburg, L 1-2 (WP: A. Voth; LP: G. Ynoa; SV: R. Benincasa)
9 @ Harrisburg, W 3-1 (WP: R. Lara; LP: J. Simms; SV: C. Satterwhite)
10 @ Harrisburg, W 3-0 (WP: S. Matz; LP: J. Simmons; SV: R. Fontanez)
12 vs. Erie, Postponed: Rain
13 vs. Erie, L 4-7 (WP: J. Ferrell; LP: G. Peavey; SV: A. Nesbitt)
13 vs. Erie, L 6-8 (WP: B. Augenstein; LP: A. Cuan; SV: R. Robowski)
14 vs. Erie, W 9-4 (WP: D. Alvarez; LP: S. Smith)
15 @ Reading, W 8-7 (WP: C. Huchingson; LP: C. Murray; SV: C. Satterwhite)
16 @ Reading, W 2-1 (WP: D. Matsuzaka; LP: J. Biddle; SV: J. Velasquez)
16 @ Reading, W 7-3 (WP: T. Pill; LP: A. Loewen; SV: R. Fontanez)
17 @ Reading, L 0-1 (WP: H. Milner; LP: S. Matz)
18 @ Erie, W 11-4 (WP: G. Peavey; LP: J. Ferrell)
19 @ Erie, L 0-7 (WP: W. Palacios; LP: M. Fulmer)
20 @ Erie, W 8-5 (WP: G. Ynoa; LP: J. Turley)
22 vs. Akron, W 12-3 (WP: T. Pill; LP: N. Maronde)
23 vs. Akron, W 5-1 (WP: G. Peavey; LP: D. von Schamann)
24 vs. Akron, W 5-2 (WP: S. Matz; LP: W. Roberts)
25 vs. New Britain, W 4-1 (WP: C. Huchingson; LP: E. Ibarra; SV: C. Satterwhite)
26 vs. New Britain, L 1-5 (WP: J. Berrios; LP: G. Ynoa)
26 vs. New Britain, W 3-2 (WP: P. Sewald; LP: A. Salcedo; SV: D. Alvarez)
27 vs. New Britain, L 7-11 (WP: D. Turpen; LP: A. Kolarek)
28 vs. New Britain, L 3-5 (WP: E. Ibarra; LP: C. Satterwhite)
29 @ Richmond, L 1-2 (WP: A. Mejia; LP: S. Matz; SV: H. Strickland)
30 @ Richmond, L 6-7 (WP: C. Alvarado; LP: R. Fontanez)
31 @ Richmond, L 0-1 (WP: E. Quirarte; LP: J. Velasquez; SV: S. Okert)

September

1 @ Richmond, L 4-12 (WP: C. Blackburn; LP: T. Peterson)

3 vs. Portland, W 8-5 (WP: C. Satterwhite; LP: N. Ramirez)
4 vs. Portland, L 0-7 (WP: J. Haley; LP: G. Peavey; SV: W. Boscan)
5 @ Portland, L 3-6 (WP: A. Kurcz; LP: P. Sewald)
6 @ Portland, W 11-4 (WP: R. Lara; LP: M. Augliera)
7 @ Portland, W 8-5 (WP: G. Ynoa; LP: L. Diaz; SV: C. Satterwhite)
9 @ Richmond, W 5-2 (WP: T. Pill; LP: C. Blackburn; SV: C. Satterwhite)
10 @ Richmond, W 5-1 (WP: G. Peavey; LP: A. Mejia)
12 vs. Richmond, W 2-1 (WP: C. Satterwhite; LP: S. Okert)

Appendix C. Twitter Handles and Walk-Up Music

Twitter Handles: Some contact and anecdotal information for the 2014 Eastern League Champions. Twitter handles courtesy of the B-Mets Booster Club; walk-up music courtesy of the Binghamton Mets. Players are listed in alphabetical order.

- **Chasen Bradford:** @cbBaseball29
- **Gavin Cecchini:** @GavinCecchini2
- **Darrell Ceciliani:** @DCintheplace2b
- **Darin Gorski:** @darin_gorski20
- **Chase Huchingson:** @NaturalState89
- **Kyle Johnson:** @Kyle_Johnson_KJ
- **Jack Leathersich:** @LeatherRocket
- **Steven Matz:** @Smatz88
- **Brandon Nimmo:** @You_Found_Nimmo
- **Greg Peavey:** @GregPeavey*
- **Kevin Plawecki:** @kplawecki26
- **Matt Reynolds:** @ReyRey_5
- **Cody Satterwhite:** @casatter70

Walk Up Music for Batters:

- **Jayce Boyd:** *Comatose* by Skillet and Vinz AND *Survival* by Eminem (both used first part of the year) AND *Am I Wrong* by Nico & Vinz (used for a few months in the middle) AND *Theme from American Horror Story* (used second half of the year)
- **Brian Burgamy:** Never had an official walk up song; team used various rock songs, like *Seek and Destroy* by Metallica, *Crosstown Traffic* by the Jimi Hendrix Experience, and *Bulls on Parade* by Rage against the Machine.
- **Xorge Carrillo:** *X Goin' Give It To Ya* by DMX
- **Gavin Cecchini:** *You Can't Stop Me* by Andy Mineo

- **Darrell Ceciliani:** *That's My Kinda Night* by Luke Bryan AND *The Outsiders* by Eric Church AND *Drink To That All Night* by Jerrod Niemann (all 3 first half of the year) AND *All-American Middle Class White Boy* by Thomas Rhett (used second half of the year)
- **Juan Centeno:** *La Pregunta* by J Alvarez AND *Se Cree Mala* (Con Letra) by Plan B
- **Travis d'Arnaud:** *The Way I Live* by Baby Boy Da Prince
- **Blake Forsythe:** *Song of the South* by Alabama AND *Whiskey On The Rocks* by AC/DC
- **Kai Gronaeur:** *Wasted* by Tiesto
- **Dilson Herrera:** *Changes* by 2Pac AND *Como Tu No Hay Dos* by DJ Buxxi (used for like, a week before being called up)
- **Kyle Johnson**: *My Life Be Like* by Grits AND *Cruise by Florida Georgia Line (both used early in season) AND* Ball Cap *by Glen Templeton*
- **Dustin Lawley**: *Sweet Home Alabama* by Lynyrd Skynyrd (used early in the season) AND *When the Credits Roll* by George Strait
- **Cam Maron:** *Get Some* by Chevelle
- **Brandon Nimmo:** *The Outsiders* by Eric Church (used for most of his stint with us) AND *Manifesto* by The City Harmonic (used at the end of the season/playoffs)
- **Kevin Plawecki**: Intro by The XX AND *Ghosts N Stuff* (Nero Remix) by DeadMau5 (both used early in the season) AND *Double Bubble Trouble* by Mia (used after he got hot)
- **Matt Reynolds:** *Bottoms Up* by Brantly Gilbert AND *This Is How We Roll* by Florida Georgia Line
- **TJ Rivera:** *Deja Vu* (Uptown Baby) by Lord Tariq & Peter Gunz AND *Push It* by Rick Ross
- **Travis Taijeron:** *Guys Like Me* by Eric Church AND *Way Out Here* by Josh Thompson (both of these were used throughout the season), AND *Mary Jane's Last Dance* by Tom Petty and the Heartbreakers (used towards the end of the season) AND *Bad Boy For Life* by P. Diddy (used only early in the season)
- **Wilfredo Tovar:** *Bailalo A Lo Loca* by Jowell y Randy AND *Del Envidioso Me Rio* by Arcangel AND *Estamo Aqui* by

- Arcangel AND *Gucci Boys Club* by Arcangel (added after returning from injury)
- **Cory Vaughn:** *The Payback* by James Brown (used early) AND *I'm Back* by T.I. AND *Vato by YG* AND *Too On To Be Off by Problem* (used these 3 rest of his stint)
- **Eric Young Jr.:** *Forever Young* by Jay Z

Walk Up Music for Pitchers

- **Hamilton Bennett:** *Follow* by Breaking Benjamin
- **Matt Bowman:** *Don't You Worry Child* by Swedish House Mafia (very early in season) AND *Boneless* by Steve Aoki (most of season)
- **Chase Bradford:** *Welcome Home* by Coheed and Cambria
- **John Church:** *That's The Only Way I Know* by Jason Aldean
- **Angel Cuan:** *La Historia De Cristo* by Roberto Orellana
- **Ryan Fraser:** *For Those About to Rock* by ACDC
- **Darin Gorski:** *Wretches and Kings* by Linkin Park
- **Matt Koch:** *Back It Up for Bobby* by B.O.B.
- **Adam Kolarek:** *End of the Line* by Metallica
- **Rainy Lara:** *Si Yo Estoy Con Dios Quien Contra Mi* by El Alfa (used before his injury) AND *Demasiado by Vakero* (used after injury)
- **Jack Leathersich:** *Cherry Pie* by Warrant
- **Steven Matz:** *Call Me The Breeze* by Lynyrd Skynyrd (most of season) AND *Lift Your Head Weary Sinner by Crowder* (used only on Game 3 of the championship series)
- **Cory Mazzoni:** *Trampled Underfoot* by Led Zeppelin
- **Greg Peavey:** *Tell The World* by Lecrae
- **Tyler Pill:** *I Am Broken* by Pantera (used early in the season) and *Running* by David Dallas (used most of season)
- **Hansel Robles:** *Flor Palida* by Marc Antony
- **Cody Satterwhite:** *God's Gonna Cut You Down* by Johnny Cash
- **Paul Sewald:** *Tsunami* by DVBBS & Borgeous
- **Jon Velasquez:** *100%* by Big Pun
- **Gabriel Ynoa:** *Aqui No Hay Miedo* by El Batallon

Notes

*Final **Author's Notes:***
  I. All web sites listed in this book were current as of this printing.
  II. All prospect ratings are from *Baseball America's Prospect Handbook,* unless otherwise noted.
  III. The primary source for statistics quoted are from the baseball-reference site (www.baseball-reference.com)
  IV. Most of the player quotes in this book occurred during Tim Heiman's pre-game radio show. Other sources included Lynn Worthy's reporting for the *Binghamton Press & Sun-Bulletin*, and the author's numerous conversations with players. On field conversations paraphrased from author's notes.

Chapter 1. From Binghamton to the Big Leagues

1. *You just knew.* Wegmann's remarks during a panel discussion during "Baseball and the Arts" First Friday event on October 1 2014.
2. *Leave me alone.* Darling, Ron, with Daniel Paisner. "The Complete Game: Reflections on Baseball, Pitching, and Life on the Mound." (New York: Alfred A. Knopf 2009) P. 7.
3. *Breaking his run.* In January of 2015 Natera was once again named the B-Mets hitting coach!

Chapter 2. Six More Wins

1. *We're just in shock.* "Suspect's Neighbors: We're in Total Shock," *Binghamton Press & Sun-Bulletin.* (April 1st 2014.)

Chapter 3. April: Our Team, Our Town, Our Pride.

1. *"Greenberg Gardens" to "Kiner's Korner."* The Pirates moved the left field fence at Forbes Field 30 feet closer to home when the team acquired Hank Greenberg from the Tigers after World War II. After Greenberg retired, this area became known as Kiner's Korner, in honor of Kiner's home run power.
2. *I never say 7:15 Anymore…* Grant, Jim, with Sabellico, Tom & O'Brien, Pat. "The Black Aces: Baseball's Only African-American Twenty Game Winners." (Farmingdale, New York. The Black Aces, LLC. 2006) Page 320.
3. *Turning Traditions into a Gaming Casino.* The selections came in later than October, in early 2015 and *Traditions* was not selected. Traditions now supports the application of *Tioga Downs* to become a full-fledged casino.

Chapter 5. The Art of Pitching

1. *My philosophy is just to attack …* (www.Metsmerizedonline.com).

Chapter 6. "Big Plaw's Gonna Get a Double"

1. *Not being able to…* (www.Milb.com)

Chapter 7. Hunting the Sea Dogs

1. *He's the real deal.* Petanick, Mitch. "Where is the Love for New York Mets Prospect TJ Rivera?" Mets Merized Online. (http://metsmerizedonline.com/2013/10/where-is-the-love-for-new-york-mets-prospect-t-j-rivera.html/)
2. *I was really excited.* Pre-game interview before Game 102 with Tim Heiman
3. *Raised in the Bronx.* In addition to T.J. Rivera, Jon Velasquez also was a native of the Bronx.

Chapter 8. A Town, A Team, and A Rebound

1. *At the end of the 1800's.* Smith, Gerald R. "Cigars, cure-alls in our industrial history." The *Binghamton Press & Sun-Bulletin.* December 28, 2014.
2. *Explained SUNY Broome President Kevin Drumm.* Staff Report. "SUNY Broome Approved for Start-Up NY." The *Binghamton Press & Sun-Bulletin.* July 31 2014.
3. *You want to feel that.* Tracey, Sarah. "Transports, Business Create College Towns." The *Binghamton Press & Sun-Bulletin.* October 2 2014
4. *This will stabilize.* Roby, John R. "Award Starts Clock Ticking on 50 Front Street," by John R. Roby (jroby@pressconnects.com). *Binghamton Press & Sun-Bulletin.* Monday, December 22, 2014.
5. *Public Art Strengthens Communities.* Brockett, Megan. "Art Enlivens Ramp's Walls." *Binghamton Press & Sun-Bulletin.* October 31, 2014
6. *These cities offer…* (https://www.aier.org/american-institute-economic-research-unveils-2014-2015-ranking-best-us-cities-college-students)

Chapter 11. A September to Remember

1. *It's easy now to say.* Worthy, Lynn. "Be-Mets Boosters Deserve a Piece of the Championship." *Binghamton Press & Sun-Bulletin.*(September 26 2014)

Epilogue

1. *They treat us like family.* Heiman, Tim. "B-Mets Named Affiliate of the Year" December 19 2014. (Bmets.com)

www.ingramcontent.com/pod-product-compliance
Lightning Source LLC
Chambersburg PA
CBHW060821050426
42453CB00008B/526